FROM SUFFERING TO JOY

About the Author

Sri Prem Baba is a master teacher in the Sachcha spiritual lineage of northern India. Born and raised in Brazil, Prem Baba worked as a humanistic psychologist, yoga teacher, and shaman before his arrival in India.

Prem Baba offers a method of self-discovery he calls "The Path of the Heart," which bridges psychology and spirituality, East and West. Through self-investigation, the path works towards purifying and integrating the lower self, until one is able to sustain joy. Prem Baba is dedicated to helping people become channels of divine love by sharing their talents and gifts with the world and thus fulfilling their true purpose in life.

For several months a year, Prem Baba offers daily satsangs and blessings at ashrams of the Sachcha lineage in India, especially at Sachcha Dham, the ashram of his beloved master Sri Sachcha Baba Maharajji in Rishikesh. He continues his work in Brazil, where he has built the Sachcha Mission Ashram near São Paulo and offers spiritual intensives. He also travels extensively around the world, giving talks and intensives to an increasing number of people from all backgrounds and religious traditions.

FROM SUFFERING TO JOY

The Path of the Heart

Prem Baba

SelectBooks, Inc.
New York

This edition published by SelectBooks, Inc.
For information address SelectBooks, Inc., New York, New York.

Third printing. Certain additions and modifications have been made since
the previous edition.

ISBN 978-1-59079-234-6

Library of Congress Cataloging-in-Publication Data

Baba, Prem.
    From suffering to joy : the path of the heart / Prem Baba.
    p. cm.
    ISBN 978-1-59079-234-6 (pbk. : alk. paper)
    1. Peace of mind. 2. Self-knowledge, Theory of. I. Title.
    BF637.P3B33 2012
    294.5'44--dc23
                    2012001387

Manufactured in the United States of America
10 9 8 7 6 5 4 3 2 1

I dedicate this book
to my beloved Gurudeva,
Sri Sri Sachcha Baba Maharajji,
who opened my eyes
with the torch of knowledge.
With faith and deep devotion,
Prem Baba

Contents

Foreword

Albert Einstein once asserted that the most important question in life facing any of us is to decide whether or not the universe is friendly. It is my privilege to introduce to the reader someone with whom I personally have learned to answer Einstein's question in the affirmative. For that, and much more, I want to register my deep gratitude to Prem Baba.

MEETING PREM BABA

I have had the pleasure of knowing Prem Baba for over thirteen years. I met him first in São Paulo, Brazil, having just returned from a brief anthropological field trip to the Amazon. Prem Baba, or Janderson Fernandes, as he was known then, was a psychologist and yoga teacher with a keen interest in Amazonian shamanism. As an anthropologist, I was curious to learn more from him.

Two years later, on a return trip to Brazil, I renewed my acquaintance with Prem Baba. This time, my interest was deeply personal. Over the course of six months, I had experienced a series of personal shocks, losing my mother to cancer and my younger brother to drowning, and watching my infant daughter struggle for life and health through multiple surgeries. My wife Lizanne and I began to work with Prem Baba in a quest to understand what we could learn from these difficult life lessons and to begin to heal our emotional wounds. I was deeply touched, first by Lizanne's remarkable recovery and then later by my own slowly dawning understanding.

Over time, I learned to integrate bit by bit these personal insights into my work life. I had long observed in my studies and practice of negotiation that perhaps the single biggest obstacle to success in negotiation is not the other, however difficult they might be. It is ourselves. The true difficulty lies within – in our all-too-human tendency to react – to react impulsively out of fear or anger. The foundation of successful negotiation, I have found, is learning how to "go to the balcony" – to a mental and emotional place of perspective, calm, and self-control. How can you possibly hope to influence others if you cannot first influence yourself? While this concept may be easy to grasp, it is nonetheless difficult to put into practice. How exactly can you go to the balcony, with all the emotions and thoughts racing through your head and heart in the midst of heated negotiations?

It is here where I have learned a great deal from Prem Baba – a way to steady myself and to remember what truly matters, even in the midst of the conflicts and wars in which I occasionally became involved as a third party. In this sense, I have slowly come to appreciate just how much work on inner peace can facilitate work on outer peace.

What I ultimately discovered, thanks to my studies with Prem Baba, is that I had a somewhat limited view of reality. My world revolved in good part around what might be called *external reality* – the material reality of objects and the social reality of human beings moving around and interacting on this planet. Then there was *internal reality*, of course, the world of thoughts and feelings, perceptions and beliefs. My life revolved around these two realities – external and internal, physical and psychological, body and mind. My sense of identity was captured pretty well by Descartes' dictum, "I think therefore I am," with the corollary, "I do therefore I am." My time with Prem Baba helped convince me that I had radically underestimated reality and myself. There was yet another reality behind the other two realities, which might be called *core reality*. I had experienced glimpses of it many times before, mostly in nature, often on high mountaintops. My studies with Prem Baba helped me appreciate that these were not just evanescent moments of wonder, but that perhaps here lay my true enduring identity. "I think therefore I am" gradually gave way to a dawning recognition of "I am therefore I am."

PREM BABA'S JOURNEY

It may be useful for the reader to have a little understanding of Prem Baba's personal journey that led him to the teachings he conveys through word and presence.

Janderson Fernandes – that was his given name – grew up in a simple family, modest in means, Christian in belief, raised by a grandmother with a deep faith and a powerful intuitive spirit. As a young boy, he recalls asking questions early on, seeking to understand the universe and God, not satisfied with the answers he received from those around him. In his early teens, he discovered yoga, became passionately interested, and studied until he became proficient enough to become a yoga teacher himself. He also studied healing and bodywork. His spiritual quest took him through many mystery schools, including Gnosticism and the shamanism of the Amazon. More formally, he studied humanistic psychology and became a psychotherapist. Over time, he found himself with a dedicated group of regular students and clients, engaged in deep inner work. This work bridged psychology and spirituality, East and West.

Despite all his success as a teacher and therapist, Janderson felt a gnawing dissatisfaction. He had the courage to recognize that he himself was not fully congruent with his own teachings about love and freedom from fear. He was not able to sustain his connection with happiness and inner peace. So began the surrender of his pride and the quest for a teacher to whom he could entrust himself. After a considerable search, he found just such a wise teacher – Sri Sachcha Baba Maharajji – living in India along the banks of the Ganges in the foothills of the Himalayas. After three more years of internal struggle, Janderson was able to take responsibility and to recognize clearly that the real obstacle to "waking up" and remembering his true identity was only himself.

The real reason he was unable to sustain happiness was that part of him did not want to. Part of him wanted to stay mired in the muck. Only when he realized this was he able to let go and wake up. In recognition of this inner awakening, Janderson began to be called by a new name, Prem Baba, which in Sanskrit means "father of love."

Love, in fact, is the essence of Prem Baba's teaching. The only sin, as he likes to say, is not to love. Interestingly, the biblical word "sin" comes from ancient Hebrew and Greek words that mean "to miss the mark," as when an archer misses the target with his arrow. Not to love means to miss the mark. Prem Baba does not deny the existence of evil in the world. On the contrary, he urges us to have the courage to look inside and see the bits of evil that lurk within each of us – evil in the form of meanness, envy, revenge, jealousy, and bitter wrath – all ultimately rooted in fear. Evil is the absence of human empathy, the extreme lack of kindness and compassion. Just as darkness can be understood as the lack of light, so evil can be understood as the lack of love.

To help others make the journey from fear to love, Prem Baba has developed a methodology he calls "O Caminho do Coração," the Path of the Heart, which he discusses in this book. This method, derived from his personal quest, integrates the insights of Western psychology and Eastern spirituality and includes practices ranging from meditation and yoga to intensive psychological exploration of what Jung called the "shadow," the denied impulses that often govern human behavior. The greatest challenge facing human beings, says Prem Baba, is to sustain happiness.

I find myself sometimes called unduly idealistic for believing that it is possible for human beings, no matter how deep their differences, to get along and live in peace with one another. Yet here is Prem Baba having the audacity to go even further. While my studies have persuaded me of the possibility of outer peace, his studies have persuaded him of the possibility of inner peace. Like many teachers of old, Prem Baba holds out the perennial hope that all human beings have the potential to live in love together. He believes that our human essence is love.

Perhaps most important, Prem Baba, in my experience of him, embodies his own teachings. He radiates the love of which he speaks. Prem Baba's teaching is integral to his life, and that, in my view, makes all the difference.

MAKING THE MOST OF THIS BOOK

In your hands is an organized and edited collection of talks (called *satsangs* in Sanskrit) given by Prem Baba during his sojourns at Sachcha Dham Ashram in Lakshman Jhula, India. I hope that they will give you a good sense of the remarkable teachings of this remarkable man.

Imagine yourself for a moment in this setting midst the foothills of the Himalayas, right along the shores of the Ganges, a wide rushing river filled with boulders and rapids. It is a place where hermits and seekers have gathered for millennia to sit quietly, meditate, and pray. From the room, you can hear the sound of the river and the prayers of a dozen temples and ashrams.

There are several hundred people sitting on cushions on the floor, drawn from all over the world, with perhaps half from Prem Baba's native country of Brazil. Prem Baba sits in a chair and speaks in his native Portuguese in a clear and resonant voice, with an English translation provided. He uses no notes, speaks spontaneously whatever comes to him in the moment, often in response to questions from the audience.

These talks, ably translated and edited by Christian Modern, Abraham Gutmann and Alegria Demeestere, are organized so as to introduce you to the Path of the Heart. The sequence of chapters leads you generally from the inside world to the outside world of relationships, society, and nature, and from the "lower self" of egoic struggles to the "higher self" of altruistic service.

If I may offer a word of counsel to the reader of these pages, do not take any of these teachings at face value. Try them out and see for yourself if they help you. Don't accept them as beliefs – that would not do justice to them. Treat them rather as working hypotheses to be tested out in your daily life. Have the courage to try, to fail, and to try again until you find something that works for you.

This book calls for a different kind of reading than perhaps what is usual. It helps to read it slowly, put the book down often, and ruminate. The words may seem strange – as if you were visiting a foreign land. You may not understand every word. You may not agree with all that is said. You may find some concepts strange. I certainly did at first, but then gradually came to appreciate that it was not about agreement but about welcoming whatever was useful for my own understanding and inner work. If there is one gem in here that serves you, that helps you on the path from suffering to joy, that helps you understand who you truly are, then it is more than worthwhile.

I encourage you to listen to what is behind the words. Listen to what the words point to. They are signs to a world that is inside you. Let them, if you will, inform the path that is yours alone to travel. These teachings are intended to awaken your own inner guide. For in the end, the teacher is inside you.

I wish you peace.

William Ury

Chapter Summaries

PART ONE: Introducing the Path of the Heart

1. Eight Keys to Inner Peace

Inner peace is the most elevated of virtues, and the secret yearning of all beings is to be at peace. Inner peace is a deep acceptance of what is. It can be attained only by letting go of the ego, by not opposing anything or anyone.

2. Realizing Truth by Recognizing Illusion

We look at the world and at ourselves through tinted lenses. We need to remove these colored glasses to perceive spiritual reality. Spiritual reality is what truly exists, without distortion, without any interpretation of our minds, which are loaded down with acquired knowledge.

3. The Yogas of Knowledge, Devotion and Action

Each person brings certain gifts and talents to this world. You have to give what you came here to give. You brought the gifts – are you going to hide them away in the closet? *Karma yoga,* the path of service, means giving your gifts away with love and tenderness.

PART TWO: *The ABC of Spirituality*

4. Stages in the Transformation of the Lower Self

Through this questioning process you liberate the repressed feelings that sustain negative patterns. An alchemical transmutation occurs: pride transforms into humility, lust into devotion, and fear into trust. The transmutation and integration of these personality distortions is the meaning of the word purification.

5. The Mask of Withdrawal

The tendency to shy away from others is a distortion of the divine attribute of serenity. When we aren't yet ready to manifest real serenity, we end up falling into this repetitive pattern of withdrawing from people as an accessible substitute for authentic serene non-attachment.

6. The Nine Matrices of the Lower Self

There is a specific reason why we do not want to critically examine the ways we fool ourselves. We may be getting some pleasure out of it. Even though this is negatively-oriented pleasure, it is pleasure nonetheless. It makes us continue to hold onto the self-deceit even though it brings us tremendous suffering to do so, for this may be the only kind of pleasure we know.

7. Pride and Humility

Unchecked vanity travels with its henchmen, stubborn self-will and fear, and this trio conspires to sustain a false self-image. The commander is vanity, the favorite son of pride. Vanity is distraction. Maybe that is why it is so dear to the devil: because it prevents us from reaching that seventh *chakra*, the center of enlightenment.

8. Adversity: The Forgotten Guest

If this challenge is on your doorstep, it was surely addressed to you. This gift is *personal* and *non-transferable*. If you try to get rid of it, it will come back with a vengeance ... then the troubles will only increase in kind, frequency and degree until you accept the challenge.

9. Gratitude through Forgiveness

Gratitude brings about the reorientation from suffering to joy – but this kind of gratitude needs to be heartfelt. This teaching will be fulfilled when we can not only honor, but truly be thankful for our birth and our parents. Such gratitude emerges when we are able to forgive them.

PART THREE: Transforming Relationships

10. The Quest for Exclusive Love

The need for exclusive love distorts our perception. It prevents us from recognizing the gifts and talents we have brought to this world. When we feel ourselves to be occupying our rightful place in the world, we start taking delight in giving, instead of only wanting to receive.

11. On Intimacy

Relationships are among the most advanced courses we take in life. One of the major subjects in the course is intimacy and mutual revelation. This class is a prerequisite for even more advanced courses in life, because as we reveal ourselves to a partner, we also overcome our own defense mechanisms.

12. Spirituality and Sex

Sex is like a thermometer to measure our inner state. Don't hold a grudge towards the thermometer because it told you the real temperature! Why sex? Because there is no other such thermometer available. This is *the* measuring tool. To avoid using this thermometer is to avoid evolution.

13. Marriage for a New Era

In the new kind of marriage there is no lying and there are no secrets. Rather, there is a constant intention of transparency. You are open to receiving both the gifts and the truth that the other has to offer – even if some of those truths may be hard to swallow. Love includes the ability to see the sleeping potential in the other, and to awaken it.

PART FOUR: Transforming the World

14. Finding Yourself in these Times of Change

If your conditioning leads you to treat pleasure as an enemy, you are probably having a tough time and are feeling severely threatened with the changes happening in the world. These times are easier for us if we are attuned to freedom and ecstasy.

15. Money and Spirituality

Money is not in any way anti-spiritual. What *is* anti-spiritual is attachment to money, and to regard money as being an end rather than just a means to a greater goal. As we mature spiritually, we discover that learning how to deal with money is a key teaching in this great school of life.

16. Raising Children to Become Conscious Adults

We can be of particular service to the world by working with children, by giving them an education based on spiritual values. Such child-rearing could prevent children from acquiring the deeply entrenched conditioning from which it takes adults so much effort to free themselves.

17. Honoring the Feminine and Mother Earth

The sacred feminine manifests itself in many ways: in your mother, who gave you life; in women in general; in your physical body; and in nature itself, with all its manifestations. If you want to know how a nation is doing, observe its relationship with the feminine in all its forms. Do you sincerely honor the feminine?

18. Selfless Service and the Promise of Our Lineage

The fifth pillar of our *sankalpa* is "to awaken God in all, with the goal of putting an end to the play of suffering, and bringing light to the play of joy." In a single sentence, this is the true goal of all our work here.

PART FIVE: Higher Consciousness

19. The Transition from Lower to Higher Self

In the second stage, after some progress, we direct our will towards establishing a connection with the spiritual realm. Our prayer will be, "May our connection never be broken. May I eternally be a channel of Your light." Soon, duality disappears;

you no longer need words in your prayers, because you and God are One.

20. Four Keys to Sustaining Ecstasy

When we start noticing synchronicity leading us towards fulfilling our destiny through various "mysterious coincidences," we rescue our long-lost faith. We are in awe as we behold a higher intelligence that guides us and guides everything in the world.

21. Putting God in First Place

Always remember that awareness of the divine presence is your real goal; so do not waste your life simply attempting to accumulate a lot of stuff. When we die, we will not be able to take our bodies, or even a single grain of dust with us. All that we take will be our consciousness, and the net weight of our positive and negative karma.

22. Sanatana Dharma: The Path of Enlightenment

When the Divine touches you, there is no going back. As much as karma may dictate that you work for a corporation and take care of a family, if you have been touched by the mystery, you will feel compelled to solve the equation. This happens to each person in their own time; it happens naturally.

PART SIX: Master Teachers

23. Rama, Sita, and Commitment to the Truth

Rama represents commitment to the truth, whatever the truth may be. In the face of this greater truth we have to confront lesser, disagreeable truths about ourselves. Rama is the quintessence of integrity and of complete loyalty to the truth. He is the personification of *dharma*. If you emulate him you will experience inner peace and love.

24. The Inner Mysteries of Shiva, Ganga and Durga Devi

Shiva is inside and outside – He is everywhere. Shiva is cosmic consciousness itself, which deliberately chooses to manifest itself in a specific form out of compassion. Shiva is the transformational power of the universe alongside Brahma, the creative power, and Vishnu, the power of preservation. Shiva means grace, good fortune, and prosperity.

25. The Bhagavad Gita on the Struggle between the Higher and the Lower Self

The higher self has triumphed when you, the person in evolution, finally realize who you really are. Until then you continue battling in an *ascending spiral:* your enemies become ever fiercer, your victories ever bigger. If you persevere, at some point you will be able to recognize your inner divine being.

26. The Essence of the Teachings of Jesus Christ

In my view, Jesus Christ is the power of forgiveness. He is the power that cures us of all the negative characteristics which we carry in our psyches and hearts. He unties the knots that bind us to our karmic burdens. Forgiveness and gratitude give us access to this healing; and we can only open our hearts once we are healed.

PART SEVEN: Challenging Questions

27. Is this Religion?

My religion is love. It is the path of enlightenment. If you let me, I can guide you until you are able to free yourself from all dogmas and concepts, from all acquired knowledge; so that only the purest truth blossoms in your heart.

28. What about all this Devotion?

The way of the heart is the simplest of all paths. The children of God dance in divine madness, for they know that God takes care of everything in their lives. I know it's scary to lose control. This is how it goes on a personal level too, isn't it? When you fall in love, you melt like ice cream. So can you imagine falling into divine love?

29. What about the Guru-Disciple Relationship?

The guru is like an oasis in the desert, a window to the heavens, a bridge to eternity. The emergence of a true guru is a rare occurrence, but the same can be said about true disciples: they are hard to find. A true disciple is that extraordinary being who has developed spiritual receptivity.

PART EIGHT: Concluding Meditations

30. Redefining Enlightenment

Maybe we need to redefine the goal: if enlightenment means realizing our true nature – which is love and light – then behaving with disrespect or indifference is a sign that we are nowhere near our goal.

31. Becoming a Channel of Light

Through the healing silence, take refuge in your true inner being, who is guided by the compass of love alone. There is no power on earth greater than love. It can heal all wounds, dissolve all separations, and resolve all conflicts.

About the Glossary

For the reader's benefit a glossary is offered with definitions and explanations of the most common psycho-spiritual and Sanskrit terms used by Prem Baba. Being familiar with them will help the reader get the most out of this book.

FROM SUFFERING TO JOY

PART ONE

Introducing the Path of the Heart

Through this process of inner cleansing we discover many truths about ourselves. On this path of the heart we come up against obstacles that need to be moved out of our way, and we learn how to identify and remove them. With every piece of junk we get rid of, we open up the channels for our love to flow freely.

1
Eight Keys to Inner Peace

Inner peace is the most elevated of virtues, and the secret yearning of all beings is to be at peace. Inner peace is a deep acceptance of what is. It can be attained only by letting go of the ego, by not opposing anything or anyone. Peace is born from profound trust in God. It emerges when we surrender completely and allow the inner voice of God to guide us.

Looking back at my personal story, I can see that my search for inner peace began at a very young age. I was barely a teenager when I joined a school of spiritual knowledge. I remember that the teacher once said, "People call themselves human, but in truth they are but humanoids: big-brained, two-legged creatures, posing as human beings. In their present condition people are unable to perceive what they really need. They believe they will be happy if they obtain this or that object or title, but all that grasping shows they are still too immature to understand that real happiness only arises from peace in one's heart and mind."

After hearing such a stark indictment of humanity, my first response was, "Could he possibly be referring to me?" Up until that point it had seemed that I could only attain peace once I had mastered my material surroundings. To hear this devastating assessment of mankind, and to suddenly perceive, in the deepest recesses of my heart, that it was true, was like a knockout blow. But that teaching opened the doors of truth to me.

It took me quite some time to realize that the mastery I had been seeking outwardly was but a symbol of the love I wanted to receive. It took me a while to comprehend that I would only attract the love I so fervently sought into my life once that same love was flowing freely from me. By "comprehend," I mean understand in the deepest way with our hearts rather than just with our minds. I eventually realized that I had been walking in exactly the wrong direction; the world itself was the real school of life. If the goal was to love consciously, I would have to learn to give rather than always wanting something in return.

Recognizing that I was walking in the opposite direction of inner peace, I was able to turn around and take my first step back towards it. I realized that living one's life often boiled down to an attempt to force the other to love us. We can waste our whole life in this futile pursuit. We find plenty of reasons to complain that we are not receiving enough love, since we sense deep down that forced love is not love at all. And so we find ever more reasons to distract ourselves and to get sidetracked from our goal of attaining inner peace.

Inner peace is only attainable by freeing ourselves from the need we feel to be loved exclusively, a need that is programmed into us from childhood. When you free yourself from this conditioning, you feel that you truly belong. When you feel this sense of belonging, you experience inner peace. But you will only feel connected once you are able to look beyond appearances and perceive the being that lies behind them. Identification with appearances causes us to compare ourselves to others. It makes us crave whatever we think someone else has and we don't. It took me a while to understand the words of that teacher and to realize that I am not my appearance or my physical body, just as you are not your body.

As time went on, I discovered that there are certain keys that open the door to peace. If you can remember to use these keys, it will be easier for you to embody peacefulness.

The first key to inner peace is to **cultivate silence**. Creative acts are born of silence. When we understand this, we naturally seek to cultivate silence in our daily lives. But for the most part, our minds are constantly busy making noise that we call thought. We think compulsively because we believe Descartes' erroneous conclusion that, "I think, therefore I am." It seems that we can only live well if our minds stay in charge. When you comprehend that compulsive thought is humanity's great illness, you will be able to observe the stream of random thoughts passing through your mind without identifying yourself with them. As you focus ever more on the empty space between one thought and the next, you will remain in a deep state of stillness. Only then can you begin to listen to the inner voice of your higher self.

The price for divine realization is solitude. It is crucial that you learn to be alone and to remain in silence. If you prefer, you may call this practice meditation, but don't worry about conceptualizing what meditation means. Simply withdraw into yourself and remain in silence – that is the essence.

The second key to inner peace is **truth**. Please understand that truth does *not* mean that we go out and tell people everything that pops into our head without considering whether they are ready to hear it or how it might affect them. Rather, truth means to follow the calling of our heart. If there is discomfort and suffering in your life, it is because there is still a veil of illusion enveloping you. So summon up the courage to look squarely at your self-deceit. Identify how and why you are still not able to be honest with yourself and with life, how and why you are wearing masks, and why you cannot be spontaneous and natural. Why is it that you need to pretend to be something that you are not? Take a good look at the various areas of your life: only with courage will you be able to face the truth. This is very demanding work, but you will see that it's very fulfilling.

The third key to inner peace is **correct action.** This has nothing to do with morality: correct action is not dependent upon corroboration from the outside world. You are not following an instruction manual of right and wrong, so throw away your "should book." Correct action is what the heart dictates – it is truth in action. It is having the courage to be you, to be authentic: this is treading the path of the heart.

The fourth key is a natural consequence of the previous one: **non-violence**, the hallmark of egoless action. Non-violence comes from purifying our consciousness of any and all brutality.

It means that we make a firm intention not to be a channel for destruction and evil that may cause suffering to others, whether on a tangible level or on a more subtle level. By "evil," I mean a defensive response, arising from numbing, that is destructive to ourselves and others.

It is natural then that we manifest the fifth key, which is the ***constant remembrance of God***. God is in everything and in everyone. Our life is transformed into a prayer. It becomes an offering to God. By using this key of remembrance we are able to look at others and see beyond outward appearances to perceive and revere God in all. This is the sincere *namaste:* "The Divine in me greets the Divine in you."

The sixth key is ***presence***. Presence is the master key that illuminates all darkness. Even though this is the master key, not everyone is ready to handle it. People's minds are still identified with various imprints and games. In order to be able to embody presence, one first needs to go through a process of purification. This is the work of the transformation of the lower self. Focus on this until you are ready to manifest presence.

In the process of cultivating presence, we can use the seventh key, ***conscious love***. But to do so, we first need to recognize our lack of love. What are the situations and people you are still unable to love? What is keeping your wellspring of love from flowing forth? What lies behind this need to keep your heart closed?

Through this process of inner cleansing we discover many truths about ourselves. We learn how to identify and remove the obstacles that emerge as we walk the path of the heart. With every piece of junk we get rid of, we open up the channels for our love to flow freely.

Then we are ready for the eighth key: ***selfless service.*** This is love in action. It occurs when we give ourselves to another person sincerely, without wearing masks, without the need to please them, nor worrying about what would be considered the right thing to do. We become love, always flowing in a positive direction.

If you use these eight keys in your life, you will inevitably experience peace. I am only sharing with you what I myself have experienced.

2
Realizing Truth by Recognizing Illusion

Let us speak a bit about spirituality and awakening consciousness. I use the word spirituality to refer to reality in its most objective sense. Another possible synonym for spirituality is Truth – the irrefutable Truth, that which is. Truth is what remains after removing all beliefs, concepts and prejudices, after removing any type of imaginative interpretation. By imaginative interpretation here, I do not mean the creative process that gives rise to inventions, art and beauty. I am using it to mean that screen of judgments, concepts and labels that prevents us from objectively experiencing what we are seeing. Imagination in this sense is a constant background chatter in our minds, be it fantasy or delusion, that distorts reality. The human mind often invents stories about what it sees. This self-deception happens when you let your imagination run away with you – you dream in a waking state. People constantly imagine all sorts of things regarding their personal identity and about what the future has in store for them:

but this personal fantasy inevitably causes suffering. Spirituality is contact with reality, contact with existence beyond the realm of imagination. This awareness of reality frees you from suffering. When all this imaginary thought is removed, Truth remains.

It is intrinsically challenging to speak about Truth, because Truth is an experience, and thus it is always difficult to translate into words. For example: how can we express the experience of love in words? How can we spell out joy or ecstasy? How can we explain compassion? Truth seems too great and words too small for the job. Nevertheless, we may use words as a bridge to the experience of Truth. We use words to transition from the state of mind to the state of no-mind, which is a state of stillness and absence of obsessive thinking. As your questions get answered, your mind slowly becomes less agitated and begins to quiet down, so that it becomes more receptive. It is then flooded by consciousness, which ultimately gives way to the experience of Truth.

The mind seeks to understand the Truth. It wants a rational answer, and it gets all worked up in search of that answer. But real answers can only come when the mind quiets down. With a quiet mind we deeply *comprehend* rather than just superficially understand Truth. This profound comprehension allows us to *experience* Truth, and only through experience can knowledge transform itself into wisdom.

For example, your mind may get distressed seeking an understanding of love. You may ponder many theories, or even propound your own theories about love; but you will only know what love is when you start loving. You have to live this experience. As long as we remain in the mind and the intellect we will just be acquiring knowledge; but sooner or later we need to start letting go of this knowledge, because it is just a collection of thoughts. Even if this knowledge helps guide us at first, there comes a point when it will have to be abandoned in order to make room for experience. Experience transforms knowledge into wisdom. If knowledge does not become wisdom it poisons us rather than making us wiser.

We sit together in a *satsang*. *"Satsang"* is a word with several meanings: to sit in good company; to be together with an enlightened being and receive teachings; it also means an encounter with the Truth. In a deeper sense, *satsang* is the *experience* of Truth. To sit with an enlightened being or even to receive knowledge is a kind of game, but a divine game that is conducive to the experience of Truth. Truth is only realized through direct experience. In other words, enlightenment begins when imaginary thought ceases. By sitting in *satsang*, your mind quiets down so that consciousness can reveal itself. I cannot give you Truth or even tell you of it – no one can. What I *can* do is clear a path; but only *you* can actually walk this path and experience it. You take that journey all by yourself.

When you recognize your true nature, you feel whole. You experience joy for no apparent reason. You find an enduring inner peace that is not dependent on external events. And this enlightened state is what you have been looking for; this is what every human being seeks, even if they are not always aware of it.

For imaginary thought to cease, clean up the garbage that clutters your mind. This garbage is composed of concepts, prejudices, beliefs, ideas, and suppressed feelings. At some point certain thoughts transformed themselves into feelings that were later denied. These in turn act as dams that prevent your divine consciousness from flowing abundantly.

BECOMING PRESENT

We human beings are fascinated by our own stories, by our imaginary self-images. This enchantment gives rise to our personal fantasy. We do not want to wake up from the dream, even when it's a bad dream and a part of us really wants to wake up. When we are dreaming, we believe the dream to be reality. Isn't this how it goes? Only when we fully wake up do we discover that it was just a dream. This is why you, who are a spiritual seeker in search of peace, should dedicate all your energy towards waking up from this dream. Direct your energy towards letting go of your personal fantasy, which means waking up. This is only possible when the mind quiets down, when you become completely present, here and now. You then become a silent witness of everything around you. This silent witness does not judge what it sees, it simply observes. Thus, observation is the main entryway to the state of no-mind. Allow yourself to experience being the observer; then transform that observation into wisdom. The ***practice of observation*** is the first step.

When we look at something, we automatically transform this image into words and thoughts. In between us and what we are seeing is a screen of judgments, concepts and labels. This prevents us from objectively experiencing what we are seeing. We look at the world and at ourselves through tinted lenses. This is what I refer to as "imagination." We need to remove these colored glasses to perceive spiritual reality. Spiritual reality is what truly exists, without distortion, without any interpretation of our minds, which are loaded down with acquired knowledge.

The second step is ***wholeness in action***. We make ourselves whole by acting through our body, by sharpening the awareness that we inhabit our body. This is how we can quiet the compulsive thinker, the one who translates everything it experiences into words. Through observation and wholeness in action we expand our perception. This sharpening of perception in turn decreases imaginary thought. This is the essence of spiritual practice.

If you notice yourself falling into the trap of repetitive thinking, pay attention to the content of your soundtrack. If it repeats itself, there is something in your past that you have not accepted. You will then need to do some healing work to get in touch with past hurts and the resentment they generated. You should work through these denied feelings until you have integrated them into your being. By quieting those soundtracks that play in a never-ending loop inside your mind you may free yourself from the past.

The path of meditation frees us from the grip of mental soundtracks. This path is divided into two practices: first, *investigative* or ***analytical meditation,*** which confronts those denied aspects of ourselves buried in the dungeons of the unconscious. Secondly, ***meditation focused on emptiness,*** which anchors presence through observation and wholeness in action. The former practice is a work of healing, purification and transformation of the lower self, sometimes referred to as "the wounded child."[1] These practices together comprise the path of meditation. Some people let go of imaginary thought and realize peace by following this path; others release such fantasies and realize peace through the path of love, the path of devotion.

Letting the Love Flow

The essence of the path of devotion, or ***bhakti yoga,*** is the renunciation of the fruits of one's actions: it's to make a prayer of each and every action. For such surrender to be authentic, it is vital first to have a glimpse of God, which might be through a spiritual master teacher or through another manifestation of divine consciousness. The path of love means that you work unceasingly to surrender yourself to this manifestation. It is a love affair. Your love grows until you melt into one with the Divine. Everything that you do, you do for God: waking up, showering, getting dressed, cooking, eating, working, singing – all for God … and you do so because you have glimpsed the eternal Truth, and have chosen the path of devotion. If you were moved to such

---

[1] See glossary of psycho-spiritual terms for an explanation of the "lower self" and the "wounded child."

a degree that you recognized a master teacher, you will naturally turn your heart and mind towards him or her. Since the master teacher is liberated, your mind and heart will naturally liberate themselves if you connect yourself with him or her. Devotion is the most direct path, but to walk this path, it is essential to have a glimpse of the Divine; otherwise you won't get anywhere. Without this glimpse, you will merely create mystical fanaticism, and get lost in the labyrinth of your runaway imagination.

At some point the path of meditation and the path of love inevitably intersect. This union happens because, when we awaken, we become a silent witness. As a silent witness, we love everything and everyone, and we know that we are born to serve that aspect of the Divine that awakened our faith. By doing so we experience *Sanatana Dharma*, by which I mean the combination of love and selfless service that is the essential nature of life.

We will then seek to use our gifts and talents as vehicles for the expression of this love. When we serve the Divine, using our talents for the other's awakening, we experience joy, and we feel fulfilled. This satisfaction arises because we have a reason to wake up in the morning. We feel joy in waking up. The joy comes from this deep fulfillment. As light passes through us to the other, we experience peace.

The key aspect of imaginary thought created by identification with the false self is the mistaken need to receive love, attention and recognition from the outside. Only when this illusion of neediness is recognized as such and we realize the Truth, do we discover that peace only comes from giving, not from receiving.

Great joy lies in realizing that you are an endless source of generosity and love. Due to the influence of our imaginary thinking we believe we always need to be on the receiving end of others' giving. In this fantasy, we are needy children who have nothing, and are dependent on the charity of others. We cling to this figment of our imagination because our minds are fixated on the past. Our emotional body acts like a child who desperately needs exclusive love. When we free ourselves from this childish need we can realize that we already have everything we need. We have it in abundance, so much so that we can share it freely with others.

The need for exclusive love is the main pillar of your personal fantasy. It is born from the identification with the false self. This demand that the other love *only* you is like a disease – a serious illness – and you need to be cured of it. This illusory need for exclusive love causes all types of turmoil and distress, games of accusation and guilt, which are the main causes of the world's suffering. We only cause ourselves misery by averting our gaze and distracting ourselves with the faults of others; we do not want to acknowledge our identification with this idea of scarcity, this idea that something is lacking, and that someone else needs to give to us. Possessiveness and neediness are illusion, not spirituality.

SPIRITUALITY = REALITY

Spirituality is synonymous with reality. To walk the path of spirituality is to walk the path of reality. Spirituality is the process of continually expanding our perception of ourselves until we recognize that we are the source of love. By acknowledging this truth we attain the inner peace we seek.

We spend our lives trying to become the most precious gemstone – and we want the other to recognize and acknowledge our great value. We do not realize that we are *already* a diamond, the most precious of gems. It is only due to this personal fantasy of neediness that we think we are a mere pebble. We spend our lives pursuing the goal of becoming the most precious jewel that we already are. You don't have to do anything. Indeed, your challenge is to stop doing.

Even meditation and devotion are but tools to help you stop compulsive thinking and doing. I know that you are still in need of these methods, because the language of silence and spontaneity has been forgotten. May you recall that you already know this language, and may you understand it once again. May you expand your awareness ever more, to the point where you think of yourself as none other than an endless source of generosity. ***You are the source of all that is good, joyful and prosperous.*** I pray that these words may echo in your hearts. May you put them into practice, and thereby transform this knowledge into wisdom. You can only receive my transmission if you put it into practice; otherwise it all simply returns to me.

There comes a time in a seeker's life when the need for spiritual experience becomes so great, when the thirst for God becomes so intense, that one lets go of everything to spend time with a master teacher, or to be in a spiritual school, an ashram. If you are drawn to the spiritual life, but your karma does not allow you to follow through on your intentions, you will suffer. You suffer because you need the water of life, but you will not go to its source to get it. This is why I am here: to quench the thirst of seekers, who may in turn help others.

3
The Yogas of Knowledge, Devotion and Action

I would like to help you overcome obstacles to embodying presence and light. Some of you have already experienced grace, and through it have been transformed. Others require knowledge to dissipate the clouds of confusion and let the sun shine through.

There are three factors that promote expansion of consciousness. They are: **jnana yoga**, or *self-knowledge*, a key feature of which is *investigative* or *analytical meditation;* **bhakti yoga**, or *devotion;* and **karma yoga**, *selfless action.* These are the three pillars upon which a harmonious life can be built.

SELF-KNOWLEDGE

In our personal lives, we may engage the first pillar, self-knowledge, *jnana yoga*, through our daily spiritual practice, our *sadhana. Sadhana* is a tool that unites us with God through sharpening the awareness of who we are. It is a process of self-investigation by which we remove layer after layer of self-deceit, until we arrive at an understanding of who we really are. This is the first step in the process of self-discovery that we refer to as the "ABC of Spirituality." We ask the questions, "Who am I?" and "Who inhabits this body?"

You will progress in this practice only when you recognize that you are an embodiment of divine love, in the form of *Atman*, Divinity itself. *Atman* is the life that speaks through all mouths and lives in all bodies. You can recognize yourself beyond your name, beyond your body, beyond your story. You realize that you are of the divine presence that emanates eternal bliss and joy. You are happy without any external reason because you are the source of happiness. This is you. This is your true identity.

Jnana yoga, the method of uniting the soul with the Absolute through self-knowledge, leads to the realization of the real you. However, for this true identity to manifest, you first need to become aware of your identification with illusion. It is important to realize just how much you still identify with your name and your body. Notice just how much you are still fascinated by your own story, believing yourself to *be* this ego. As long as this false identity remains, your true identity is obscured. This is why the first step in *jnana yoga* is to *identify your identifications* so that you can release them.

We undertake this recognition of identifications through self-observation, the main technique on this path. We identify layer upon layer of illusion. These layers are mind creations, thoughts that we feed with much attention, until we believe that they are actually true. Certain thoughts act as autonomous complexes, as if they were independent entities. We may feel as if we are possessed, that alien entities are acting through our psychophysical system. This is indeed happening, but it is only a manifestation of our obsession. We have fed so much energy to our runaway imagination that it has acquired a life of its own and acts on its own whim. So in the beginning of your self-observation process you identify these layers of illusion that you have believed to be you, until they fall away. This continues until, at the propitious moment, Truth reveals itself.

One should not neglect this aspect of *jnana yoga*. You should dedicate yourself to the practice of self-observation until you recognize yourself as *Atman*. You have made progress on this path when you stop becoming distracted by the outer world and by thoughts from the superficial defense mechanisms of the ego. These thoughts make you believe that the answers lie outside of you, that the negative situations in your life are caused by external circumstances, that *others* are to blame.

Don't be fooled by your compulsion to blame – simply do not waste your time with such distractions. The process of self-discovery is demanding. You'll find that you are identified with many negative traits that are not pleasant to look at. This realization may cause shame and the desire to escape the confrontation. Remember that what you observe is only an identification, not your ultimate reality.

One of the challenges that arises while shaking off numbness and ignorance of these identifications, is that people begin to think of themselves as terrible monsters. This is but a trick of your ego: it is that same identification coming in through the back door. That boogeyman is not you. You simply recognize your identification with it.

Remember that if you haven't realized that you are a manifestation of love and light, there is still a layer of deception in your system. Your work, your prayer, is to focus on overcoming your propensity to identify with illusion. If you run into arrogance, shame or stubborn self-will, persist. Commit yourself to looking at it, even though it may offend your personal vanity and wound your pride. From now on, if you find yourself in conflict, recognize and acknowledge *your* responsibility in the matter.

Gradually you notice that your identification with destructive games is weakening. You understand that they are just thoughts, just clouds passing by. The clouds may be light or dark ones, but remember that they are just clouds. *You are the sky that observes the clouds.* Once you observe the transitory without becoming identified with it, you will be close to realizing your true identity.

DEVOTION

The second pillar is the path of devotion, known as *bhakti yoga.* If you are able to practice this way of devotion, it indicates that a transformation has occurred. This transformation is a consequence of your work on the first pillar, *jnana yoga.* Love takes root once we transform lust into devotion. On the path of devotion we redirect all our energy towards the manifestation of the Divine that awakened our faith. We put the Divine in first place and dedicate our lives to it. We keep God in our minds and hearts at all times. Everything that we do is done for God. We dedicate our lives to God so that every act is a prayer to our Beloved.

This love begins to arise subtly as knowledge illuminates our minds. As we disassociate ourselves from images, random thoughts, and the false self, we allow the light of love, our true self, to emerge in very subtle ways. In the beginning, the spring is just a trickle, because our energy and our love are still occupied with our various identifications: our need to quarrel, to compete, and to struggle for power. We are still lost in games of lust. By "lust," an old term, I do not mean moral sin, nor do I mean merely strong sexual desire. Rather, I am referring to the manipulative use of sexual desire to obtain power over another person. More starkly, lust is the use of sexual energy to take revenge on a partner or someone who may feel attracted to you. As we identify these tendencies, and distance ourselves from them, the spring of devotion becomes a brook that then overflows its banks, until it becomes a great river flowing towards the ocean.

As this river of divine love flows, we are truly taken with the Divine, like Mirabai, who was completely in love with the Divine in the form of Krishna. She renounced a kingdom, renounced everything for her devotion to Krishna. She had her Beloved in her mind and heart at all times, until one day she became one with him. With this unity, the river became the ocean; two melted into One. This is the path of devotion.

SELFLESS SERVICE

The third pillar is *karma yoga,* love in action, or selfless service. You practice this yoga of action by dedicating yourself to becoming an instrument of the divine will. You can only practice *karma yoga* perfectly when you are able to clearly see your identifications during your self-observation, and understand that this is not you. You disassociate yourself from the ego that always needs to take credit for its achievements and receive the fruit of its actions. The ego constantly bargains with life and wants something in exchange for everything it does. We might witness this in our constant need for reassurance, or in our hankering for material gain, a simple look from someone, or anything else we might desire.

The perfect *karma yogi* resolves desire into his or her being – there remain no more desires. Everything one does is done out of love for God. Like Mirabai, one sees God in all and serves God in all. This is the essence of service: to put your gifts at the service of the Divine, at the service of goodness itself. The quintessence of goodness is to use your talents towards seeing others happy. You truly take pleasure in seeing the other shine, without concern about whether or not you are shining. Service means using your gifts to bring out the best in others, always moving towards selflessness.

I am speaking about love in action, in the service of goodness. I am speaking about the purpose of life itself, the purpose for which you have been born. What do you think you are here for anyway?

Each person brings certain gifts and talents to this world. You have to give what you came here to give. You brought the gifts – are you going to hide them away in the closet? *Karma yoga,* the path of service, means giving your gifts away with love and tenderness. In this way you fulfill the purpose of your birth. This love takes you to God.

PART TWO

The ABC of Spirituality

Note of Acknowledgment: In this section and throughout the book I use a number of the terms and insights that are presented in the Pathwork lectures given by Eva Pierrakos and beautifully codified in the books *Fear No Evil, Creating Union* and *Surrender to God Within*, published by Pathwork Press.[2] For further information about lectures and courses, please visit the Pathwork website www.pathwork.org. I am immensely grateful to this deep and wise work.

[2] Pierrakos, Eva, and Donovan Thesenga. *Fear No Evil: The Pathwork Method of Transforming The Lower Self.* Charlottesville: Pathwork Press, 2000. Print.

Pierrakos, Eva, and Judith Saly. *Creating Union: The Essence of Intimate Relationship.* Charlottesville: Pathwork Press, 2002. Print.

Pierrakos, Eva, and Donovan Thesenga. *Surrender to God Within: Pathwork at the Soul Level.* Charlottesville: Pathwork Press, 1997. Print.

4
Stages in the Transformation of the Lower Self

Question: During the retreat last week I saw everything so clearly and felt like I really understood the workings of the lower self. Now I have returned to a state in which it is more difficult to identify the false selves. That day's realization seemed overwhelming, but now I miss the clarity of seeing my true inner workings. How can I permanently establish the clarity to identify and renounce those false selves?

Prem Baba: This forgetfulness is a natural phenomenon of the process of purification. You may remember and forget again many times. In the process of purification and transformation of the lower self, which is the ABC of Spirituality, there are *four stages of the evolution of consciousness*. Here I am drawing upon the insights that were received by Eva Pierrakos and that are beautifully summed up in the book *Fear No Evil*.

In the *first stage* the person in evolution is *sleepwalking*, living in the present moment without knowing it. The person merely follows the dictates of their senses and is dominated by unconscious impulses, both positive and negative. This unconsciousness sabotages happiness. It is a defense mechanism created as a response to painful events. We feel jealous or envious and are overwhelmed by that emotion. When we are so possessed, we are not present. Who am I at such a moment? Jealousy, envy? At that moment we completely identify with that little particle of our identity. At this stage we may get angry and frustrated with ourselves for being this way, but can't do anything about it yet. The possibility of behaving differently may not even cross our minds.

In the *second stage* of the development of consciousness – the first stage in the process of awakening – we begin to realize that we aren't that random impulse passing through us, that the *lower self is not our ultimate reality*. We now realize that jealousy, anger, fear, and pride are just visitors that we invited in, but who will eventually leave. We can distance ourselves from our reactivity once we observe these false selves and the destructive manifestations of the ego's masks. We start to observe ourselves objectively. At this stage we are awake enough to realize when we have been possessed. We realize that this too shall pass, for it isn't our final reality. It is just a current passing through us.

When we mature to the *third stage* of evolution, we *make a conscious choice whether or not to allow a sensation or impulse from the lower self to proceed into action.* For example, if you operate from an "I" dominated by pride, you always want to have the last word, to defend your point of view, and assert that your truth is better than another's. When you recognize this "I" coming, there is a moment of decision. You may choose just to go the other way. Conscious choice is a valuable tool in the *yogic* process of redirecting the will.

The question that was asked at the beginning pointed towards the third stage of this psycho-spiritual phase of the journey, when you employ your will to act differently. But you lost the light of awareness that helped you choose. Know that when your defenses are down again, clarity will return and light your way. Life moves as a wave. Sometimes you are up on the crest and sometimes down in the trough. When you are in the trough, don't fight it. Relax, because in a little while you are going back up again. That is how life is.

During the third stage it is really an epic struggle, as you are trying to recapture the throne. The *jnana* method of self-inquiry is the yoga that is the most appropriate for the process of the ABC of Spirituality. At this stage you need firmness, determination, discipline. At the same time you need a lot of gentleness to deal with the lower self. Indeed, beyond going easy on yourself, you need a sense of humor to work with your lower self. If you just fell in that same old hole yet again today – okay – tomorrow will bring another opportunity to act differently. The experience you acquire in this process prepares you to use the method of *Tantra*, the path of total acceptance. Further along the way you no longer even need those practices: you will do nothing but simply witness life and watch the river run.

The *fourth stage* is the integration of the aspect of the lower self that you have encountered on these steps of your journey: you transform this destructive pattern into wisdom. You are illuminated by the light of understanding, and so you perceive the cause-and-effect relationship. You are able to view the pattern from a distance, and ask, "Where does this impulse come from?" and "Why does it come up in me?" Through this questioning process you liberate the repressed feelings that sustain negative patterns. *An alchemical transmutation occurs: pride transforms into humility, lust into devotion, and fear into trust.* The transmutation and integration of these personality distortions is the meaning of the word purification.

A Tibetan lama once told me that the evolution of consciousness is like walking down the street and falling down a manhole. You remain in the sewer a long time. You don't even remember how you fell into the hole, much less understand why. One day you climb out, but you don't even know how you got out. The next day you walk down the same street and fall into the same hole. But this time you start to think about how and why you fell in. You focus your memory on how you climbed out before, and recall what worked. The next day you walk down that same street and you fall in that same manhole, but you climb out rapidly. One day you stop just short of the hole. I say that the process of purification is complete only when you walk down another street altogether.

I am trying to express the inexpressible here. Words are small containers for such a vast and ineffable reality. These stages are real, but they aren't stagnant pools – rather, the different stages always overlap each other. It is possible that you have already reached the fourth stage in one area of your life, while in another area you may still be at the first. It is also possible for an area of your life to fluctuate among the stages. Use this map for reference, but navigate the reality.

5
The Mask
of Withdrawal

Question: In looking at myself I have realized that I am stuck in a repetitive pattern: the tendency towards introversion, which makes me repeatedly withdraw from the world. This compulsion to withdraw has been at the root of all my problems, especially those that have emerged in relationships. It's hard for me to figure out the cause of this reluctance to interact with others because I am so totally locked up inside that it's difficult to feel any kind of emotion.

Prem Baba: The tendency to shy away from others is a distortion of the divine attribute of serenity. In the process of growing up and evolving, you came to believe that serenity would be a solution to the disquiet you felt when problems arose. But when we aren't yet ready to manifest real serenity, we end up falling into this repetitive pattern of withdrawing from people as an accessible substitute for authentic serene non-attachment.

THE GUARDIANS OF FEAR AND PRIDE

Withdrawal from human companionship is a response to your feelings of alienation and isolation. You won't let anyone touch you emotionally just as you do not allow yourself to touch another in a deeper way. You may have some superficial interaction with people, but when it comes to sharing a deeper part of yourself you run away. No one can get close to you, because, if they do, your inner alarm system is set off and warns you of approaching danger, the danger that you may stand exposed as you reveal yourself. So you are only willing to show people the introduction to your book, or maybe sometimes a single page somewhere in the middle. However, if you continue to develop your ability to observe yourself, you will be able to distinguish the presence of fear. *This fear reveals itself in your constant need of being in control.*

In particular, you are in need of controlling what you allow others to see, and so you express yourself only through the filter of conscious thought. You spend your time thinking out and planning every interaction down to the finest details. By doing this you hope that you will remember only to reveal that part of you that is likely to be accepted, and to hide the part you suspect will be judged unworthy. By sticking closely to the script you remain in control, hoping to look good in the encounter. In this way you show the other person that you are in charge of the situation.

If we are persistent in our self-observation, we will perceive that behind this fear lurks a symptom of pride known as shame.

Even if we do not quite know what exactly we are so ashamed of, this shame unavoidably limits us and makes sure that we remain mostly a closed book. The voice of shame warns us that it is extremely dangerous to venture beyond the protective wall of our introversion. When we are dominated by shame, we believe that safety can be guaranteed if we only reveal that specific part of our book that we know will be accepted. We strongly suspect that, if we reveal certain other pages, we will be rejected.

FORGOTTEN SECRETS

Usually it happens that the greater the drive to withdraw from the world, the more traumatic the incidents of humiliation or exclusion the person must have experienced on their journey through life. This is often the source of the urge to withdraw from the company of others. So next we should ask ourselves the following questions: "What do I have to be so ashamed of?" "What am I hiding within myself that is so ugly that I can't let it be seen?" "What could be so dangerous for the other to discover that would make it worth isolating myself?"

So you may have built a high wall and were ready to hang a big sign on it saying, "I don't feel anything." But that sign made you uncomfortable because it was a bit too starkly honest, so you scrapped it and instead painted one that says, "I have risen above having feelings." And whenever this claim is challenged, you make use of all the tools and ingenuity of the mind to justify your isolation.

The most extreme introverts are excessively uncomfortable around people, but sometimes relieve their isolation by making a friend. That's alright as long as the new friend is an acquaintance and has not yet discovered the footlocker full of un-confronted issues that one is trying to hide. As soon as the other begins to understand this, one finds a reason to quarrel with the would-be friend to escape from the possibility that, in the process of growing closer, one may have to open up that Pandora's box.

What are we so desperately trying to hide inside that box, even from our own eyes? Since the other is but a mirror of ourselves, we are trying to avoid looking at something we have still not accepted from our past. If we are withdrawn and isolated, it is because our mind is imprisoned by the past. In the present moment there can be no withdrawal, because presence reveals our true nature in a natural and spontaneous way. If we are still unable to be spontaneous, and are hiding behind a wall, it is because we are using withdrawal, this distortion of the divine attribute of serenity, to flee from something. Without realizing it, we live with the constant fear of being found out.

LETTING FEELINGS OUT

It's a sign of progress that you have identified and articulated what's going on in your psyche. In so doing, you have identified a common denominator to your personal issues. By observing your daily life and identifying the moments in which you were swallowed by unconsciousness, you have recognized this pattern of withdrawal.

The next step is to ask yourself, "What do I carry inside that is so ugly that I have to hide it and lock it up with multiple keys? What am I fleeing from? What in my life brings me such shame?" Perhaps what has been bothering you are merely ghosts: the root of the problem may have nothing to do with the current state-of-affairs of your life. But these ghosts may continue to haunt you nonetheless, since you have not been able to come to peace with them. Usually these ghosts do come from the past, and you may still carry them inside in a very tangible way.

Am I making myself understood? I will say it once again: *we will only be able to free ourselves from the past when we have come to peace with it.* We may choose to run wherever we like: we may go to the North or South Pole. We can flee to the center of the Earth, or even to another planet, but we will continue to carry these ghosts with us. We can only exorcize them through acceptance. It is imperative for your spiritual progress that you attain acceptance, or your light will be extinguished and you will live in darkness, haunted by ghosts from your past.

If this transmission somehow fits you, you should seek to understand what you are running away from. Imagine that all your secrets, every last one, were being laid bare and exposed to the group in attendance here today. Picture us making a circle and putting you in the middle of it. We don't even have to actually create the situation I am describing – just imagining it is enough to help you identify what it is you do not want anyone to find out.

I have had the opportunity to help people with this withdrawn personality type overcome the inability to let feelings through. In the process they discovered and worked on some very significant traumatic images from the past. A person comes to mind who had grown up in extreme poverty, and he experienced shocks of exclusion from friends whose families were better off. Another example is of a woman whose mother was considered crazy, and as a child this girl was very ashamed in the face of her neighbors' pity and mockery. Yet another person experienced painful childhood episodes related to her mother, and even after many years of therapeutic work she is still strongly ashamed of the mother she had. These are but a few examples to illustrate the kinds of traumas that can lead to introversion and isolation, and I hope that bringing them forward may aid you in your personal inner research.

What have you been unable to accept in your life? If you have not accepted the past, you have not accepted the present. In such a case, the practice of anchoring presence is made more difficult. The key is acceptance: but for that acceptance not to be just another thought, we must identify what is causing us shame. We must first identify the ghost so that we can then open ourselves up to accepting it, and ultimately let go of it.

Comment: I feel that before I can accept this part of myself I need to first scream a lot, let myself go and become the angry monster I feel within.

Prem Baba: You are coming closer to this dark area that has become an autonomous complex. The wounded child does not want to expose itself, but you can let it give voice to its pain and watch the process of catharsis as a witness. Allow the child to kick and scream. Allow your hatred to express itself. What does it want to say? You can do this inside yourself. Keep your observer present as the cleansing takes place. Continue to ask for help from the Divine Self to sustain you and prevent you from being swallowed by the fear and hatred you are facing. You must do this to keep your consciousness awake during this intense cleansing process. You will heal these wounds by allowing the catharsis to happen while simultaneously observing it without judgment. This is a very valuable technique, and it can be of great use during the earlier phase of the work, which is the purification and transformation of the lower self.

6

The Nine Matrices of the Lower Self

Question: Could you speak about deceit, and especially about self-deceit?

Prem Baba: Deceit is the ninth "matrix," or aspect, of the lower self, also called the wounded child. In the course of a human life, the wounded child acquires many layers of self-defense as a response to shocks of exclusion, rejection, abandonment and other emotional traumas. These defenses develop into varying degrees of selfishness and destructiveness.

Spanning a spectrum from most dense to most subtle, these matrices manifest themselves as the following urges:

Gluttony – any kind of compulsion: for example, the compulsion to eat, to speak, to buy or do things. This encompasses all types of voracity, including that of compulsive thinking.

Sloth – paralysis in confronting what needs to get done. Sloth or laziness is not a moral issue in and of itself: it's caused by frozen feelings that prevent a person from doing what they need to do. Sometimes sloth can actually impel a person to work hard and exert a lot of effort, but any effort done sloth-fully is by nature misdirected. Such effort cannot accomplish what actually needs to get done.

Greed – the desire to accumulate, to own things, to possess all the things that one covets. Through greed we get completely focused on outside references, but we can get greedy even about subtle internal experiences.

Envy – the impulse to destroy whoever possesses the object of your desire or to destroy the object itself. This can also mean putting the other down so that he too may experience the misery of your wretched state.

Wrath – the destructive impulse itself, in all of its manifesta-tions. It ranges from cold indifference to explosive bouts of hatred.

Pride – a particularly complex and intricate matrix, but this colonel most frequently appears escorted by its favorite lieu-tenants of vanity, shame, and bloated self-image.

Lust – the distortion of love, whereby you use your sexual energy to obtain power over the other in order to dominate them.

Fear – one of the primary defense mechanisms known to humans. Fear is the vigilant guard of denied feelings and manifests itself in numerous ways, especially through doubt and skepticism.

Deceit – is the last and trickiest matrix of the lower self. It enables us to convince ourselves and others that all of these compulsions are not our problem at all: "Not me!"

LAYERS OF DECEIT

The spectrum of matrices moves from dense to subtle: gluttony is indeed the aspect of the lower self that is the most apparent, while deceit is the ninth matrix because it is the most subtle, the most difficult to peg. It is important to notice that the subtle layers also permeate the more tangible ones. Looking specifically at deceit, we see that it is present in all the denser matrices.

Beyond this wider gradation, each matrix itself has aspects that vary from dense to subtle. The most obvious forms of deceit are when we lie to others. For instance, we may lie to our spouse or children so as to exalt ourselves and avoid criticism – deceit in the service of pride. These forms of deceit are blatant and more easily observable. Even if we ignore them, the feeling of guilt that they elicit will be unavoidable. Deeper than these forms of lying we may also discover a more subtle aspect of deceit called the delusion of self-sufficiency. This is the myth that you are a separate autonomous being, a story in which you believe that you know exactly who you are, and are sure that you are able to control life.

Until you see yourself as an embodiment of divine love and light, it means that there is still a veil of deceit enveloping you. This mainly takes the form of efforts at reaffirming the idea that we are the droplet rather than the ocean, that we are in control of our own destiny. So we make an effort to build a house and to accumulate possessions, because each new conquest reinforces the idea that we are a separate autonomous being. This very subtle layer of deceit can take over our very identity.

There are many small acts of self-deceit that sustain the over-arching illusion that you are a being separated from the whole. One such self-deceit makes us imagine that the things we need are lacking in the world. This fear of scarcity makes us want to grab, to take things by force. In this way we pressure nature to give beyond its capacity.

We force life to flow where we arbitrarily think it should flow. To fight against the current we need to fill up our lives with compulsive doing, and we exert much effort that only ends up causing us to suffer. This is because everything we do is based on the big lie of self-sufficiency. We think we know who we are and what we need. In this way we continue going around in circles, creating karma and imprisoning ourselves ever deeper inside this dream created by the veil of illusion, *Maya*. Why do we entangle ourselves ever more in the spider's web of *Maya*? Because we want to do things our own way. But this way is a dead-end, because we do not know who we are. All our efforts are designed only to reaffirm the myth of self-sufficiency.

If we can't see ourselves as the ocean itself, it means that we are still enveloped by a veil of illusion. Everything we do fails. We work so hard, and we even achieve some progress, but at some point we inevitably fail. We fail because what we are doing only strengthens the voice of this false self-sufficiency. At the deepest level we still want to prove something to some-one, someone who lives deep inside of us. This little someone personifies a frozen image from our past. We want to prove to our mother and our father that we are competent after all.

We want to prove that we can accomplish what they think we should be striving for.

TRUSTING IN THE TRUTH

Observe how you move through life. Do you act from trust or from fear? Are you able to trust in the truth that God gives you exactly what you need? God is life itself. Life gives you what you need to reach your goal, to fulfill the role your higher self is calling on you to play. As long as you keep trying to do things your own way, you will continue to stray from your real purpose in life, which is to acknowledge yourself as an embodiment of divine love and light.

The new building we are adding to the ashram here in Rishikesh is a good example of the call to surrender and to service. I did not want to build a hall, to undertake such a massive project; but I simply saw myself facing a situation where there were too many people to all fit into the hall we were using. I told Maharajji what was happening, and asked what to do. He said, "Build another hall." I told him that I did not have the money to build one. He said, "Don't worry, God will provide." Okay, if this is what you want, I will do it; by your grace it will be possible. Now the hall is being built, but it is really God building it. People give their donations and it is going up before our very eyes.

We come towards truth by following the way of the heart. There is no difference between what the guru says and what our intuition suggests. The teacher is one and the same. It does not matter whether the master teacher is the guru, our higher self, or life itself – the teacher is one. There is only one Truth.

Here we are in a guru-disciple relationship, as I am with Maharajji. We are fortunate to receive support directly through the physical presence of the guru, constantly helping us to sharpen our intuition. That is why we speak so much about surrender and trust. You will only surrender yourself if you feel that this guru really is mirroring your higher self. When delusion takes possession of us, when we are at the peak of suffering, we really need the guru's help. But if at that crucial moment we are unable to trust even the guru who awakened our faith, we will once again feel alone and isolated.

So the main way you deceive yourself is by convincing yourself that you are just the water droplet: you buy into the misguided concepts of "me" and of "mine." If you see yourself as a droplet, you will also view others as droplets. You will measure yourself against them, attached to the notion that you are inferior or superior to the other droplets. This in turn awakens all the matrices of the lower self, which further feed this competitive mindset. With this mentality we start feeling envious or jealous, start believing that the world will not give us what we need, and get trapped in a cycle of negativity. This sense of estrangement gives rise to humanity's dominant disease – neediness. Neediness generates the idea that we must receive exclusive love.

You are truly an embodiment of divine love. You are the very source of love itself. If you remove the veil of illusion and recognize yourself as being pure love, love will gush forth from you. You are an inexhaustible fountain of love. As long as love is flowing freely from you, it is natural for you to receive it back in abundance – but receiving is not your motive. You receive simply as a consequence of the law of cause and effect. You won't be waiting around to receive anything in return, because you are always in the eternal here and now. You realize that you are one with everything. In this way you will inevitably experience *ananda* – bliss – because you are a channel of divine love.

EXPOSING THE BIG LIE

Until we eliminate this self-deception about scarcity, we will not recognize the truth of abundance. We will continue to think of ourselves as needy. We believe we are empty and need to be filled. We believe all love and attention must be turned only towards us because there might not be enough to go around, and we are desperate to ensure our own supply of the good stuff. We want our personal vision of scarcity to be acknowledged as valid by all, and we actually seek out those prepared to confirm that our self-deception is indeed true. So we validate each other's illusions; but if the other simply looks away at the wrong moment we already feel slighted and pick a fight. We spend our whole lives clamoring for this recognition. If the other does not acknowledge us in the way we expect to be acknowledged, it means that they have let us down. As you can see, illusions can be piled on top of illusions.

The isolated water droplet feels desperately vulnerable, empty and inadequate. This spurs it to create another more superficial layer of delusion to convince itself that it is very important indeed. This outer layer of personal fantasy can only be sustained with the collusion of another person. Sometimes, for example, you might believe yourself to be ugly, even though that idea is a distortion of reality. You then naturally create another layer of distortion by making yourself believe that you are beautiful. You become enslaved to anyone who comes along and confirms that indeed you are beautiful. If they were ever to say that you are ugly, even out of spite, you are liable to fall apart. You have yet to deal with the misguided beliefs you maintain at this deeper level, where you consider yourself to be ugly. You need to look at this until you fully comprehend the truth that beyond beautiful and ugly, *you are beauty itself.*

Until you are able to feel health, prosperity, and joy flowing abundantly in everything you do, until you are able to feel that your life is full of light, it means that a curtain of illusion still envelops you. It may be a very thin veil, but it is still there. Spiritual practice, *sadhana,* will only be valuable if we use it as a means to confront delusion, whether it be the myth of false self-sufficiency or the myth of neediness. Without this self-confrontation we will only be fooling ourselves. And it is possible to misuse spiritual practices in order to feed a personal fantasy rather than overcome it.

An appropriate prayer for help in such a situation might be as follows: "May I be able to perceive my self-deceit, and may I

truly be able to overcome it. Guide me from falsehood to truth."
We will be guided to say this prayer consciously when we are able
to catch ourselves falling into the destructive patterns of our personal myth: "My self-deceit is a dream; awakening is the truth.
My self-deceit is darkness, and darkness has no existence in itself;
it is merely the absence of light." As soon as we turn on the light,
darkness dissipates. We need to acknowledge that we have been
sitting in the dark before it even occurs to us to turn on the light.
We may recognize that we are in the dark through the symptoms
of discomfort and suffering we feel.

There is a specific reason why we do not want to critically
examine the ways we fool ourselves. We may be getting some
pleasure out of it. Even though this is negatively-oriented pleasure, it is pleasure nonetheless. It makes us continue to hold onto
the self-deceit even though it brings us tremendous suffering to
do so, for this may be the only kind of pleasure we know.

People are also taken in by pride. Pride is another aspect of
delusion. Pride blinds us to the possibility of acknowledging that
we have ever been mistaken. The only time we go beyond our
personal mythology so we can experience the truth is when our
suffering becomes intolerable. When reaching such a low point
we need to recognize that there is something wrong, and admit,
"It's not possible that the whole world is wrong and that only I
am right."

We may be determined to maintain the big lie. This means
that we are not yet prepared to face the truth – so maybe we need
to suffer a bit more. Okay, this is part of the play. It will go on

until we get to the point where we are ready to say the following prayer: "Please, reveal to me the truth I have not yet been able to see. Even though it may wound my vanity, I still want to see it. I am committed to seeing it." In this way we are asking to be helped to realize that we are still in the dark. With that realization we may turn on the light and move from delusion to truth.

7
Pride and Humility

Question/Comment: I was inspired by what you said about the fear of death being related to the attachment to bodily image and vanity. I feel that I sincerely desire to be an instrument of the divine will, to be part of the divine peace project that you are working to establish through the Sachcha Mission. I felt humbled by the description of what I am being called upon to be. But as I was processing your words I ran up against an old dilemma, a paradox I can't get my head around: sometimes humility seems to get mixed up with feeling bad about oneself, and self-confidence confused with pride. How can we feel good about ourselves without becoming smug? And how can we become humble without hating ourselves?

Prem Baba: Only when we have achieved significant progress in freeing ourselves from the tyranny of pride can the Divine guide our steps. Only then can the Divine make us vessels worthy of carrying the nectar of the divine peace project to the world. It takes authentic humility for a person to make use of the power of prayer to ask truthfully: "Please, guide me.

Direct my steps so I may become an instrument of Your holy will. May I be one with You: may our connection never be broken. Give me strength, that I may fulfill the duty You have asked me to carry out, until the day comes when You and I become One."

SPIRITUAL VANITY

There are specific challenges connected with the opening of each energy center of the human body. As consciousness climbs its way through each *chakra*, surrender becomes ever more crucial. Giving oneself over to guidance is like being in the front hall of enlightenment. At this stage the seeker is already quite an enlightened person with many *siddhis*, or spiritual powers. The seeker may even be guiding others. Even when the *kundalini* energy rises as far as the third eye, the seeker can still fall from this elevated state. This is because the challenge of the sixth *chakra*, of the third eye, is precisely the one you have identified in yourself: vanity.

Vanity can seize and commandeer our spiritual achievements. A line from a movie I once watched stuck with me: the character of the devil said, "Vanity: definitely my favorite sin."[3] Why would this be? Vanity involves believing that we already know. Consequently we believe that we don't need to challenge our assumptions. Vanity protects the false self. It can manifest itself as obstinate stubbornness, as a fanatical adherence to our

---

[3] *The Devil's Advocate*. Dir. Taylor Hackford. Regency Enterprises, 1997. DVD.

own points of view. Unchecked vanity travels with its henchmen, stubborn self-will and fear, and this trio conspires to sustain a false self-image. We use this self-image as a layer of protection to hide who we truly are.

In your case, you found that the commander is vanity, the favorite son of pride. Vanity is distraction. Maybe that is why it is so dear to the devil: because it prevents us from reaching that seventh *chakra*, the crown *chakra*, or center of enlightenment. When the ego, which is the conscious self, distracts us through its own vanity, we set ourselves up as someone who "knows the path." Then we cling to, and proclaim authorship of our good actions. The power of this self-importance drains energy from others, and this energy feeds the false self. Self-importance is a defense mechanism that is activated by vanity and its supporting actors fear and stubborn self-will. This bloated self-image is an obstacle to raising the energy all the way up to the crown *chakra*.

The way to the last *chakra* remains blocked because of the pain circulating in your psycho-physical system. If you have been the victim of some abuse of power, then that can present difficulty in surrendering yourself to the flow of life. Perhaps your father or some other authority figure mistreated you. You project this situation onto life, feeling that you are a victim. In your mind, life is unfair, therefore God abuses authority. This false idea of life as punishment, with God as an arbitrary dictator, generates fear of being hurt again. We fear revisiting the haunted house. We fear reopening the superficially-healed wound.

A DROP OF HUMILITY

The treatment for your third eye, the figurative "third-eye drops" I like to joke about, can only be applied when you perceive what is really happening, and then clear the blockages that obstruct the crown *chakra*. What do those third-eye drops contain? A dose of effortless clarity, an unassumingness that leads to humility. This clarifies our vision of the distortions caused by vanity, fear and obstinacy. Humility comes when we free our mind from past confrontations with authority and from pride in our own story. But we will only be free of this defense mechanism of self-importance when we forgive, and can be thankful for the past.

Simplicity emerges when we are able to renounce the past. This renunciation allows us to disarm our defense mechanisms, which use fear, stubborn self-will and vanity to guard us against what life might throw in our direction. Only through forgiveness and gratitude can we free ourselves from our own past. When we have progressed in dismantling these defense mechanisms, we open up space for a spark of humility to emerge. This spark can kindle the blaze of true prayer. When the miracle of prayer occurs, we are able to say "yes" to life and everything it sends our way.

Until we are freed of the "no," and as long as our defense mechanisms are active, even a simple prayer such as, "Please guide my steps" is going to be countered on the subconscious level with the retort: "*I* guide my *own* steps and know what is best for *me*, thank you." That subconscious "no" resists the flow of life. It even reverses the flow. When we progress in the purification of our own past, we confront the "negative intentionality" that acts like a fierce general commanding the forces of resistance to our spiritual journey. "General No" is the guardian of the seventh *chakra*. Vanity, obstinate self-will, and fear are under the command of this negative willpower. When we free ourselves of the past we will finally be prepared to battle this great general of our negative intentionality. Our greatest weapon will be this spark of humility that emerged. Humility allows us to eliminate the remnants of the stubborn self-will that was leaching the strength of our conscious willpower. Only those beings who have developed unshakeable willpower are able to activate and sustain "positive intentionality." Doing this will then enable us to utter something like the following prayer, truthfully and with utmost sincerity:

"Lord who resides in my heart, I am tired of this game of ignorance. I'm sick of walking around in these circles of suffering. Everything that I have tried to accomplish by my will causes me to get trapped in immature love. Even the very idea of individuality is strengthening this delusion. Oh Lord, please don't try me anymore, for I am tired of fighting. Please, illuminate me. Pour your grace upon me. It is your very play to illuminate me. How then could I possibly be without your light? Please Lord, make me One with You. Free me of these products of karma, of so many foolish actions in the pursuit of happiness. I have tried to be the author of my actions in order to receive a little crumb of recognition from the other: free me, Oh Lord, free me from this misery!"

When you can thus pray for freedom with all your heart, you will be free. When you call upon God wholeheartedly, your prayer will be answered. One aspect of surrender to God is that you open the gates of living simply, of acceptance, and of giving yourself over to the flow of life. Surrender means being receptive to what is offered to you. If you are still protecting yourself, you won't receive the elixir that is being given. If your cup is full, how can nectar be poured in? To surrender or to give yourself over to God means emptying yourself. The subtext of this emptiness is "May Thy will be done." Only through such receptivity does your cup run over with divine love. The Divine wants to make you an instrument of healing and love. But all of the resistance by General No and his colonels is meant to keep you in the army of the lower self. They try to use you as an instrument of conflict and hatred by reactivating your past imprints.

A SIMPLE LIFE

What does it mean for a person to live simply and attain humility? A truly humble person is not a submissive person — for submission is but a distortion of humility. True humility is a great power of the soul that reveals itself once we become free of the past. This authentic humility unfolds when we are illuminated by forgiveness. Until we can forgive, our lower self will use pride as a defense mechanism. False simplicity and submission are faked humility: they are but another aspect of pride. But when our path to enlightenment is opened by forgiveness, and we are able to thank the past, we won't have to wear a mask anymore. We won't have to pretend to be someone we aren't as a means of relieving the pain we feel. We no longer need to please others to receive constant recognition as a substitute for the acknowledgment we didn't get from parents and others who have disappointed us.

Real humility can be attained when we heal these wounds, and thus gain authenticity. An authentic person lives in simplicity. Only through such unassumingness can a person surrender to the flow of life, which could lead anywhere. A person who exudes simplicity has been freed of the idea of being different from others. In our forms we may be separate, but inside we are all the same. When you realize this unity that underlies duality and multiplicity, you can surrender to the flow.

First you have to let go of authorship, which is the main product of negative intentionality. The hankering for acknowledgement distracts us with the desire for publicity. We feel the need to attract attention by bragging. We cling to this need of authorship because we want to be seen. Each individual needs a specific medicine to help in their healing process. Some people really need their names in lights and to receive the Oscar, so that the world can recognize their lofty accomplishments. That's alright, because this aspect of the personality might need to be solidified before it can be cut apart and dissolved.

There is still a needy little child inside. How do we deal with the wounded child, how do we help it grow up, or at least allow *us* to be grown-ups? We must find out what is blocking up our systems. We need to shed the tears that weren't shed. We need to give voice to the protests that weren't expressed and bring out any repressed emotions. Those actions free us from the past and bring fresh air to the stuffy room. Getting in touch with your emotions in this way will allow you to be illuminated by deep comprehension and by holy wisdom. Then you understand why this game needed to be played in the first place. When you understand why it all had to be exactly as it was, when you can really accept the past, your heart opens and you can forgive. This opens the way to gratitude, not just through the words of your mouth, but coming from the deepest recesses of your heart. This acceptance frees us from the habitual need to project past conditions onto present situations. It frees us from the need to defend ourselves with fear, stubborn self-will, and pride. In this way we will be truthful and authentic. Through such simplicity and humility we won't have to struggle so arduously in an attempt to author our own life.

When you surrender to the Great Mystery, it can then use your talents and gifts to fulfill its plan. Who or what is the Great Mystery? None other than your true being, than love itself. Devote yourself to love. Devote yourself to the project of world peace whose goal will be brought to fruition by opening the hearts of humankind, until the whole world is ruled by the heart. May you be an instrument of this love by walking the path of the heart. May all your gifts be at love's service, rather than carrying out the whims of the wounded child who feels the need to take revenge upon the world. When you put your talents into the service of love, you will feel that you belong and are able to occupy your rightful place in life. Then you feel fulfilled and experience the joy of waking up in the morning that service brings us. Without this joy it's not surprising that so many people don't even want to wake up in the morning. To just wake up to the same old misery, to the same war, fought over and over again is a drag. However, if you wake to love, the dawn breaks sweetly.

8
Adversity:
The Forgotten Guest

Question: How do we trust in God when facing the difficulties that life deals us, such as a great financial loss, the death of a dear one, or a child who is born with special needs?

Prem Baba: Not a single leaf falls from a tree by chance. If this challenge is on your doorstep, it was surely addressed to you. This gift is *personal* and *non-transferable*. If you try to get rid of it, it will come back with a vengeance. If at this stage the only way you can learn is through suffering, then the troubles will only increase in kind, frequency and degree until you accept the challenge.

WELCOMING THE GUEST

You sent out an invitation to guests and then forgot about it; but time did not forget. Now the first guest has arrived for your party and has caught you off-guard in your pajamas and with the house a mess. You may deny that you ever sent the invitation and say, "Party? I don't know about any party. I didn't invite anyone," but you look and sound ridiculous because the guest has your invitation in his hand. Thinking that you are just clowning about, the guest continues to stand at the door, waiting for the party to start. If you continue to deny that there's a party, he'll think you're just disappointed because only one guest showed up. He'll leave and come back with others that you invited, so that you don't feel so alone, saying, "The invitation says you really want to party, so I brought more guests to get you in the mood. Let's party!!"

There is one law on this material plane that you cannot escape: the law of cause and effect. It is not a moral, but rather a mechanical law. Isaac Newton described it in his third law of motion, setting the foundation for the study of physics: "Every action has an equal and opposite reaction."

We refuse to open the gift sent to us because of a trick of the mind: this trick makes us believe that we are victims of the world's injustice. The truth is that we are not victims – except maybe a victim of our own minds, which has us firmly in its clutches. These apparent catastrophes are not the playing out of some kind of injustice, but rather the natural outcomes of the law of cause and effect. We are responsible for the fact that the guest is standing at our door. We sent him the invitation.

Summon the courage to cope with the situation. First, take full responsibility for your plight. You apparently forgot that you had sent out invitations, so you need to deal with the situation as the guests arrive. Ask the guests to wait in the front hall or out in the yard while you get ready and deal with your real-life circumstances. Pick up the phone, order the pizzas and drinks, and start cleaning up calmly but efficiently. Put on some music, take a deep breath, open the door and invite your guests in. Do not put this challenge off. The party brings forward a great new opportunity for spiritual evolution. Free yourself from the idea that the universe is conspiring against you. As long as you continue playing the victim you will remain stuck in your childhood traumas.

We don't take responsibility because we don't want to grow up. Like children, we want to keep playing at the playground. Little Johnny is not yet ready to go home for dinner, so he throws a fit. It's like we are still tugging at our mom's skirt or pestering our dad, saying, "I want candy! I want ice cream!" Physically and intellectually we may have grown up, but not emotionally. We are desperate to avoid the anguish of taking a good hard look in the mirror. We lose the potential for growth by fleeing from life's challenges. We insist upon playing the victim so we can cling to the excuse that life has been unjust to us.

These situations are gifts life presents us with. Summon the courage to open the gift! There may be a daunting challenge inside, but also a stimulus for your personal growth. I have seen certain challenges emerge that instigate a great leap of personal evolution. But we deny that the gift is at our door. We tell ourselves that if we could just forget about the gift, it would somehow disappear. However, if we try to ignore it we will continue to attract this type of gift, for we have not yet integrated the imprint inside of us that is attracting them in the first place. Thus, breathe deeply and call for firmness; ask God, in the words of an Amazonian song, for "strength to carry on, faith to not falter, light to see, and love to offer thanks." This challenging gift gives you the opportunity to take a huge step forward, to resolve your karma, and to evolve spiritually.

LEARNING THE LESSON AT HAND

Until you learn the lesson at hand, similar situations will repeatedly present themselves to you. This will happen indefinitely if necessary; and the intensity of the challenge will increase each time, until you can no longer stand the suffering and your resistance to the lesson crumbles.

This is how the *school of life* works. This is how the teacher makes sure that the lessons have been understood – the teacher in this school being the Great Mystery. This method reveals how to overcome our identification with the mind's creations, since the idea of victimhood and grievance are ultimately nothing more than the mind's projections and have no real existence. The good teacher is helping us free ourselves from the grip of our personal fantasy. This good teacher, the Great Mystery, manifests by various means: through life in general, in the form of a guru, or in the form of the inner master. By guru, I mean an enlightened master teacher who has the ability to guide others to enlightenment. By inner master, I mean your own higher self who guides you in the direction of the light.

Question: Which responsibility is more important for a man to accept: to care for his own child, or to follow his heart beckoning him towards freedom?

Prem Baba: If you are responsible for bringing a child into this world, it is also your responsibility to care for that child. *You are responsible for that child until he or she is capable of independence.* It is not only your responsibility, but your karma: one way or another, you shall reap what you have sown.

A man arrived here last year with a child showing symptoms of schizophrenia. He wanted to leave the child here at the ashram, saying, "I think he would really benefit from staying here for a while." Then I asked him where his son was. At that very moment his son was playing in the construction site of the new hall and balancing on a concrete pillar that was 60 feet in the air. He was in extreme peril. The man pleaded with me, "I'll pay someone to look after him." I told him: "No. If you don't accept your responsibilities in this life, maybe in the next life you'll have to deal with twins with special needs, not just one. You have to embrace your task and summon the courage to reap the harvest."

9
Gratitude through Forgiveness

The situation of the incarnated human soul is similar to that of a knight walking around with his armor on. We spend our lives stuck inside suits of armor. We get so accustomed to it that we believe ourselves to *be* that armor.

The coat of armor is the idealized self-image we create along the course of our lives, and we come to accept it as our real identity. Denied feelings sustain this false identity, and we only begin to remove the armor when life shows us that something is not quite right. Only when we become aware of the negative and destructive repetitions that occur in one or more areas of our lives may we take responsibility and decide to do something about our clunky armor. This is how many people decide to follow a path of self-discovery: by becoming either curious or miserable enough to need to uncover the truth beneath that hard shell.

The armor only falls away after we have completed a journey of initiation. This involves solitude and a long hard look in the mirror of our souls. When we face ourselves in that mirror, cracks appear in our armored facade. Then those cracks split apart bringing tears of regret, and rays of love begin to illuminate our lives. This is the beginning of a miraculous transformation: the miracle of learning a new way of seeing things. Whereas our attention had been focused on what was lacking, causing us grief, upset and suffering, now we concentrate on what we have in abundance: the gifts that God has bestowed upon us. When we can do this, we will be truly thankful.

FEELING GRATEFUL

Gratitude brings about the reorientation from suffering to joy – but this kind of gratitude needs to be heartfelt. Gratitude is the first virtue the soul reveals. We sense it when we feel grateful for life, for the sun, the moon, the stars, for the forest, for the sea, for the earth itself.

If you can feel genuine gratitude for the existence of all beings, you will be truly thankful for the blessed moment of your birth. You will sincerely thank your mother and your father, the vessels that brought you to this world. Once you are able to acknowledge the divine nature of your own parents, you also recognize that you are a child of the mystery of love.

You will only leave your finite personality behind once you truly thank the Divine. You will only be ready for transcendence when you can truly honor your birth. By honoring your birth and your parents you also honor your extended family and departed ancestors. If you still maintain any point of hatred towards any member of your family you will feel imprisoned on Earth. I realize that the word "hatred" is a strong word to employ. By "point of hatred," I mean a powerful anger often accompanied by a desire for revenge, resulting from childhood wounds, that may be suppressed because it is unacceptable to others and even to yourself. If you still harbor such strong rancor, you will be unable to free yourself from your personality, for it will still have something to teach you regarding the mystery of love.

This teaching will be fulfilled when we can not only honor, but truly be thankful for our birth and our parents. Such gratitude emerges when we are able to forgive them. This forgiveness emerges once we deeply comprehend the reason behind the hardships we suffered as children. This profound comprehension takes root only when we understand that all those hardships were actually opportunities for healing and growth, rather than being misfortunes. As long as we believe that life is against us, our gaze will focus on what is lacking. As long as our vision is distorted, we won't be thankful. We won't even respect people, and of course we'll be entirely unable to love them. Our hearts will remain closed, and the result will be suffering. This is why we pray for deep, enduring comprehension: "May I be bathed in the light of awareness." Only through such sincere prayer will you approach devotion. Continue your self-discovery until you feel you are a blessed child of the mystery of love. Gratitude will spring forth profusely. You will then be ready to forget your name and personal story. You will recognize yourself as the divine being you truly are.

LOCATING WHERE YOU ARE

Contemplate the depth of these words: if you do not realize your own divine nature, it means that ingratitude is still present. Some unforgiven grievances, some points of hatred remain in your psycho-physical system. These points may seem small, but they are like tiny specks of a toxin that can infect our whole system. They imprison us in the past and generate all types of negative patterns because we don't yet understand the mystery of our birth. We end up holding on to the resentment and hurt produced by difficult experiences.

I have just given you a map to locate where you are on your journey and to examine how far you must yet travel to reach your goal. If you can't recognize yourself as a divine being, do the following exercise to help pinpoint exactly where you are on this map: visualize your mother and father, and sincerely tell them, while looking them in the eye, "Thank you very much; I am eternally grateful to you." Offer a heartfelt *namaste* ("the Divine in me greets the Divine in you") and a *pranam* (reverence) to those beings who brought you into this world. You need to forgive them regardless of their personality flaws.

Until we sincerely feel this gratitude, we will be imprisoned by our past and by our finite personality – we will still be fragmented. These points of hatred that permeate us arise from grudges and resentment. They persist because we don't understand that they prevent us from experiencing unity. Because of this rancor we may find it difficult to abide in our higher selves.

Rather we remain identified with the wounded child whose needs were not met, who was not loved the way it needed to be loved.

We recreate these childhood wounds in our adult life through our relationships with the partners we choose, who are often merely projections of those dysfunctional parents. If we have not yet recognized this pattern, we will unconsciously look for our incognizant parents when choosing our partners. We naively hope that this time it will be different: "This time I will be loved. This time I will succeed in pleasing them." Thus we repeat all the games of rejection, dependence, co-dependence, control and domination.

All this arises due to our identification with the wounded child who wanted to receive exclusive love, but did not. This is why, when people seek to abide in the higher self, they fail. They are unable to retain even a tenuous connection to it because these feelings poison their emotional bodies, which still need healing. We all may heal our emotional bodies through deep comprehension, which allows gratitude to emerge.

The Emergence of Gratitude

To summarize, the main remedy for the emotional body is gratitude, but this gratitude cannot be forced. Until it emerges, you should continue getting to know yourself. Understand why you had to be born into this particular family, with this mother, this father, and these siblings. When you deeply understand the divine mystery behind your birth into your family, you become free of hatred. You begin to feel gratitude and love.

Only through gratitude will you move your focus from the small to the universal family. This gratitude emerges if we eliminate the points of hatred, the resentment and sorrows that permeate and poison our minds. Only when we accept, and can even be thankful for that beating we received, even for that most cruel act of un-love, can we honor the teaching of Master Jesus: "Father forgive them, for they know not what they do." Forgiveness was the core teaching of Master Jesus.

This is the starting point, the ABC of Spirituality. What is the transformation of the lower self if not this inner house-cleaning of old hurts and lingering points of hatred? What practice other than this purification enables forgiveness and gratitude, opens the heart, and makes us want to give rather than receive?

As long as we identify with our wounded child, we will want exclusive love from all. We remain entrenched in a scarcity mindset because in the past we perceived something to be missing or awry, and our minds are still fixated on that event. And so we are convinced that everything is lacking: "No one loves me. No one wants me. Life does not agree with me. Things don't work out for me." As a consequence of embracing this distorted belief-system our minds create and sustain the feeling of scarcity. This attitude attracts even more scarcity into our lives. So we confirm that for us, *everything* is lacking. Clearly, this is a vicious cycle.

When you liberate your mind, express gratitude, and identify yourself with the Divine, you discover that you are the source of love itself, the source of everything. There is no deficiency in the world of God. You and the source of love and prosperity are One. Once you have made this transition, you are no longer identified with your personality. Your personality is merely a vehicle through which you move yourself in the world: it is an extension of the body. This body was once born, and one day it will be returned to the earth. But the *Self*, your spiritual identity, never dies: it is eternal. When the body gets old you simply let it go and take another.

I am here to help you understand how you function, to give you a map so you may know where you are and what you need to do to arrive at your destination. I pray that this knowledge may give rise to wisdom in the lives of each and every one of you. Knowledge becomes wisdom only when you put it into practice.

PART THREE

Transforming Relationships

Relationships are among the most advanced courses we take in life. One of the major subjects in the course is intimacy and mutual revelation. This class is a prerequisite for even more advanced courses in life, because as we reveal ourselves to a partner, we also overcome our own defense mechanisms.

10
The Quest
for Exclusive Love

All of us are born free, but with rare exceptions, we die as prisoners of our mental conditioning. We put on armor just to survive the challenges we undergo during our early lives. It is unavoidable. These challenges may be shocks of exclusion and abandonment, humiliation and rejection. Such shocks shut down the child's natural spontaneity and establish the habits of neediness and selfishness. Bit by bit the developing human being becomes indoctrinated with societal beliefs concerning right and wrong. We are given rules, discipline and training to make us fit inside socially correct norms. All this detracts from spontaneity and our inherent state of freedom.

MASKS OF SUBMISSION, AGGRESSION, AND WITHDRAWAL

We create a mask of submission or conformity, with the child becoming an obedient adult; we confine ourselves to acting within the framework of the rules imposed upon us. Alternatively, we may create a mask of aggression; we rebel and join a sub-culture, turn to crime, or become an outcast, refusing to follow the path that society deems correct. Or, thirdly, we may build a mask of withdrawal or indifference, whereby we are "above" all this.

Regardless of which of these three approaches a person uses, one's mind still remains completely fixated on the other. The other is the reference point. Such a person is desperate for others' recognition, praise and love. One's whole life is dedicated to the effort. A life so dependent on another is artificial: it is a life lived disconnected from the heart. One becomes a victim of the compulsion towards perfectionism, of the need to do everything just right for the sake of approval. This perfectionism becomes so automatic that we believe that such mechanical behavior is our natural state. Then, we can't understand why we are in anguish, why we feel so depressed, irritated, and incomplete. People are so deeply identified with the perfection-mask that they don't notice that the root of their discomfort lies in their inability to be themselves.

Denied feelings sustain the identification with this idealized self-image. That image is created by perfectionism and driven by the need to please. Fear is the gatekeeper guarding the dungeons of these feelings. We fear shaking off our conditioning, and having to walk without our crutches. I am not implying that there is anything wrong with any person's evolution: this is how things go. But it is important that we recognize that we are in transition. During this transition, we must realize that although all the knowledge once given to us, all the rules imposed and all the conditioning were somehow necessary for the evolution of consciousness, most of them will ultimately need to be abandoned.

A child needs limits, just to ensure its survival. Since we live in society, we need rules. But we need to evolve one more step in our relationship with society, to the point of being able to teach our children that someday they will have to abandon many of these rules. For one can only find freedom when one frees oneself from the dependence created by having to please the other. By freeing ourselves from this dependence, we develop equanimity. We will then remain unshakable in the face of whatever may happen externally. We remain the same, not because we are numb or indifferent to outer circumstances, but because we have found our center. We turned inwards and discovered our own being: we found the source of consciousness.

In this way, we free ourselves from the dramas caused by not being centered in who we are. Until we find the true center, we will identify with a false center, which is the mask and our self-image. The mask is only viable if we can find at least one other person willing to reaffirm its validity. If we are identified with the mask – that is, if the mask is the center of our self-image – we get so needy that we become "beggars of attention." Our whole life becomes a huge effort to draw the other's gaze, and to try to force the other to love us. People waste their lives in useless conflicts, for they want others to confirm that they are indeed the mask that they are wearing. Life becomes a masquerade, where one constantly demands that others pay attention to one's mask.

The Need for Exclusive Love

This need for exclusive love distorts our perception. It prevents us from recognizing the gifts and talents we have brought to this world. These gifts and talents are the channels through which the higher self flows. When we feel that we are occupying our rightful place in the world, we start taking delight in giving, instead of only wanting to receive.

Since the veil of illusion, *Maya,* obscures people's vision, they believe they have nothing to give. When they do get a glimpse of their intrinsic generosity, people do not trust the insight because they have habitually protected themselves through neediness and selfishness. We fear letting go of this distorted psychological complex because it gives us a sense of security. This becomes a vicious cycle of self-defeating selfishness.

What we most desire, to be loved, will only happen when the love we crave flows from us in abundance. This is not an intellectual process. It is a phenomenon that occurs in the realm of the soul, in the realm of the heart.

We open ourselves to this healing love by honestly examining whether we do indeed play this dark-side game of demanding to be loved to the exclusion of all others. Be aware of whether you try to force the other to love you. Ask yourself whether your ego is using your whole repertoire of acquired knowledge to force the other to give you what you want, when you want it. If not, congratulations. If so, then it is time to recognize this strategy of the ego so that you can, at this very moment, choose to change.

This picture of co-dependence is like an x-ray of one of the circles of hell. Nonetheless, this is where the great majority of humanity finds itself. You who are spiritual seekers are part of a select group of aware people in the world who want to escape from prison. Even if you only want freedom from those chains to ease the pain, still, it indicates that your intelligence is awakening. You have shown that you want to move beyond conditioning, beliefs and acquired knowledge to embody your true nature.

TUNING INTO YOUR HEART

You can begin to undo this negative conditioning by attuning yourself to your heart. Your heart is like a sun that can illuminate everyone in the world. Its light is never extinguished. As this transformation begins, you notice that you have gifts and talents that you no longer use to please others and satisfy the lower self: you instead use them to help you become a channel of divine love. You understand that your talents give you a role in the divine project of love and world peace. We spread this message, this song, so that others ready to awaken may hear the music.

We can shed this limiting conditioning when we deeply comprehend the past, forgive, even give thanks for every difficulty we experienced, however painful. We accept that a rose also has thorns. We give people the freedom also not to love us. When we accept that this is how the game of life is played, we stop resisting it, and we quit trying to take revenge. We are finally able to shift from negative intentionality, the absolute *no* to happiness, to positive intentionality, a *yes* to life – a yes to all that is good, joyful and prosperous. Then we celebrate life continuously. We make a prayer of each moment. In this way we rescue the sanctity of living. Let us revive the holiness of inhabiting this body, and of living on this planet. We can then embody these words from the Amazonian tradition:

> *I live here in this world*
> *I do not owe anyone anything;*
> *I live in the world of God*
> *Where God abides as well.*

I wish from the bottom of my heart that every being may awaken from this dream in which they seek what they need outside of themselves. Everything you seek is inside of you. Your heart is the source of all love. But in order to find this source, you have to cultivate solitude – you have to meditate. You have to be willing to live this great adventure, which is to unveil the mysteries of the heart.

When we awaken, we also awaken the others around us. This happens naturally. Only in this way are we truly able to help. But for that, we need to have something to offer. Only a happy person can help another become happy.

Today a Baba came to visit us. He left us the following message: "Life is short, so fix your minds on God. Time is passing quickly, and your death approaches. Open your third eye, awaken. Everything is possible. God bless you."

Blessed be each and every one of you. Receive the blessing that helps you celebrate each moment of life.

11
On Intimacy

Question: I would like you to speak about revealing oneself to God and revealing oneself to a partner. How can we sustain love in a relationship? Are all relationships doomed to endless misunderstandings and boredom, or can the act of revealing oneself feed the fire of love?

Prem Baba: God already knows who you are even without your revelation. But you and your partner need this mutual revelation. You especially need what such deep disclosure brings with it: the overcoming of pride, fears and stubborn self-will. It is through revelation to a partner that you reveal yourself to God.

Intimacy is a word I often use regarding the relationship between partners or between master teacher and disciple. You might not know my intent when I use the word intimacy, because it has multiple meanings. For some people, intimacy just means a sexual relationship – but that is not what I mean. A couple may spend years having sex but still not enjoy the slightest intimacy. A couple may spend their whole lives together, may have children, and may have built a life together, but still not share real intimacy.

Seeing our partner naked is not intimacy. We are often so identified with the body that we believe that to expose our bodies is to reveal ourselves. We may think that the body is the ultimate reality, but the body is just the surface. At the surface people may caress each other, but this does not mean that their hearts come together.

It is very common for bodies and personalities to meet and touch each other; but the inner selves usually remain untouched. There is quite a security system protecting the headquarters. This protective barrier arises in a unique way in each person. It may be built of shame, fear, pride, or other negative emotions. Often, there is a whole set of electric fences – a triple perimeter or more. For instance, superficially, your barrier may be made of arrogance and false self-sufficiency, but behind this layer there may be fear, and behind that may yet lie shame.

We are ashamed of things we have not quite understood, and of which we may have no conscious recollection. We are ashamed of what we erroneously believe ourselves to be, and are afraid that our partners may discover what we are hiding. People are ashamed of their past, of their family and of various traumas they have experienced. They may also be afraid of their partner revealing their inner being because that would imply that they will also have to reveal themselves. Revealing oneself to a partner is just as vital for one's own inner discovery process as it is for one's partner. We are fleeing from ourselves. We avoid anything that might disturb our denial.

Relationships are among the most advanced courses we take in life. One of the major subjects in the course is intimacy and mutual revelation. This class is a prerequisite for even more advanced courses in life, because as we reveal ourselves to a partner, we also overcome our own defense mechanisms.

The personality has four main levels of expression: physical, emotional, mental, and spiritual. According to each person's conditioning, one will either find it easy or difficult to reveal oneself at each level. Conscious love within a relationship emerges when union has occurred at each of these four levels. We might have great difficulty revealing ourselves physically, due to sexual repression. Or, depending on the way we were raised, we might have great ease revealing ourselves physically, but this openness still does not amount to intimacy.

Real love is eternal. Let's make a clear distinction between the authentic item and the cheap imitation in wide circulation. Love is a word that no longer means anything. You may say, "I love you," but often you don't feel it. Moreover, we often confuse love with sex, with passion, with neediness, or even with extreme selfishness. Sometimes one may even confuse love for the deepest hatred. This severe distortion of reality has even led people to the deluded conclusion that they need to "kill for love." Love can never kill anything. Love is a power that makes everything grow and prosper.

THREE FORCES THAT BRING YOU TOGETHER

In relationships, there are three forces that promote intimacy and ultimately lead to union. The first is **sexual energy**; the second is Eros, **erotic energy**; and the third is **love**. These are three distinct energies, but they are often jumbled together in people's minds. This three-way distinction I draw from the work of Eva Pierrakos.[4]

Sexual energy is vital energy and a natural instinct. It is an impulse of the body that comes from our animal nature. Sexual energy is the most primal expression of the one and only energy that moves the body. It is primitive in the sense of being basic, being at the root. But don't react against the word primitive, nor against sexuality itself. Sexual energy is none other than life energy. This energy manifests in varying ways as one draws it up the spine. It is the same energy that manifests in the astral world, the mental world, and the spiritual world.

Love is the ultimate goal of our quest, but it is still a rare phenomenon in this world. Love is the experience of life and of union. It is an indescribable experience.

Eros, or passion, is much easier to speak of: Eros is what's commonly called "falling in love." It is the bridge that takes you from sex to love. Eros has a well-defined purpose: it guides us towards the experience of love. Eros can be active in a sexual or in a platonic relationship. Sometimes Eros manages to guide you

---

[4] Pierrakos, Eva, and Judith Saly. *Creating Union: The Essence of Intimate Relationship.* Charlottesville: Pathwork Press, 2002. Print. For further information please visit www.pathwork.org.

to love. Sometimes it dies unfulfilled. The erotic fire in a relationship might last a day, a week, or longer; but within three or four years it usually either burns out or it kindles a new fire – you now start on the journey that leads to the experience of mature love.

If we are married or are in a long-term relationship, and Eros has fled, we live a life devoid of passion. We keep trying to find a way to escape our boredom. Some people find themselves lovers; others wait for death to bring a solution to the problem.

Usually passion dies but the couple stays together and continues to have sex from time to time. By now this is mostly mechanical sex with a superficial orgasm that brings no satisfaction. It is tedious to the extent that people often prefer to masturbate rather than have intercourse with their partners. It is more pleasurable to masturbate because at least then one can go deeper into intimacy with oneself. Through our fantasies we forget about the stranger living under the same roof. How is it possible to keep the fire of Eros lit after being together for several years? Everyone wants an answer to this question. One keeps the home fires burning through mutual revelation. Adventure feeds Eros. What adventure could be more exciting than to explore the world that is your partner?

When you begin a relationship, you may be enthusiastic about getting to know your partner – Cupid's arrow pierces your heart. But you may have actually fallen in love with the image the other has allowed you to see. You may in turn have shown your partner a tailored image of yourself. It becomes clear that you are both maintaining facades once you start to live together and have to interact daily. This process brings challenges to the surface. You may find out that you are not so motivated to reveal yourself to the other. You may be ashamed of something and you are afraid it will be exposed.

LOOKING INTO THE MIRROR

In relationships, we never go any further than a certain page in our autobiographical book. I am not referring to telling others our life's story: in fact, we sometimes tell our life's story as a distraction to *avoid* intimacy. Rather, I am speaking about truly being able to be ourselves around others – about being spontaneous, about being whole. We cannot be whole when there are parts of us that have been denied and repressed. We do not want others to see these parts because *we* do not wish to see them. These are the parts of our personal story that are top secret. They are off limits; we do not dare reveal them to anyone. All this holding back makes us believe that our partner also has no further mysteries to reveal. At this point, Eros starts to recoil: we begin to lose our admiration for our partner. We begin to believe they are no longer interesting. We feel this way because we have only gotten to know them up to page four. We stopped there. If we had read further, there might have emerged a danger of exposure. We protect ourselves in many ways, and one of them is by extinguishing the erotic fire.

What we usually do is to find ourselves a different partner to escape real intimacy with the one we already have. We do this because our current relationship demands revelation. Being in the relationship demands that we overcome our imprints of abandonment and rejection. We could use our vulnerability to overcome pride, stubborn self-will and fear. All this seems extremely threatening to the lower self.

These are difficult challenges. We may have chosen exactly the person who will bring out both the best and the worst in us. When the worst comes out, we think we need to change partners so we can find a mate who brings out our best. We are only kidding ourselves: if there is conflict outside, it is because there is conflict inside.

Our partner is a mirror: they show us what is inside ourselves, what still needs work. If you have not done inner work, I doubt that you will find a satisfactory partner. You may find a different body. The introduction to their book might sound like a new and interesting read, and in the beginning it may really seem different, but after a few pages you will notice that you just got married to the same person. Our big mistake is thinking that making exterior changes alone will do the trick, when we have not been transformed within.

We might look for another and yet another person – sometimes serially and sometimes simultaneously – with whom we can once again go up to page four. This continues and our frustration mounts until a time comes when we rationalize that we are not meant for the world of relationships. We lose all hope of uniting sex, Eros, and love. Sometimes we try to go deeper, but do so by only showing different pages of our book to different people, and thereby expose ourselves only in a piecemeal fashion.

We manage our fear of revealing ourselves while still easing our sense of isolation. Understand this: you fear revealing yourself to anyone because you are afraid of revealing yourself to *you*.

When you truly transform these imprints and shadows, it is possible to love everyone. In this way you don't pit one relationship against another – you actually love all of creation. You do not love one person in order to hurt the other. Love simply flows, just as the sun shines on all.

Question: Is love not conditional upon a guarantee?

Prem Baba: All guarantees that people seek in exchange for revealing themselves, so that they can then experience intimacy, are precisely the obstacles that prevent love from blossoming. Love already exists. It is the natural manifestation of your spiritual body. Your higher self is already present. Its expression is love, but it is covered by many layers of thoughts, ideas, and beliefs, all of which act as defense mechanisms.

THE PATH OF SPONTANEITY

Question: What is your opinion regarding the control of sexual energy during *Tantric* sex, with the non-ejaculation of the male partner?

Prem Baba: Generally I encourage people to follow *Tantra* – but *Tantra* is a word that has been widely misconstrued to be only about sex. When I refer to *Tantra* I mean spontaneity and a natural way of life that may involve sexuality. On this path of love we work to transform sex into devotion. At some point the sexual energy may be directed inwards and upwards through *Tantric* techniques.

But before trying out any techniques, ask yourself whether this need to manage the natural flow comes from a healthy place within you. Ask yourself, "Who inside of me wants control?" I always insist: do not try to rush (or dam up) the river, for it flows at its own pace. As you dedicate yourself to the practice of self-observation, you may discover that this wish to control the sexual experience arises from a need to rule over your partner. In such a case, you should then ask yourself, "Who in me wants to dominate the other?"

You can make use of certain techniques that will indeed help you; but they will be beneficial only if your objective does not turn into a need to control. Rather, the sole purpose of these techniques should be to remove the garbage that clutters the river, allowing it to flow more freely.

Recently a man came to speak to me regarding the difficulties he was having in sustaining loving relationships. He longed to experience *Tantric* sexuality, but he could not overcome his fear of relating to women. The man's isolation caused certain habits like compulsive masturbation, which always brought with them intense feelings of guilt that plagued him. So I told him to forget all about *Tantra* if he wanted to take a genuine step towards the feminine world. Authentic *Tantra* blossoms naturally from union and love, as the fruit of the tree of consciousness ripens. But the flower will blossom only after the seed of normal sex has been planted. And to have a healthy sexual life,

I told the man that he first needed to identify the hatred he still harbored towards women.

Only after a person has freed themselves from fear and hatred towards the other, and thereby stopped engaging in manipulative games and power disputes, can they experience *Tantric* sexuality as a natural blossoming.

The way to free ourselves from the bondage of karma is to create intimacy. If you are already in a relationship, forget about elaborate techniques; instead, look into the eyes of your partner and begin to breathe together. Have the courage to remove all masks, so as to reveal yourself, and embrace your partner's revelation. In this way, you move from the surface to the heart-center. When your heart meets the other's heart, something magical takes place: true *Tantra*, the path of spontaneity arises. When two heart-centers meet, time stops: you have no further reason to reach anything or anywhere. Certain rituals naturally emerge as part of the sexual act, but they are renewed with each encounter. The power of love sweeps you away, and the walls of separation between masculine and feminine fall apart. A circle of energy is created as masculine and feminine melt into one. Rather than down-and-outwards, the energy flows up-and-inwards, and orgasm happens on another level: you have a glimpse of the eternal.

The majority of humanity is destined to live this deep encounter with another soul. This experience is perhaps the most effective way to purify the personality of the addictive habit of putting the other down. It is the most direct way to unite the sexual current with the heart and to transform lust into devotion.

12
Spirituality and Sex

Many people believe that sexuality and spirituality are mutually exclusive, antagonistic opposites. For some, it is impossible to even conceptualize uniting sexuality and spirituality. My view is that spirituality means unity: if you have difficulty uniting with a sexual partner, it means that you are still fragmented within. A person who has internalized spirituality does not divide themselves into separate conflicting parts. Spirituality entails the integration of all aspects of life, including the physical, sexual energy.

It so happens that everything that exists in our psyche also shows up in our sexual expression. All that we cannot admit and confront regarding ourselves is laid bare through sex. So our sexual expression, which includes whatever sexual tendencies we have, is a vehicle through which we also reveal all that is not sexual in our psyche. For instance, let's say you harbor repressed guilt: by extension, you also repress a tendency for self-punishment. If you still can't recognize the blame game that's in effect, you will inevitably find a partner who feels the need to humiliate you. You have a need to be rejected in the relationship. You don't see its connection to your inner world, where it signals the point where you still need to heal yourself.

There is no better gauge of our spiritual maturity than our sexual expression. It provides the clue. It is the treasure map for self-discovery. People habitually deceive themselves, because the mind and the ego are very clever. You may think of yourself as a very evolved person – but sexual expression reveals your spiritual level. As long as there remains a desire to humiliate our partners or to have power over them, it means we are still harboring hatred in our systems. To cover this up people don the mask of "great goodness" or the mask of "most elevated enlightenment."

FACING OUR UNRECOGNIZED FEELINGS

The sexual current can energize one's wholesome life force or it can activate the denied shadow. Throughout human history the sexual impulse has been repressed in the hopes that denial of our animal nature would allow for an influx of elevated spiritual energy. This repression can be understood as a protective response because sexual expression was so often abused as a channel for the deepest cruelty, brutality, and animality. That was a protracted stage of human evolution during which gentleness and respect were virtually non-existent. Since there was no way of facing and integrating this shadow that manifested itself through the sexual impulse, sex was denied and suppressed, along with its cruel expressions.

This suppression happened for a long time and still happens today. Nowadays we may not get away with killing or enslaving as in the past, but we hurt the other in more subtle ways. The shadow still manifests itself through distorted sexuality.

A student of mine thought of himself as a very enlightened person because he had experienced *samadhi*, the state of unity, a few times. He could not get involved with women because every time he fell in love with one, he also felt like killing her. Hatred would emerge from the depths of his being. Since he couldn't cope with it, because it was completely irrational, he avoided ever relating himself romantically with another.

Some spiritual traditions ended up containing humanity's natural expression due to this psychological immaturity. Since sex had the potential of bringing out all the denied brutality and animality, it was prohibited in ashrams, which act as focal points of spiritual energy.

Humanity is now mature enough to face its shadow with more equanimity. The foundations are being laid for a new era in which there is no more alienation between the sexual and spiritual energies and no more hatred between the masculine and the feminine principles – indeed no separation between anything.

All guilt that we feel regarding sex is due to the "evil" that can express itself through sexuality, a viciousness that makes us desire to humiliate the other, to have power over the other, to put the other down. It is this denied shadow that contaminates sacred sexuality. It is the constant avoidance of the shadow that makes us shirk responsibility: instead, we blame the other, we mistrust the other, and we harbor negative attitudes about the other.

People often freeze up and become emotionally numb during the sexual act. That is because they already anticipate the inevitable emergence of the negative feelings. This in turn increases both their desire and frustration. To satisfy this frenetic, impulsive and repressed desire for sex one may develop addictions like pornography. Such denial and repression only create despair.

This issue touches a very deep and sensitive place. This is a conflict at the very core of the human experience. Every single human being carries this conflict inside themselves, through the conditioning bequeathed by thousands of years of the association of sex with domination. Even very enlightened people bear this internal conflict. People feel guilt experiencing any pleasure, because behind pleasure lurks an unmanifested hatred, that has not been faced, not even been identified.

This complex of unrecognized feelings causes mistrust in couples. It increases the sense of alienation between the masculine and the feminine principles. The inability to see our own denied shadow creates a character weakness that makes us recognize the shadow only in the other. For example, let's say that you cherish the secret desire to have more than one sexual partner. Because you repress this desire, you may start to project this same repressed desire onto your partner. You start to think they are cheating on you, or seeking an opportunity to do so. Your partner may indeed harbor the same repressed desires as you do, but that is his or her concern, not yours.

We get used to looking critically at others instead of having a good look at ourselves in the mirror. Recognizing this blame-game is a necessary step. It is part of the "ABC of Spirituality": until this foundation is built, one cannot construct the building.

The Disconnect between Masculine and Feminine

This is a very important stage in the unfolding of the human journey on this earth: the possibility of uniting heaven and earth, the possibility of integrating all levels of the personality. Sexuality is eminently sacred – it is a door to God. In truth, it is the expression of consciousness that most clearly embodies blending and union. But because of this denied and suppressed destructiveness, we have created strict taboos around sexuality; so much so, in fact, that some of you are getting queasy even listening to me talk about it.

I feel that sex without hatred or hostility is still a rare phenomenon in the world. Still, I am working to enable this integration of the masculine and feminine principles. Sex without hatred is the purest manifestation of love: it is a prayer. What could be more profound and beautiful than such an act of pure love? We can chant *mantras* in a mechanical way, but real lovemaking cannot be performed mechanically.

Hatred manifests itself in the form of pride, stubborn self-will and fear. These are the clouds that cover up your purest expression of the resplendent sun of love. I am working hard to help you look at, identify and dissipate those clouds. Then, perhaps one day you may embrace *brahmacharya* – conscious celibacy with devotion – as a natural phenomenon, as an expression of your true being. This occurs once you have elevated your life energy and sex no longer makes sense for you. It is not that you oppose sex, for you are not *against* anything; rather you see beauty in everything.

Know that this disconnect between the masculine and the feminine principles in the outer world is a reflection of the estrangement of the masculine and the feminine inside. The possibility of union has been undermined by the linkage between brutality and sexuality in the past. Even with all the evolution of culture over time, this negative association has been reinforced just the same. This happens in a more subtle way nowadays than in the past, but it is always recreated through beliefs and prejudices that separate and alienate us from the opposite sex. We learn at an early age to separate ourselves from the opposite sex in one way or another, according to the dictates of the culture and the family conditioning we inherit. For example, say that your family taught you that men are worthless. You learned that you cannot trust men and therefore you have to protect yourself from them. This may have come about because your mother had been hurt by a man, and accordingly taught you that men are not trustworthy. As a child, you internalized this idea. You created an image of the irresponsible male, a stereotype according to which no man is worthy of your trust. This sort of erroneous generalization results in the reinforcement of the historical disconnect between the masculine and feminine energies.

Sex as an Expression of Spirituality

Sexuality can and should be an expression of spirituality. There is no conflict between sexuality and spirituality. Sexuality is a path towards love. At the right moment sexuality can transform into love. Two become one – there is no more separation, and duality ends. The denied shadow causes separateness and alienation to dominate; but sacred sexuality can end duality. This is the path that eventually may lead to conscious loving celibacy, which is the authentic solar *brahmacharya*, a phenomenon of the soul. *Brahmacharya* is the last stage in the evolution of the sexual current. It brings about the experience of the real. But a person can actually experience reality only when this *brahmacharya* is also real, and not an escape from oneself. *Brahmacharya* can also be a healthy approach when an authentic guru suggests it to a disciple as a specific practice for that disciple's current stage of evolution.

Sex is like a thermometer to measure our inner state. Don't hold a grudge towards the thermometer because it told you the real temperature! Why sex? Because there is no other such thermometer available. This is *the* measuring tool. To avoid using this thermometer is to avoid evolution. We deny ourselves the possibility of evolving because we are attached to suffering. So we just avoid using this measuring tool by not paying attention to our sexual tendencies because, if we did, we would hear the message that life is trying to tell us. Thus we deny those aspects of our personality that are imprisoning us in the cycle of negative and destructive repetitions. We are stuck because we won't take an honest look at our denied feelings. It's as if the disasters just happen, and we are unable to control them. When things spin out of control, the habit of negativity may manifest itself in an argument or a destructive relationship, a professional or financial failure, or even an inability to meditate.

Question: In the example you gave, where the mother teaches that men are worthless – say she teaches this to her son: what does that cause?

Prem Baba: This will vary on a case-by-case basis. Each one will recreate the experience according to their specific *sanskaras* or karmic imprints. But in a more general way, this can cause impotence and a general sense of self-loathing, because such a man does not recognize his own value, his own strength: he has been castrated. In other words, that mother is saying, "You are worthless; I have no trust in you."

Question: You cited an example of a person who would feel hatred whenever he fell in love with anybody. I think this happens a lot, but more subtly, so that most of us just don't notice what's really going on. Could you describe, in a more practical way, how one can notice this hatred by the extent to which one still wants to possess the other?

Prem Baba: When we realize that we still want to possess the other we should understand that we are fooling ourselves. Though we may wear a mask of "the loving one," we do not want someone to love: we want a slave who will do our bidding. If that person does not comply with our wishes, our vengeance can be awful. We "love," but if the other moves even an inch from the line we have drawn, Beauty turns into the Beast. All that love disappears, and the monster of our loathing emerges from the depths of a dark murky lake.

In truth, what is commonly called love is just egoism disguised as love. When this hatred arises after having been long repressed, it causes that person much trouble. For example, the student I mentioned, the one who resisted relationships because of the hostility he had towards previous partners, is now angry at me as well, and he does not want to hear any mention of my name; and he has furthermore conceived a hatred for God.

He wanted to become enlightened, and he wanted me to provide him this enlightenment. I told him, "Yes, all in good time, but first you have to do some inner house-cleaning." Then, following this logic, I said, "Find yourself a girlfriend." As soon as he did, all his suppressed hatred emerged. He responded by concluding that I had been a catastrophe in his life. It will take a few years for him to be able to sort through all this hatred. During his childhood, his mother and his sister had mistreated him severely. As a result he carries a lot of hostility towards women. This process is not an easy one. He does have the potential of becoming enlightened, but first he needs to purify himself of this hatred, because enlightenment is unity. You cannot become enlightened and be estranged from the masculine or feminine principles – there would be no sense in such "enlightenment." Before you are able to sustain cosmic bliss, you need to have integrated your shadow enough to sustain the ecstasy of an intimate encounter.

How do you expect to be able to look at the light of the sun if you are unable to look even at the light of a candle? The more mature you become, the more unified you become. You unite yourself with all and everything.

Sex is the seed, Love is the flower, and Compassion is the flower's perfume. If we disdain the seed and refuse to plant and water it, there will never be a flower, and there will be no perfume. But at man's current stage of evolution, this seed is still being widely condemned. We need to plant and water the seed – we do that by freeing up the seed. We need to re-establish the paradigm of harmony between the masculine and the feminine. You are the vanguard of this new knowledge, of this divine project for planet Earth. This project, though, will still take years to become established, because it requires more purification of the hatred that is stored in the psycho-emotional system.

Understand well what I am saying: as long as there is still a desire to dominate and to humiliate the other, or even to dampen the other's spontaneity, there is still malice in our hearts and minds. The guilt we feel is because we still deny this and still blame someone else. But as soon as we take responsibility for our own antagonism, the guilt dissipates. By assuming responsibility you really accept that it was none other than you who wrote your own story. Taking responsibility frees you from guilt.

So, once again, the invitation is for you to dive inside yourself. "Know thyself" – and may you really want to know yourself! We are afraid of loneliness, and of really facing our own dark side. But when we develop the willingness to look at it, we will notice that this sight is like a beam of light that dissipates darkness. As soon as we identify the lower self, we can de-identify ourselves from it. The first step is to identify it, but in order to actually see it for what it is, you must truly *want* to see it. This process begins by identifying the symptoms of your own dark side: anxiety, depression, irritation. Another symptom is repetitive conflict in a relationship, or even the failure to establish a relationship at all. I am not speaking of a mature choice to be in solitude. Rather, I speak of isolation, of the fear of relating to another, because we fear that the other will mirror what we do not wish to see. Do you want to remain numb and hide from the world, or do you dare to see yourself? This resolve to see ourselves forms the cornerstone of the ABC of Spirituality. Nature does not take leaps – do not think that you can trick God and arrive in heaven with all this malice still inside you. The gates of heaven are very narrow, and none of these false selves that you carry with you may enter. Only you can fit through.

Allow this subject to resonate inside of you. Some of you are feeling grateful that I broached this subject, others are feeling uncomfortable – okay, just let it sink in. Let me shake you up deep down inside. The shaking will help you wake up.

13
Marriage for a New Era

Question: You have identified the usual kind of unconscious marriage based on fear, jealousy, and the control mechanisms of the lower self, but what would a new kind of healthy marriage look like, the kind of marriage that would be suitable for the new era?

Prem Baba: From all that I have explained so far regarding the normal, distorted kind of relationship, it should be clear that this new kind of marriage for a new era of higher consciousness would require emotional and spiritual maturity. Such a state of preparedness will usually not emerge early in life. It is only in very rare instances that a person is ready for deep connection in a lasting relationship or marriage during the earlier part of their lives.

TAKING RESPONSIBILITY

Even among more mature couples there are few examples of conscious marriages. They remain rare because the new kind of marriage is such a deep encounter: it is a process of blending and fusion that requires complete transparency. Both partners must have the inclination and the sincere intention to unite sexuality with the deepest heart connection. To reach the state in which such union is possible, one must first have purified oneself to the point of being able to sustain the power of this connection without having to run away when things get challenging. Both sides must have matured enough to be capable of humbly assuming responsibility for the ups-and-downs of energy that are bound to occur in a relationship.

This ability to take responsibility for conflicts that emerge is a sign of maturity in a relationship. When people are still immature, no matter their age or the length of their marriage, they still need to blame the other for their own inability to love or to be happy. Often people blame their partners automatically and without ever cultivating the ability to step back from their need to always be right. They don't attempt to understand whether the other is actually at fault, or whether, just maybe, the fault might lie at their own feet.

In the new kind of marriage, this blame game no longer has any appeal. When the energy of reciprocity flowing at all levels starts to fluctuate, each partner will take their own share of the responsibility for the situation. Each one must have the humility to admit their fear of this intense current of love that is flowing through them, and to just let it flow, instead of fleeing and accusing the other.

If you have not yet experienced union between sexuality and the heart, the union of the currents of life energy, it may be difficult for you to understand what I am talking about. I am referring to that same power that manifests itself during mystical ecstasy. This ecstasy is so intense and potent that it threatens to crush the person who has not yet completed the work of purifying and raising their consciousness. If one has not yet matured enough to admit one's own fears, one will escape – and the best escape route is by blaming the other. If one's partner does not have an obvious flaw to pick on, one is perfectly capable of inventing something to fault. Thus, a person may find ample reason to make their body go cold, and their partner may find reasons to stop loving them and to find themselves another lover.

The marriage of the new era is imbued with intimacy. Each partner maintains the sincere intention to reveal themselves and to open up to receive the other's revelation. This is not simple to do if the soul has still not been able to dissociate itself from the dominant role the wounded child plays in the psyche of the unawakened man or woman. Your partner holds certain truths inside himself or herself that are difficult to accept, just as you fear to speak the truth because you are uncertain of the other's reaction. ***In the new kind of marriage there is no lying and there are no secrets.*** Rather, there is a constant intention of transparency. You are open to receiving both the gifts and the truth that the other has to offer – even if some of those truths may be hard to swallow. Love includes the ability *to see* the sleeping potential in the other, and *to awaken* it. Love brings the willingness to nurture higher consciousness in both partners.

The Key to Personal Development

The blending of essences at this deep level also involves all of one's physical energies. Sex becomes a sacred and creative act. Love and a sense of connection are renewed with each encounter: lovemaking becomes a prayer to the Divine, for it is the experience of unity. Here, one is in no hurry to finish the act, for one is not striving towards any goal. One does not need to flee the encounter through projection. Whereas sex is often nothing more than the meeting of two surfaces, here two centers come together and merge. When these centers meet, the energy flows freely: the mind stops and the ego is no longer in command. You have a glimpse of the eternal, of absorption in unity or *samadhi*.

This encounter points in the direction of *brahmacharya*, of uniting the masculine and feminine within oneself even without a partner. The next step is to live the experience of ecstasy alone, through meditation. However, this ecstasy will not visit us in our meditation if we are still holding onto the idea that our partner is our opponent. We may even experience ecstasy through spiritual practices, but we will be unable to sustain it, because we are still clinging to duality and opposing ecstasy within ourselves.

This marriage of the new era can thrive only within the framework of spiritual development. Such a union will naturally generate conditions favorable to the evolution of higher consciousness, as transforming two into one is a potent spiritual practice. Until we have reached this stage, however, it is important for us to focus on examining and purifying old negative patterns in our life. It is essential that we understand that, romantic notions and sentimentality aside, relationships are great teachers. They provide the opportunities we really need to evolve. From this standpoint, even a challenging and somewhat problematic relationship can be better than isolation, because at least we get the opportunity to see ourselves more clearly. Please note that I am not saying that people should remain in a truly hellish relationship.

Relationships are the means by which most people may develop spiritually. There is also the exceptional case that occurs when remaining single is a conscious choice. We make this choice to create conditions conducive to diving deeper within ourselves. We clean up our inner abode in a solitary way. But you should honestly evaluate whether you really need to remain single to create the right conditions for your inner journey, or whether you are just fleeing from this intense encounter between souls. You already know the answer: it should be quite apparent to you whether you are running away or whether you have made a conscious choice to remain alone so as to go deep within yourself. Divine love is only possible after you have experienced the marvels and the miseries of human love. We return to that basic law of the spiritual world: you are only ready to depart once you have arrived.

Transforming the Wounded Child

One of the greatest obstacles for evolution within relationships is pride. Each person has undoubtedly experienced many difficult situations in life that have left imprints of abandonment and exclusion. In order to shield ourselves from the pain of those shocks, we may make use of the defense mechanism of pride. This pride prevents us from evolving. Pride is a very complex entity, and has hundreds of psychological forms and derivations. One of the most prominent of these is shame, which prevents us from revealing ourselves and from showing ourselves to the other.

Another important component of pride is the idealized self-image, which is the collection of masks that we have so ably crafted and worn throughout the course of our lives. It took herculean efforts for us to develop this false self-image, but even so we did it, because we are so afraid of the truth. We fear that the rending of these masks will reveal what's really underneath. We are terrified of this exposure, for when our masks disappear it may seem that nothing remains, because we don't yet know our real selves. Thus, where there is pride, fear is lurking in the background. Behind this fear lies stubborn willfulness: we are still trying to control life and to do things our own way, so as to maintain our personal status-quo. We try to do this to avoid surrendering to who we really are, the unknown "I am."

To suppress these unpurified and distorted aspects that still exist in most people, some religions have prohibited marriage and loving personal relationships for those who are in search of

God. The belief was that intimate relationships could open the door to "evil" and darkness and lead one astray from following the path of transcendence. If you wanted to elevate yourself, you had to eliminate altogether the possibility that this door be opened.

Until very recently in history, people were entirely unprepared for the deep work required for transforming the inner shadow through relationships. But I feel that the new kind of marriage does not inhibit spiritual evolution. On the contrary, it is an essential part of any real progress: it can be a form of spiritual practice, *sadhana*. This can only be possible if we have freed ourselves from the erroneous beliefs and mistaken concepts created by the mind in response to societal conditioning. Those concepts make us view a partnership in the framework of the old-style dysfunctional marriage.

To put it simply, in the traditional marriage, two wounded children are meeting each other – and so it is often but an encounter of neuroses. However, this too plays a role in the process of evolution. Depending on your karma and your evolutionary path, you may need this experience of immature love to learn and integrate what still needs to be assimilated in your psyche. In contrast, the new kind of marriage is an encounter between two adult human beings. This encounter is a "clean energy source" that will not only illuminate your personal journey, but also the journeys of many people around you. I feel this kind of marriage to be a path towards liberation, for the unification of the masculine and the feminine inside of you.

Question: Could you speak about homosexuality, and how it plays a part in spiritual life?

Prem Baba: Both homosexuality and heterosexuality are the search for the complementary part that is experienced in a partner, but actually resides inside yourself. Through the loving physical relationship you continually evolve until you find what you were looking for, and your search is over.

Question: So you stop searching for the other once you have found yourself?

Prem Baba: Precisely. Your search is complete when you find, inside yourself, the counterpart that you thought was missing. The masculine principle is in search of the feminine principle, regardless of the type of sexuality. The search ends when an inner marriage occurs between the masculine and the feminine principles, *Shiva* and *Shakti* (the manifestations of the divine masculine and feminine). This is when lead is transformed into gold: you have found the philosopher's stone. The fountain of youth is the ecstasy created by this fusion.

It is not my purpose here today to make you feel discouraged at how far away your relationships might be from the new era ideal I speak of. I have simply answered your question, and my intention was to show you the way forward. As far as you may feel from this new kind of marriage, it is important for you to be able to visualize where you want to go. Where are you today in regard to this subject? Are you alone? If so, are you alone because you consciously decided to be alone or because you are isolated and afraid to relate to a partner? If you are in a relationship, what moves you inside this relationship? Are you in it to see yourself, to grow in love and in union, or to give way to your destructive impulses?

If you feel that you are far from this goal, I do not want you to feel as if I am pointing the finger at you. Rather, wherever you may be on your evolutionary path, I want you to have the courage to admit that you are not there yet and to face up to your current circumstances in an objective way. I know that you have the ability to move forward and improve the way you experience life. This subject deeply bothers many people. I have been traveling the world over, and I see that the need for a clear understanding of what is possible in relationships is a key point in many people's lives.

Many seekers are also still influenced by the dim view of marriage taken by some religions, where any spiritual search cannot happen alongside sex and married life. At some point you may even renounce marriage, but such renunciation cannot be forced. It may happen naturally when you have reached complete non-attachment and a certain degree of transcendence. I like the example of the child who has played enough with her toy and does not feel like playing with it anymore. It is not that the child opposes the toy: it just remains on the shelf. If some so-called "higher law" insists that, in order to grow spiritually, we are no longer allowed to play with that specific toy, our interest in that toy is guaranteed to be revived even if we repress our desire out of obedience and guilt. It will literally be staring at us from the shelf. This desire, in turn, will make it much harder for us to untangle our feelings from societal conditioning. Everything that is prohibited is desired all the more. The path is not that of repression, nor renunciation born of guilt or shame. The solution is transcendence.

In conclusion, perfect union is the entrance door to spiritual initiation. The first step towards achieving this state of oneness is being in union with another; but that's not the last step, for the price of realization in God is solitude and the transcendence of attachments to objects that stimulate the senses. But keep in mind that nature does not take leaps. This movement of awakening consciousness occurs in a natural and organic way, as we progress from one *chakra* to the next.

PART FOUR

Transforming the World

*The mission of the divine project for the planet is to have every insti-
tution function solely in order to instill this new spiritual paradigm.
It is a radical departure from the status-quo. Imagine an economy
being motivated by love instead of by fear. It sounds crazy, doesn't it?
But who are you going to serve, divine love, or hatred and fear? You're
going to have to choose. Choosing light doesn't mean that you automatically become a channel for divine love. You still have an internal
housecleaning to accomplish; but this commitment to spreading love
becomes the guiding beacon of your life.*

14
Finding Yourself in these Times of Change

Miracles are happening: hearts are opening and wounds are healing. Some are grateful for what is happening, while others are still going through deep transformational processes. They are experiencing the growing pains of change. I see that many of my beloved friends are going through very intense times. This intensity is particularly strong within couples' relationships.

Previously we spoke about elevating the vibrational frequency of the planet and reviving the forgotten language of freedom and ecstasy. If your conditioning leads you to treat pleasure as an enemy, you are probably having a tough time and are feeling severely threatened with the changes happening in the world. These times are easier for us if we are attuned to freedom and ecstasy. We feel the changes are natural. We experience them as a smooth ride because we are immersed in the joy that gratitude brings.

We are living in a time when people's traditional roles are falling apart. What you thought was your castle is crumbling back into sand. This is a time of deep and radical change. It is time to open one's arms to accept the planetary changes. We have entered a new era with new "codes" of freedom and pleasure.[5] Such joyful freedom is the natural expression of being, but has been forgotten and repressed throughout history. This blissful language of being is now enjoying a revival as our inner worlds are redefined, and our outer world is shaken up by the evolutionary transformation of the world's institutions.

At the heart of traditional social structures lies the institution of marriage. Whereas real inner marriage embodies the process of fusion between masculine and feminine, the outer institution of marriage has created various fantasies inside our psyches throughout the ages. These fantasies prevail within most couples, whether they are formally married or not. These distortions of reality now need to be re-examined.

The time has come to meet God within. We can no longer flee this encounter. But the cost of admission is solitude. We pay this price until real love is the only force that draws us to another person. When we are mature, only love inspires our attraction to another, nothing else.

At this moment, many are feeling pressured and threatened because this teaching is a figurative sword pointed directly at our possessiveness and attachment. In the larger picture, what is happening is that more light is streaming into the world, threatening our false identities.

---

[5] See glossary of psycho-spiritual terms for a definition of "code."

Proceeding from Fear to Trust

If we identify with a thought, we actually believe that we *are* that thought. Thoughts of possessiveness, jealousy, insecurity and fear belong to the realm of the shadow. When we get identified with them, we start to believe that we actually are that shadow. The moment the light shines, we experience the terror of annihilation because the nature of light is to dissipate darkness.

You are not the mental construction you think you are. If you suffer, it is because you identify with that image. This false self-concept is not your final reality. You are just dreaming, or quite often, having a nightmare. When you are inside your nightmare, you believe it to be real. I am giving you a wake-up call: it's time to awaken from this nightmare. Focus your awareness on your breath. As much as you may believe in this mirage; as extensive as its influence inside you may be, there is always a thread of awareness remaining to remind you that you are only dreaming. You can use this awareness to breathe softly and deeply, to return to your center. Through this awareness you will try to remind yourself, "I am dreaming; I need to stop with this destructiveness." Just go for a walk, drink some cold water or take a shower, until you can again return to your center. Once you come to your center you will see with more clarity.

A change in orientation is happening. You are moving from one extreme, where you are addicted to receiving exclusive love, to the other where you are able to give love. The first extreme is based on fear and a belief in scarcity, but now you are moving towards trust, towards self-confidence, and the outlook that there is nothing lacking in this world.

We will only embody the experience of freedom and ecstasy when we re-establish self-trust. Until we trust ourselves, we will not be able to sustain freedom and ecstasy. We will continue suffering inner conflicts.

Everything in our lives happens by divine grace to help us re-establish self-confidence. If our intrinsic trust in ourselves is buried beneath many layers of self-doubt, it remains hidden and inaccessible. We will encounter more work and challenges ahead. It is natural that our vices, destructive games, and other bad habits become more apparent at this moment: we will be able to identify them with much greater ease. Based on this identification, we will be able to make the intentional choice to change course.

Learning to trust ourselves facilitates the union of the masculine and the feminine within. For this union to come about, one first needs to heal the estrangement of the polarities within oneself. It is because of this disunion that things are so intense in people's lives. The intensity happens in order to help us identify this division and its cause.

THE VOICE OF FEAR

During this process of healing, do not lose faith in union and in love. We often experience an unconscious primal dread that manifests itself more superficially through various symptoms, the main one being fear. Right now there is a sword pointing directly at this fear, because fear is the emotion that prevents us from trusting ourselves. Through self-confidence we can receive and embody the divine messages of freedom and pleasure that are being sent to this planet. Fear troubles us through our doubts, our skepticism, and our tendency to talk ourselves out of sustaining love. The self-fulfilling prophecy of failure makes us believe that God is against us and that the world is out to get us.

Identify the voice of fear. Know that it stems from your lower self. Once you have recognized it, do not pay it any heed. Continue diverting energy from self-loathing to self-confidence, until you cross this bridge of self-doubt. Even when the lower self has taken over your mind, maintain the understanding that there is an impostor at work – someone has taken possession of your house, and is squatting in it. Remind yourself that, "This is illusion. God is my best friend. Life is in my favor. If I am undergoing a trial period, it is because I need to learn something by it. Please Lord, grant me humility so that I may learn what You are teaching me."

If fear is in command, pride and stubborn self-will are its lieutenants. All these negative emotions are like a military junta, but in spite of all their power they are mere lackeys of the lower self. The lower self occupies our minds and demands that the higher self step down. This coup can only be successful if we fear change, if we are afraid to experience this newfound freedom, since it brings the unknown. With this fear also comes pride, which makes us think that God is clueless, or an unjust tyrant.

This is an erroneous image of God: it is a mere projection of our negative parents. God is the one and only life. God is the creative intelligence that manifests in everything and everyone. God is love. Sometimes, love needs to wring us out in order to cleanse us, so that we may become a pure channel of divine love. We need humility to undergo this experience. Only through humility will we experience acceptance. Only when we accept love can we surrender to love.

LETTING GO OF THE DESTRUCTIVE GAME

Meditate upon these words. Look deeply within yourself. Where are you in this divine play? What destructive game do you need to abandon? What addiction or bad habit do you need to break? What clutter is blocking your heart and needs to be removed?

If you do not know the answer to these questions, tell your higher self: "I want to know; please, show me. I am committed to seeing clearly." It will not help writhing in your own agony. Even if you try to get somewhere, you will be walking around in circles. What will help is answering the following questions: What are you hiding that makes you keep beating yourself up? You guard the very rock that blocks the way to your heart. Why do you let this rock obstruct the way? Why do you protect this addiction or bad habit? What is the hurtful game that you want to keep playing? What do you gain from maintaining it? There must be some pleasure in your self-defense, otherwise you would not keep acting this way!

Set the intention to recognize the obstacles in your path, and to discover how they take you over. Dive deeply within yourself to understand how you act and react in the world. One way to dive deeply is through prayer and meditation. Through this process you receive inner knowledge. When this knowledge arises, you will have to make a choice, and you may have to take some difficult actions. You may have to renounce something, such as a bad habit or a destructive game. But for this renunciation to be true, it must come from a place of deep understanding and insight. For that, you must first truly want to understand your situation; yet often you actually do not want to see it. You avoid taking a good look at yourself, and instead look critically at other people, convinced that the other is responsible for your suffering. You use this avoidance mechanism to protect the destructive game to which you are addicted. The time has come to delete this ancient piece of software from your system, and yet you protect it as if it were a treasure, because you are addicted to it.

Why do we so stubbornly resist letting go of our destructive games? The light of truth is like our inner cop, chasing down and trying to arrest the robber who is hiding in your house with his cache of stolen goods. The items are not even worth all that much – it's a misdemeanor, not a felony – but instead of handing them over to the policeman and facing the consequences, your inner robber cowers in fear and is willing to risk his life over them. The lights on the police cars of our higher self are flashing, and its voice is calling to us over the bullhorn, saying, "Come out, for God's sake. Such drama over a few stolen knick-knacks!"

Your house is under siege. It is up to you to surrender your bad habits and your harmful games. It is up to you to align yourself with joy, with love and with light. There is no way out – I can guarantee you that. You will inevitably reach happiness. You may hide wherever you want, but you have already been caught. You can put up a fight, or you can go crazy – but there is no way out. You will be happy. You will dance, sing, and celebrate life. I am completely committed to this: this is my *sankalpa*, my promise, my heartfelt intention.

Your destiny is to realize the Truth, and the Truth is that you are free. You are an embodiment of light and of divine love. As much as your conditioned mind may want to believe something else, the brilliance of true reality will come shining through. You will wake up from this dream of scarcity in which you believe yourself to be a powerless wounded child, insecure and never good enough. Wake up from this nightmare! It is but a layer of illusion that covers up the reality that *you are trust itself.* Meditate upon this. Affirm to yourself: "I am divine. I am love and light. What could I possibly be lacking?"

Put all your fears to rest. Your house is the abode of the golden light of God. The house I speak of is your body. Your body is a temple of divine light. This transformation is inevitable. You only need to redirect your willpower. This will happen if you make the intention, because the reality is that *you* are divine light. Your body is a channel of that light. All negative feelings are superimposed layers that come from our identification with repetitive implanted thoughts and childhood conditioning.

These beliefs make us accept the myth that something is missing. Because of this delusion we feel a compulsion to grab what belongs to others. We are being invited to abandon that game. We do not need to take anything from anyone – we just need to give. Instead of always focusing on your own needs, you will long to inspire the best in the other, forgetting yourself altogether. The more you focus on making the other shine, the more you yourself will shine.

Keep these words in your hearts today.

15
Money and Spirituality

Every human being longs for happiness. Many believe that they will attain happiness through fulfilling desires, acquiring material goods, or through grasping for future security by saving money. People invest all their time and energy in the pursuit of these goals, often subjecting themselves to great sacrifices in the process. They seek to attain an appealing yet elusive contentment by acquiring the objects of their desire. Once people acquire such objects, they experience only fleeting joy. This ephemeral happiness may last only for a few minutes. After the brief satisfaction, the person returns to his own bottomless pit of discontent and creates a new desire to pursue, a goal that will surely bring satisfaction this time … This goes on endlessly. Such a person – who we could say is still spiritually immature – believes that inner contentment can only be possible once the outside world starts playing by his rules, living up to his expectations and wishes. On the other hand, a spiritually mature person knows that happiness is not a destination, but rather a vehicle.

EXTERNAL REFLECTS THE INTERNAL

Our experience of the external world is a reflection of our internal world. To attribute any form of happiness to external events is a trick of the mind. It allows one to blame destiny, karma, God or other people for one's own failures. Whether one experiences joy or misery depends exclusively on oneself. Therefore, joy should be cultivated inside. It will then naturally blossom in one's external life. Such a state of contentment does not depend upon external circumstances, nor upon other people; rather, it is an inner phenomenon. Happiness is God, and God is your most intimate reality. By attaining such happiness you realize your true essence, and you reach the goal of your whole search. Happiness is right here, right now.

The meaning of spirituality is knowledge of oneself. Who are you? The path of spirituality takes you towards yourself. It is the path that leads back home. The immature personality could be compared to a water droplet – wearing a suit and tie, expensive sunglasses, driving his convertible, and thinking of himself as something – anything – but the ocean. This is the reality of most human beings. We have lost ourselves at a masquerade, believing ourselves to be the mask that we are used to wearing. True happiness emerges once we remove the veil of illusion that we have created and maintained throughout our lives. We may call this veil of illusion ignorance – ignorance that manifests itself in the form of our masks and of the lower self.

The lower self is a creature of transitory reality. It is but a distortion of our real being. The lower self manifests a wide range of characteristics, commonly known as weaknesses or vices, like gluttony, laziness, greed, envy, rage, pride, lust, fear and the compulsion to lie – to name just the most common. These unappealing aspects of the ego must be uncovered and embraced before they can be understood and integrated. This process enables us to reach our ultimate reality: our higher selves. But if we refuse to get in touch with the lower self, we cannot work on it so as to finally transcend it. The wholeness that results from this process is spirituality. It is the crossing of the sacred ocean, to reclaim our true identity, to remember our divine nature.

THE ENERGY OF MONEY

What does all this have to do with money? Money is neutral energy. The human beings who use that money are the ones who polarize its energy. If the higher self uses money, it acquires a positive polarity and may be used towards the greater goal of fostering a culture of peace in the world. But if the lower self uses the power of money, it lends a negative polarity to wealth, which will cause destruction and foster conflict. The lower self believes that money gives it power. This power is used to dominate others, which enables us to numb our ever-lurking feelings of neediness and inferiority.

When our consciousness is centered in the higher self – when the water droplet is aware that it *is* the ocean – the higher self becomes our energy source. On the other hand, if the illusion of separation breaks the connection with the higher self, one becomes helplessly needy of the higher self's energy. To compensate, one desperately tries to tap into the energy of others, for they seem to be something apart from oneself. The strategy of the ego is to drain the other's vital energy, like a vampire, and to make the other feel inferior.

Money is just a human symbol representing the value attached to goods or services being exchanged, but many forces attach themselves to this symbol. Money is an energy that should be treated with respect and wisdom. Ignorance, in the form of lust and greed, enslaves us to money. This lust and greed are two aspects of the lower self that make the human being more identified with the body – and as a consequence, one becomes identified with the false self.

Money can also serve as a substitute for affection. It is exceedingly common for a father who does not give his child love, to give that child money or material goods to compensate for his neglect. He says, "I don't have the time to be with you, but I'll ensure that you lack for nothing." The developing personality of the child comes to the erroneous conclusion that money is synonymous with affection. Such a child then generalizes this image of "money as substitute for affection" and tries to keep money as a close companion for the rest of his life.

When the child grows up and becomes an intellectually mature adult, he still harbors this wounded child within, with all of its mistaken conclusions about life. Such a person projects the distant, absentee father on other people, making the generalization that everyone will behave like their father. Although the person may understand with their intellect that money and affection are not one-and-the-same thing, at an unconscious level the person really does believe that the two are interchangeable. To protect the child's wound of neglect, these imprints are relegated to the depths of the unconscious mind. There they exert their influence unrestrained, hidden in the shadows of forgetfulness.

HOW MONEY FLOWS TO PEOPLE

Money often becomes the final goal of people's life journey, for they believe it can solve all their problems. This is the underlying cause of all the conflicts and coldness that permeate human life, especially in Western society. Unconsciously, we are all really searching for love.

Depending on their karma, some people will achieve material abundance. However, all the money they have acquired might only serve to strengthen their personal defenses, for that money reinforces their belief in themselves as being powerful and self-sufficient. Deep down they are well aware that their sense of completeness is a blatant lie, for they know that they are still just needy children acting inside an adult body. This psychological discrepancy causes confusion and suffering. The person has trouble distinguishing between means and ends.

If money has become a person's end goal in life, then all that person's efforts will be directed towards making money. In the efforts to become wealthy, such a person pays little attention to the nature of the work they are performing. They don't question whether it is worthwhile, fulfilling or enjoyable.

The spiritually mature person knows that their actions are governed by the heart's intent, and that money is a natural consequence of their actions. Work, often perceived as a burden, now is transformed into service and becomes a precious gift given to others from the depths of one's being. We reach this state when we serve the Divine, which is to serve one's own heart. Service brings us pleasure and fulfillment as a natural reward. Money is a part of this reward, for it gives us dignity as well as the means to support ourselves without depending on others. But money is not the primary goal of our endeavors, only the means to our ends, which are spiritual. When we develop such maturity, we are no longer slaves to money, for we have freed ourselves from attachment. Attachment is the bondage that causes so much suffering, and imprisons the human soul.

The wounded child acts through the adult body. Only through self-discovery can we grow up and start giving money a positive energy, as it begins to be used by the higher self. In our school of spiritual initiation, we regard working with the inner child as a preparatory course that is a prerequisite for a higher education in spiritual life.

People have come to associate money with all kinds of symbols and beliefs. For example, I once received a person who explained that he had much difficulty in making money. He would work a lot, and everything would be alright as long as he did not make too much money. However, when money would start to flow in abundantly, he would go into a deep personal crisis – and that would block the process of his financial gain. By inquiring into his life story, we discovered a link between money and a pattern dating back to childhood. It was a story involving pain, manipulation, control and struggle – all around money. That person unconsciously regarded money as responsible for all the discord that rocked his early family life. Money had become a symbol of that trauma. This explains his rejection of money and his difficulty in obtaining it.

It is a common belief that one needs to suffer endless hardships to deserve any pleasure whatsoever. There is a religious mindset that many of us inherited from our culture, which exalts those who are nailed to the cross. This mindset is deeply imprinted in our subconscious. The idea is that, if we wear a crown of thorns, people will finally accept us as worthy and unselfish. Another common belief, based on a misinterpretation of a saying of Jesus, insists that we *do* indeed have to be poor to be spiritual, for "it is easier for a camel to go through the eye of a needle than for a rich man to enter the kingdom of God."[6] Such beliefs inevitably limit the understanding of the spiritual role of money. They prevent us from understanding our true spiritual identity.

---

[6] Matthew 19:24

PAYING FOR SPIRITUAL WORK

Another issue regarding money and spirituality, is how people tend to look with suspicion at being asked to pay for spiritual work. It is curious to observe this mentality. People spare no effort and make few judgments when they seek to obtain material goods. We may even consider something to be expensive, but if we *really* want it we usually buy it anyway if we have the money. On the other hand, when money is required to help us work on ourselves, we hesitate. People often understand that monetary contributions are necessary for explicitly charity-based work; but people struggle to understand the legitimacy of payment for psychotherapy sessions, self-discovery workshops or personal growth retreats. This reactive suspicion is born of spiritual immaturity. Underlying this critical mindset are limiting beliefs and a lack of knowledge about the "law of giving and receiving." Mistrust arises with the idea that, "if what they offer costs money, then it can't be all that spiritual."

Deeper down, such excuses are used to flee from the conditions that would bring about the confrontation with ourselves. Such a judgmental attitude avoids responsibility for our own process. The fear of discovering ourselves underpins this apparent stinginess and reluctance to pay for services rendered.

Divine grace is like the sun that illuminates everyone equally. Divine grace and enlightenment cannot be bought or sold. In authentic spirituality, money in and of itself is not the focus. The primary focus is on the transmission of knowledge and on the fulfillment of the greater work. Money is energy that circulates among people, which finances the physical infrastructure needed for people to achieve these spiritual goals.

Still, there are many people of low character, and even some well-intentioned ones, whose conscious or unconscious focus is on making money through their "spiritual work." To those caught in this pattern, the money earned comes to represent affection. Little by little, a person's inner growth enables them to distinguish between authentic spirituality and spirituality distorted by the immature need for recognition.

FULFILLING YOUR PURPOSE

Money is not in any way anti-spiritual. What *is* anti-spiritual is attachment to money, and to regard money as being an end rather than just a means to a greater goal. As we mature spiritually, we discover that learning how to deal with money is a key teaching in this great school of life.

During our spiritual journey, we may work and earn money, but we should not waste our time or energy worrying about money. All one's attention should be towards recognizing oneself as an embodiment of divine love, and seeing the same divinity in all beings. You have not been born into this world to drive yourself crazy or ill worrying about money. And you can be sure you weren't born in order to buy goods and services. Rather, you came in order to perform the great work, which is to recognize

God in yourself and in every living being. In this way you fulfill your *dharma*, your real purpose in life. Be a sincere devotee, and your life will lack nothing. The Divine Mother always gives her children everything needed for their self-realization.

If we feel that something is missing, it's because we are identified with the illusion of scarcity, because in reality there is no lack of anything in this world. The idea of "me," which defends the tyranny of the mind over the heart, gives rise to the idea of "mine" – and thereby lays the foundations of self-deceit. We consider the illusory to be real, and we attach ourselves to that illusion. In this way we create the conditions for suffering to overtake us. The path that leads to liberation lies in self-observation. In this practice, the only question we ask ourselves is, "Who am I?" As our dedication to the path of truth grows, all our legitimate needs will be met – always.

GIVING UP THE FEAR OF SCARCITY

A person is only ready to experience real wealth when they are prepared to live in poverty without fear. Just as one can be immortal only when freed from the fear of death, so one can experience abundance only when one can live within modest means without shame or fear. Everything that is built to cover up something of which one is afraid or ashamed will crumble sooner or later.

A student of mine had prospered in the material realm. He had a company that would rake in a hundred million dollars profit a year. Then he faced an emotional crisis in his marriage, and things went badly for him in business. He lost more and more money, until within a short time he was completely bankrupt. He discovered that someone had been stealing from him without him even noticing because he had been so caught up in his emotional crisis. Having reached this awful state, he decided to seek me out to ask for help – help, that is, in reclaiming his lost riches. It soon became clear to me that he first needed to face up to his current poverty, for he had built his empire to flee from such poverty. He had grown up impoverished, but had never had the courage to look at and really accept this poverty. There is a psychic law to the effect that, unconsciously, what you fear the most is also what you desire the most. Everything the mask-identity builds will fall away sooner or later. It does not matter whether this false identity is the attachment to an empire or to a psycho-emotional state – at some point it will have to crumble.

Coveting more money than needed for a simple lifestyle conducive to spiritual realization is an illness. This burning desire for ever more wealth is a disease rooted in lust and greed, both manifestations of our absolute identification with the body. Unless we are cured of this illness, it will inevitably generate suffering. But you do not have to feel concerned if this is your case. Through self-investigation, identify your dependence on material sustenance and the feeling of vulnerability such dependence creates. Having recognized this attachment and dependence, stop agonizing over it. Open your heart instead. That practice will elevate your consciousness and lead to the resolution of your problems.

Spiritual practices do not guarantee liberation. We may perform many practices but continue to act based on the same old fear of scarcity, and so manifest the selfishness produced by such an attitude. We may be sleepwalking around in circles, but believe that we are really getting somewhere, unable to recognize that we are just seeing the same landscape over and over again. Cultivate your ability to recognize that you are a manifestation of the Divine, and that this same divine essence is alive in every living being. This vision of unity is only attainable through self-investigation. Once you can see the Divine in all, your heart opens and reveals your love, which is your true nature. You transform your actions into service to God.

Don't just fold your arms and wait for the things you need to fall from the sky. God has no hands other than your own. Since God is inside of you, you are the one who needs to get the work done. However, your actions should be dedicated to God. You should not perform them to get anything in exchange. Recognize this insistence on taking something in exchange for anything you may give, and put an end to it, for this is a fruit of ignorance.

16
Raising Children to Become Conscious Adults

Question: A few weeks ago I participated in an international conference on holistic education. I left really inspired about the new paradigm in education and about music education in particular. I would like to know your views about education, and particularly about some children I have encountered at these more progressive schools who demonstrate impressive maturity and wisdom beyond their years.

Prem Baba: This is an extremely important and complex question. It is clear to me that a new paradigm in parenting and education is the only basis upon which a new era can emerge, so that we may sustain life on this planet in the face of the environmental crisis we have created.

EDUCATION FOR A NEW ERA

I feel that we can be of particular service to the world by working with children, giving them an education based on humane spiritual values. Such child-rearing could prevent children from acquiring the deeply entrenched conditioning from which it takes adults so much effort to free themselves.

Mainstream education has failed in its mission of preparing children to live joyful and fulfilling lives, and so, we need to re-examine it. Much of education is based on fear. The child is educated to look after their own self-interest and to extract the maximum possible advantage from everyone in every situation. Isn't this the way you were educated? But it was the very emptiness created by this kind of value system that ultimately brought you here. Many are here out of love for God, but many others are also here searching for a way out of suffering. This suffering is caused by the endless karma created in your search for happiness. The mainstream educational system has been playing a strong role in keeping people stuck within this cycle of suffering, because it is oriented towards the ego rather than towards the being.

What would be the hallmarks of education for a new era of higher consciousness? It would be an education that nurtures the spirit, one based on ethical human values. It would keep the childlike spark alive in young people as they grow into adults, through the arts, music and dance as well as academics. The educational system of the new era would help children get in touch with their God-given talents and gifts. It would inculcate self-confidence and values of love and cooperation rather than competitive individualism. The emphasis would be on the practice of compassion rather than the adoption of belief systems. The goal of such education would be to guide children towards a life focused on establishing higher consciousness and peace on earth.

To establish such an educational system, educators and parents must have something to offer in terms of psycho-emotional maturity, so as to lead by example. It does no good to keep repeating admonitions from the manual, because children take in and emulate what they see you doing, not what they hear you saying.

The biggest challenge for educators and parents is to understand the importance and true nature of the spiritual side of this calling. It's really not about having the kids *become* anything; it's about helping them realize who they already *are*. Parents and teachers don't have to be perfect to do this work, but they do need to have integrity. It is essential to have developed a measure of authenticity and humility, and to be able to admit our mistakes, even in front of a child. Unless we can own up to our own fallibility, how can we expect children to love themselves and others, warts and all?

Virtually every child born into this world is trained to believe that he or she has to be perfect at all things. This pressure to excel leads to the creation of an idealized self-image. These overblown expectations are impossible to fulfill. Carrying the burden of this unattainable image of perfection, the child bends over backwards trying to conform to the expectations of society about what is "right and proper." The child is trained to conform to societal norms. As a result, they will live their lives always acting in an artificial way. I am reminded of a young man I once met who was very proud that his brother was a bank robber, and not just some two-bit mugger. I am simplifying the subject considerably; as a matter of fact the creation of this idealized self happens in subtle and complex ways that make it difficult to detect. The self-image that is impossible to ever live up to may subsist completely on the level of the unconscious mind.

Virtually everyone I come across seems to carry an imprint that prevents them from accepting their own imperfections. Even the more evolved children that are arriving in these times struggle because they are not always the best at absolutely everything. I see children getting extremely upset because they make mistakes. They are assaulted by feelings of shame, for they have been conditioned to be perfect: "Don't mess up or I'll stop loving you." Children hear this message from parents and educators in very subtle and indirect ways. It is a cruel tyranny, for through these insinuating mechanisms parents are quite effective at forcing the child to serve their whims.

BEYOND RULES

Children, as well as the emotionally immature adults they often become, struggle to stick to the script that has been written for them in order to gain acceptance from their parents, teachers, or peer group. Only occasionally do the grown-up children realize that the time has passed for observing once-useful rules, and that now they can move on to define the rules that are appropriate for them as adults.

The rules appropriate for children should arise from a loving consciousness, and be geared towards fostering authentic human values that are intrinsic to one's spiritual evolution. But few adults understand what constitutes an appropriate limit for children. Rather, children are generally trained to follow rules rooted in ignorance and enforced with an implicit threat of withdrawing the parents' love if the child does not conform to their expectations. "If I don't do what Mommy and Daddy want me to they will not accept and love me anymore," is what the child is thinking. Adults in turn find the turbulent emotions of the child to be hard to deal with because of our own conditioning. We often find the child's spontaneity to be unsettling, because it reminds us of how far we have fallen from our own real childlike selves.

A child does need limits and rules. The problem is that no one gives them any real understanding of the merely transitory importance of those limits. With such an understanding, when these children grow up, they would be free to let go of some of those limits that served to protect them from harm as children, but may be limiting or counter-productive as adults. Many of the limitations that are normally applied to children are not even valid to begin with. They are not based on eternal truths, but rather on the dogmas and beliefs of the child's family or of the larger society.

If children need some boundaries for their own safety, those limits have to emerge from the loving heart and not from the wounded child of the parent unconsciously competing with their own children. This is a huge challenge for parents, more than for educators, because of their strong sense of ownership over the child. For parents, the tendency to project is strong. What causes this is the idea of mine: "My son, my daughter, mine, mine ... everything is mine – so everything has to be done *my* way." We set ourselves up as tyrants, taking revenge on our own children for everything that happened during our childhood, and so teach them to in turn pass it on to the children they will one day have.

LOVE INSTEAD OF FEAR

This multi-generational pact of vengeance is why the world is headed towards such a deep sustainability crisis. Children feel a need for exclusive love that is impossible to fulfill. Even when children have grown up physically and intellectually, they usually do not grow up emotionally. And so, people want the earth to feed them exclusively, and teach their children to wish for the same. Comprehend what I am saying: the need for exclusive love arises as a symptom of a certain phase in the world's evolution, which is reinforced by the educational system and by the child's upbringing. This child grows up without having integrated and healed the wounded child – and so the wounded child raises the next generation of wounded children. The adult still needs to affirm himself or herself, and so takes revenge on the child in an attempt to fill their inner void. To escape this vicious cycle we need to understand the process so that we don't pass down this virus of "immature love that never grows up."

The current generation of children born in the new millennium are coming with a modified code: they have a greater ability to give selflessly. They serve as channels that come with programs that are more attuned to divine light. But although the program is already installed, it is in sleep mode, and you are the one who needs to turn it on. The only touch which will work is that of your own example.

To keep this program running smoothly, the child needs to receive an education that is based on humane and spiritual values. Through their example, educators should remind children of the purpose of their lives. Children must learn to live harmoniously in society, but with the awareness that they are spiritual beings living a human experience. The whole system should be focused on establishing and anchoring this spiritual consciousness on earth. The mission of the divine project for the planet is to have every institution function solely in order to instill this new spiritual paradigm. It is a radical departure from the status-quo.

Imagine an economy being motivated by love instead of by fear. It sounds crazy, doesn't it? But what else are we doing here? You have to choose what energies and whose second-hand ideas you allow to move through you. Who are you going to serve, divine love, or hatred and fear? You're going to have to choose. Choosing light doesn't mean that you automatically become a channel for divine love. You still have an internal housecleaning to accomplish; but this commitment to spreading love becomes the guiding beacon of your life.

Question: How can we help our preteen children make the difficult transition to adolescence and the teenage years? In the modern world there are both stress-inducing and nihilistic influences that tend to stifle the spontaneity of children. I can remember the very moment this happened with my younger brother, when he lost the joy of living that is natural to children.

Prem Baba: When children reach adolescence the conflicts of childhood are often revisited. The parents have a second chance to get it right and establish a heartfelt friendship with the being who is now coming into its own. Be a true parent-friend, open up to this being who is your equal. Listen to your kids. Enter into their world to understand what's going on with them.

When I spoke about the sacred role of a parent, I was speaking about leaving aside the role of father or mother to be a *real* father or mother with an open heart to accept and embrace the child. This is the way you can help. Adolescence can be a real challenge, because when your kids revisit childhood conflicts they might become really angry at you. They are going to poke you and step on your toes. The great challenge is to come to the realization that there is something more to you than your own wounded child, who must react in the face of these frontal assaults by your angry teenager. The key is to realize who you are identified with. Are you a channel of love, or a channel of your wounded child with its insistence on having its own way? For a while, you will continue to alternate between being identified with your higher self and with your lower self. You should persist in this practice until, bit by bit, you become only a channel of love.

17
Honoring the Feminine and Mother Earth

I have a student who recently participated in a conference at NASA where the world's top scientists met to discuss studies conducted to ascertain the situation of the earth's environment. Their conclusions about global warming, and the sustainability and natural resource crises were that it is impossible to avoid the impacts that our civilization will soon experience. It is up to us human beings to reduce our environmental footprint, to remedy the harm already done, and to adapt to the changes in motion.

WORKING FROM THE OUTSIDE IN AND THE INSIDE OUT

To this end, there are two different and complementary approaches we can take. In the first approach, we work from the outside in. This is akin to using allopathic medicine to treat symptoms of disease in the body. We can begin treating Mother Earth's affliction by taking action. There are many efforts already underway that embody this approach, and that clearly show us what needs to be done. We must curb our careless consumption of energy resources, irresponsible consumerism, and ceaseless production of toxic waste. We should also raise awareness and educate each other. Further, we need to provide feasible alternatives to our deeply-ingrained habits. We must make these changes in our daily lives, in our laws, in our business practices, and in our social values.

But as important as these efforts are, we should be aware that we are only dealing with the symptoms of the disease. We must not delude ourselves into believing that these concrete measures alone will be able to heal the underlying issue. At some point we must turn inwards and address the reasons behind our unconscious destructive behaviors.

This is the second approach, from the inside out. We must look deep within ourselves and realize that ultimately, the issue is our hostility towards the feminine. We do not respect the sanctity of Mother Earth. We dishonor and mistreat the feminine. We want to have power over her and make her our slave, thus repeating a conditioned pattern that has existed for thousands of years. But recognizing this requires a maturity that many of us don't yet have; until then, it is important to continue to effect change from the outside in, taking concrete action to minimize the harm that we cause our planet.

Sometimes people treat this whole destructive process as illusory. And yet, it really is destroying us. Even if it is illusory, we are still identified with hatred and continue to react from it.

What is truly harmful is our lack of awareness of how this hatred acts inside of us. This ignorance prevents us from admitting and taking responsibility for our destructiveness, and so we continue unconsciously wreaking havoc on the planet.

THE MASCULINE AND FEMININE PRINCIPLES

Let's look at the relationship between the masculine and feminine principles; note that this is not the same as the relationship between men and women. Any creative process can only come about through the union of the masculine and the feminine. The masculine principle is the assertive, active force, while the feminine principle is receptive, nurturing, accepting. Acceptance and trust are innate qualities of the sacred feminine; they are the greatest powers on Earth.

A seed is planted: that is the masculine principle at work. The time required for the seed to sprout and eventually blossom into a flower: that is the feminine principle at work. These principles act in all of nature, and they are acting inside of you at every moment, creating all that exists. They materialize in bodies as male and female, although each individual manifests both the masculine and the feminine principles.

Throughout human history, these principles have been misused. The activating male principle has degenerated into tyranny and brutality, so that men repeatedly abuse women physically and psychologically. As for the feminine principle, whose strength is acceptance and trust, it has been distorted into dependence and submission as a form of manipulation. Thus, instead of a healthy masculine meeting a healthy feminine to make love and create fresh, new realities, it is a distorted masculine that has been meeting a distorted feminine, causing only enmity and destruction.

This co-dependent dynamic is installed in our programming and is replayed endlessly in our relationships without us being aware of it. Some of us are starting to opt out of it: women who are working towards independence and men who are working to accept their vulnerability. But for the most part, men are not aware of the hatred towards the feminine that they harbor in their system; they may think that they value the feminine, but in reality they are numb, feeling nothing. Meanwhile there are women who think they love and embody the feminine principle, but who suffocate their men with too much attention and care. They mistake this smothering for love when in reality it is an expression of their anger and resentment.

The sacred feminine manifests itself in many ways: in your mother, who gave you life; in women in general; in your physical body; and in nature itself, with all its manifestations. If you want to know how a nation is doing, observe its relationship with the feminine in all its forms. Most importantly, whether you are a man or a woman, examine your own relationship with the feminine: How do you relate with the sacred feminine? Do you sincerely honor the feminine? Are you able to maintain the awareness that the feminine is sacred as you relate to her in your daily life?

MISTREATING THE BODY AND MOTHER NATURE

When we are careless with our physical bodies, we are careless with Mother Nature, because the body is a microcosm of nature. Your veins are the rivers; your heart is the ocean. What have you been throwing into the rivers of your body? You have likely been ingesting the same things that you throw into the earth's rivers: plastic, heavy metals, and various chemicals.

The urge to eat junk food, or what the ancient Hindu science of Ayurveda labels as *tamasic* food, also stems from this hostility towards the feminine. You feel the need to stuff the body with chemicals, dead foods, and altogether too much food in order to numb yourself and avoid feeling your emotions. You need to do this because it is dangerous to feel; because if you are not numb, you may feel hatred. You may also feel love, which is not so different of a threat.

This trash is clogging up your system just like it is clogging up the planet. We have come to a point where there is nothing that can be done with the amount of pollution on this planet. This is one of the problems we need to address in the outer world.

Another way that the hatred of the feminine is expressed is in our habit of eating meat. I know it may sound strange to many, but in a sense eating meat means "eating the mother" – fried, barbecued or roasted. You stick a fork in her, cut her up with a knife, put her in your mouth, and chew. The issue of eating meat is a deep one, because it is connected to the crisis that the earth is going through. The forests in Brazil and elsewhere are being purposefully burned down in order to raise cattle, which drastically decreases the amount of plants and trees available to transform carbon dioxide into oxygen. At the same time, these fires release great amounts of carbon dioxide into the atmosphere, contributing to global warming and making natural fires throughout the world be much more destructive and frequent. These positive feedback loops are very difficult to stop. Curiously enough, cows themselves directly contribute to the problem as they produce methane, which is a greenhouse gas that is twenty times more potent than carbon dioxide in its ability to trap heat in the atmosphere. Half of our diet-related greenhouse gas emissions come from the production of meat, which has become a mainstay of the world economy. In short, the harmful impact of beef production undermines the possibility of building a long-term sustainable economy.

The issue of deforestation is one I have first-hand knowledge of, because I often visit the Amazon rainforest in Brazil. In the past, I didn't need to go far to access the deep jungle; nowadays, I have to travel for hours because of the clear-cutting and burning done for cattle-ranching. The land is eroded and exhausted. The destruction of the Amazon forest is an attack on the lungs of Mother Earth.

I pay a lot of attention to these different issues because examining and connecting seemingly disparate problems helps shed light on some of the mysteries of life. One conclusion I have come to is that as long as we continue to slaughter animals for food, we will not be able to end hunger or establish peace in the world. This is because the meat industry is not only cruel in its mistreatment of animals, but also extremely wasteful of natural resources. Veiled by ignorance, many of us don't realize that killing animals is one of the ways that we abuse the Mother.

If it is hard for you to see the connection, go deep into your own psyche and see if you still hold resentment against your own mother. Look at her. If I ask you now, "How do you feel about your mother?" and you say, "Alright", this tells me that you feel nothing towards her. You are indifferent towards her, and indifference is a symptom of anger. Does the love flow? Does the gratitude flow? Are you able to look at her and thank her? Are you able to revere her as a divine manifestation? If you can, great. But I doubt that a person who has this level of gratitude for the mother will eat meat. They are different manifestations of the same thing. Hatred expresses itself through various forms, just as love does. When you truly love your mother you love the feminine, including nature.

HEALING THE WOUNDS

In a stroke of synchronicity, a man sent me a note today saying, "Beloved teacher, yesterday I had a very strong experience in which I confronted my mother and the hatred I have towards her, which had risen to the surface." When you tell me that you confronted your mother and noticed the hatred that lies in your inability to communicate with her, I feel that you have begun to find the path towards transforming your destructiveness.

Rationally, you may have many reasons for feeling the way you do: she used to invade your personal space and she abused you in many ways. But understand that both her behavior and your hostility are re-enactments of a pact of vengeance. One of the strategies used by the distorted feminine is to use her role as a mother to gain power over her children, causing antagonism and alienation between mother and child. This makes the child want to take revenge on his mother. Allow yourself to go deep into this hatred of the mother, this resentment towards the feminine, and really feel it so that you can begin to heal it.

Until that wound is healed, you may choose to love and revere other manifestations of the feminine such as a Goddess or Nature. But even then, be aware that this love is not pure: there are still masks there, and you are still bargaining. You are doing this for sake of appearances and because you want to receive something in exchange. Until your actions truly spring from the heart, you are not putting love into movement yet.

This healing that is occurring at the personal level is also occurring at the planetary level. The economic crisis that is taking hold of the world is the beginning of this healing process. It is happening so that we may free ourselves from this distortion, from this fear and hostility towards the feminine, and begin to live coming from trust and love. At the deepest level, this crisis is the healing of our relationship with our mother. It is teaching us how to revere her once again; how to see the Divine in her, regardless of her personality flaws. Then we will be able to see planet Earth as a manifestation of the mother.

Our planet is alive; she is a sentient being. When we wake up in the morning and place our feet on the earth, we should do so with reverence because we are touching this being that is receiving us. Each little corner of the earth is a part of the mother; each part is performing its *dharma* and manifesting its karma. And it is part of the *dharma* of this earth to awaken us, to open our hearts, to purify our bodies, to remind us of our divinity.

OFFER YOUR GIFT

We are living in a time of great changes, and there is a lot of enthusiasm about elevating the vibration of the planet. I am determined to do this; I am giving it my best. I do everything I can to help you awaken internally, so that you may exert influence from the inside out and also from the outside in.

I support many projects that help bring the paradigm of love to the world – social projects, economic projects, educational projects... I am lending my support to every positive project I possibly can. If I see that there is space for me to give support to this paradigm of love, I do. I am giving you strength so that you may share your talents, so that you may contribute your best. If your talent is to make music, I will help you to become a good musician. If your talent is to make movies, I will help you. If your talent is in gardening, I will help you become an excellent gardener.

I do this because it will enable you to bring out the best in yourself. When your soul reveals itself, the world will inevitably also begin to reveal its own soul. What is the soul of the world, if not the sum of all of our individual souls? If you give to the world that which you came here to give, the world will also give you what it has to offer.

I believe that by nurturing the unique contribution each person has to make, conditions in the world can improve: people can start to treat each other with more consideration, nations don't have to be so quick to attack or scheme against one another, and the human race as a whole may finally wake up to its collective need, and mobilize all of its creativity and resources towards protecting the planet from our excesses.

As intense as the ecological crisis may get, and as turbulent as things may be, I have unshakeable faith in the positive outcome of this healing process that we are undergoing.

18
Selfless Service and the Promise of Our Lineage

Selfless service is love in action. But such a wave of love can only be generated in this way once you free yourself from self-interest to the point of being able to take a decisive step beyond egoism. You truly put yourself in the service of the common good and of collective peace, in the service of harmony and of the awakening of all beings. *Seva*, service, or the practice of altruism, is the cornerstone of the path of *karma yoga*.

When you practice *seva* you make yourself a link in the chain of happiness, purely in order to make the other happy, or to bring comfort. You do all you possibly can to help make them shine. There is the kind of *seva* that is practiced within a spiritual community such as ours, and there is the *seva* that you do out in the world, for the benefit of the greater global community. When you practice *seva* for the benefit of a spiritual community, you become a channel for the fulfillment of the mission proposed by that spiritual lineage. Here, our purpose is to fulfill the *sankalpa*, the spiritual promise of this lineage. To keep this promise alive within us in everything we do, we pray the *sankalpa* throughout the day: in the morning or in the evening chants, during our prayers on the banks of the Ganges, and at times when we get together and sing during *satsang*.

Since it is a promise, as long as the *sankalpa* has not yet been fully manifested in the world, this lineage will continue working to bring it about. The essence of our mission was defined several millennia ago by the sage Narada, who assumed responsibility for the regeneration of humanity after the devastating War of Kurukshetra described in the *Mahabharata* and the *Bhagavad Gita*. This calling gained even more definition and shades of meaning with the renewal that was codified by Sachcha Baba. By establishing our *sankalpa*, Sachcha Baba, the Guru of my beloved Guru Maharajji, defined the course of our work for eternity.

OUR PROMISE

In the *sankalpa* we request, ***"Lord, grant us knowledge and the light of devotion."*** Through acquiring knowledge, we open the space for devotion to emerge. Knowledge illuminates wisdom. I am not referring to secular knowledge, which serves as a foundation for us to move ourselves in the material realm. I am speaking about divine revelation and the spiritual teachings that instill faith, trust and love of God in us. As knowledge transforms into wisdom, a person acquires faith. Such true faith allows our love for God to be developed and cultivated.

The second pillar of the calling of Sachcha Mission is the *"removal of the veil of evil tendencies."* Thus, we strive to purify and transform evil. The term "evil" should be understood to mean the defensive response that arises from the state of numbness and which is destructive to ourselves and to others. From a spiritual standpoint, evil is actually the sum of all the protective layers that we have built up during our existence and through which we play out our ignorance. These layers are deeply embedded in our system. They have the effect of making us numb, and when we are numb we can only behave destructively, thus creating ever more karma that binds us to the Earth. This protective armor must be removed before our true nature can reveal itself.

In the third pillar of our *sankalpa* we pray that God may *"manifest in the form of Annapurna Lakshmi, and show us the natural light of the Self."* When we have progressed in our practice of the second pillar, the removal of the veil of evil tendencies, we also free ourselves from the fear of scarcity – a thick layer of evil and ignorance that imprisons us. This great psychic mass drives us to accumulate possessions and to hide behind what we have amassed. As long as we fear that something will be lacking, we will make improper use of the power of Mahalakshmi, the goddess of abundance, who provides for what we need in order to live in this world. This goddess feeds the hungry, clothes the naked, houses the homeless, and brings harmony and balance to our spiritual and material lives. As long as this power, which corresponds to the material aspect of life, is not deeply understood and used appropriately, there will be hunger and want throughout the world. So we pray that no being goes hungry. Beyond praying, we take concrete actions and work tirelessly so that everyone may have their material needs met, and thus be free to cultivate and nurture the spiritual being that they are.

The fourth pillar of Sachcha Baba's calling is the mission of *"establishing harmony in society according to the words of the Vedas."* This is the request that everyone may discover and cultivate their God-given gifts and talents. The wisdom of these ancient sacred texts – the *Vedas* – guide people in their spiritual and material lives, so they may recognize these innate gifts.

The fifth pillar of our *sankalpa* is *"to awaken God in all, with the goal of putting an end to the play of suffering, and bringing light to the play of joy."* In a single sentence, this is the true goal of all our work here.

SERVICE AS A SPIRITUAL PRACTICE

Everyone who performs some *seva*, or service, in this ashram is nourishing this flame, stoking this fire of love, for the fulfillment of our *sankalpa* which aims to burn the world's suffering down to ashes.

I see Sachcha Mission as a big employment agency for the divine project of regenerating the spirit of the human race. It's as if there were a huge sign out front that reads, "Help Wanted," and lots and lots of listings for available positions.

Let's find out just exactly how you can become a vehicle for divine love. How does *seva* work? Here there are people with the most diverse talents: doctors, psychologists, engineers, law-yers, mediators, artists, musicians, dancers, tinkers, tailors, and candlestick-makers, even jesters ... the whole gamut of talents. And here in our *sangha*, our community, there is no caste system: everyone is equal. If there is a need to cart dirt around for the garden, then many of us chip in to get the work done. If we need people to prepare the hall for *satsang,* those volunteers are sure to come forward.

It is a natural consequence of the process of giving that you feel fulfilled by your good deed, but that is not the goal of *seva*. If you are working in a seemingly altruistic way but in reality are wanting to receive attention or anything else in return, then you are not practicing *seva*. Real *seva* is pure; it is one of the most elevated spiritual practices in existence.

Seva is a spiritual practice; the more you do it, the more you evolve in the quality of your service and the sincerity of your prayer. Your *seva* will be perfect when you are no longer concerned about anyone knowing that you are performing it or about receiving something in return. *Seva* is real when you don't do it to feel important or self-righteous. Indeed, our practice is only worthy of being called *"seva"* when the only thing that moves us is our love for God. Our service will be truly selfless when it becomes a prayer. We donate our talents, our physical and mental efforts, and seek to find any way at all that we can help. We do it all purely as a declaration of love for God our Beloved. The prac-tice of *seva*, of *karma yoga,* is going to be ever less conspicuous until it turns completely silent.

An ashram is a microcosm: we work here for the benefit of the universe. The authentic *seva* that is practiced within a spiritual community is always performed for the whole world. When you are away from a community like ours, because your karma asks that you go back out into the world, you still continue doing *seva* for the larger community that is planet Earth. You put your gifts at the service of the Great Mystery as it works towards fulfilling the great *sankalpa*: establishing peace on Earth.

When you place your heart in what you are doing, regardless of what it may be, your action becomes prayer. Such prayer draws you closer to God. When your prayer is heartfelt, it reaches heaven, and then heaven pours its blessings over you. The tears of joy of the Divine Mother wash your sadness away, so that you too come to experience joy.

PART FIVE

Higher Consciousness

Directing your will towards God will bring about a revolution in your life. Your inner processes will accelerate as you accumulate more energy. Your karmic bonds will start to loosen. New directions will emerge for you, presenting new ways for you to play the game of life.

19
The Transition from Lower to Higher Self

Question: On the one hand you say there is nothing to be done. On the other hand you advise techniques for serious self-observation. Isn't this a contradiction? And why do you keep talking about all the psychological stuff instead of just focusing on higher consciousness?

Prem Baba: One needs to get to the root of one's problems and resolve them before one can know what spirituality really is. The foundation needs to be laid before the house can be built.

The truth is that I don't plan to speak: words emerge according to the needs of the people who have come here on any particular day. If you ask me not to speak about a certain topic because it bothers you, I will have to disappoint you. I am not here to please you, but rather to awaken you, and I use whichever method I feel is most needed so that you can open up to truly receiving love. Sometimes the transmission activates higher consciousness and you feel joy and bliss; other times you may feel squeezed. I will touch on things inside you that you refuse to accept because they are part of the lower self.

A basic law of the evolutionary process states that if someone inside of us is bothered by our own flaws, and is uncomfortable with any particular subject, it is exactly that self that has to be transformed. It is keeping us from the experience of unity. We can only reach divine perfection after we accept all human imperfections, our own and those of others. We will only be ready to launch into the realm of the Divine after we have fully arrived here on Earth.

SELF-INVESTIGATION

If you observe whatever emerges from a certain distance, you will notice that the clouds that pass by are sometimes dark and heavy, but at other times are fluffy and light. My efforts are aimed at helping you remember that you are the sky that merely observes the clouds. Regardless of what the clouds are like, you remain the same.

Let's discuss my methods for leading you to the sacred abode of the heart. The evolving being is a complex energy field with several "bodies," the main ones being the physical, emotional, mental and spiritual bodies. These bodies are programmed to act in specific ways according to the imprints and conditioning they carry. The imprints are the results of shocks experienced in the past that remain in the system as frozen images sustained by the continuous denial and suppression of feelings. They are compounded by the conditioning or second-hand beliefs that also unconsciously dictate your approach to life. These complexes of feelings, memories and beliefs guide your behavior and block your vital energy.

The first phase of the purification and transformation of the lower self, which is based on *jnana yoga*, is aimed at aiding in our self-investigation. We begin with a self-assessment: "Where am I now? Where do I want to go? What needs to be done to get there?" Once we have been able to look at our situation honestly, we can start to identify the conditioning and images that are blocking us; we can start to untangle the complex knots that bind us and keep us attached to our past. This inner housecleaning initiates a healing process that liberates the feelings kept bottled up in our psyche. The release of these feelings interrupts the repetition of negative behavior that they were causing. This is the psycho-spiritual work that we call the ABC of Spirituality.

Meditation during this first stage is investigative, analytical meditation. Regardless of the specific technique being employed, your meditation practice is a self-study, and it aims to strengthen the observer. Observation is the foundational practice. Why? Because self-observation is the principal tool that enables the evolution of consciousness. Everyone on a spiritual search has already developed some ability for self-observation. But we are not able to continuously and consistently stay in self-observation; our conditioning and patterns constantly take over and distract us from this state. So it's important to deliberately, consciously direct our self-observation and strengthen our discernment. This is accomplished through practice.

Becoming the Observer

Just like seeing, hearing, tasting, touching or smelling, observing oneself is a natural sense of the body. Because this sense has not been used, it did not develop as the other senses did. Developing one's sense of observation requires discipline and a committed practice. When the purification process has been accomplished, the commitment becomes natural, and self-observation becomes a sixth sense. We no longer make an effort to observe ourselves; rather we observe in the same way that we breathe. Observation is constantly present in everything that we do.

The more we get to know ourselves, the more our power of perception increases. The focus of our identification changes. In this phase, we ask the question, "Who am I identified with?" To be identified means that instead of being in the position of the observer, we have become whatever thoughts, emotions or sense-objects were just going through us in passing. However, we can also "identify" with the ever-present observer, to the extent that we become the observer.

Until this shift occurs, we live with the symptoms of terror: depression, anxiety and panic. We continue to identify with the false self and are unable to let go of it, no matter how much we may want to, because we still believe it to be our final reality and we are terrified of being annihilated. But when we change the focus from the false self to the observer, we are no longer what we are seeing; we are the awareness that perceives it. This awareness brings understanding, and understanding brings bliss. When all this light comes in, the false self gets dissolved and the seemingly infinite primal terror of extinction disappears from our soul. We realize that we are the observer, and discover that it is an expression of our real being that is readily accessible to us and with whom we can safely identify.

In the first stage we go on awakening the observer until we are naturally guided to the second stage, which is the more important phase of the process. Although the first stage is a crucial step, it is still just a means. We are ready to move beyond it when the purification process has been successfully completed.

CONNECTING WITH THE DIVINE

The second phase of meditation is focused on emptiness, a practice that can open the way to *samadhi,* a state of unity disassociated from identification with the lower self. This is the stage of activating higher consciousness. In this stage we come in touch with our true nature, and see God in all creation. At this point we have resolved our old issues related to the wounded child and are ready to move beyond healing our neuroses. There is no more need for psycho-spiritual investigation. We are devoted to the purely spiritual endeavor of giving ourselves over to God. We practice *bhakti yoga,* or devotion, and *karma yoga,* selfless action, and continue to advance in these practices until every molecule of our bodies is at the service of the divine will. But know that this realization won't happen through our efforts alone. Rather, it comes about through communion with the Divine in the form of a guru or some other divine manifestation that has awakened our devotion.

Question: What is it like for someone to continuously abide in a state of consciousness and equanimity? How does life appear when one has arrived at the second stage? That is, when you have worked on the psychological complexes and they have been integrated and thereby transcended?

Prem Baba: In practical terms it means that if you receive a yes, that's okay, and if you receive a no, that's also okay. If the day is sunny, okay: you can make a picnic of it and take a dip in the Ganges. If it's rainy, you may stay quietly in your room, perhaps meditate or read a little. Why fight life? What is the problem with a rainy day? The sun will soon be shining again.

It is important to understand the cyclical nature of energy: sometimes it is down in a trough, sometimes up on a crest. When we can remain unperturbed and accepting through the ups-and-downs of life, then we are abiding in that which never dies: we have found immortality. It's simple: don't identify with what is transitory, and you'll find what's eternal.

In the second stage, after some progress, we direct our will towards establishing a connection with the spiritual realm. Our prayer will be, "May our connection never be broken. May I eternally be a channel of Your light." Soon, duality disappears; you no longer need words in your prayers, because you and God are One. Prayer becomes communion with nature: with the wind, with the flowers, with everything that lives.

When I tell you that there is nothing to do, that you should just connect your heart to mine and live naturally, it is understood that you have already developed the observer. Staying in that state is no longer an effort. Just as our eyes see the rain falling outside, so we see feelings passing through our bodies, thoughts passing through our minds, and the images that they bring up. When an image surfaces inside of us, we can either be swallowed by it, or we can observe it and understand the connection between this image and the negative behavior we have noticed in ourselves. By observing ourselves, we integrate the parts of the personality that are calling for transformation.

The *sadhana*, or spiritual practice, that Sachcha Baba presents us with is a movement towards surrender. Maharajji once said, "I have come to a conclusion: when you surrender yourself one-hundred percent to the Guru, you become enlightened." I have reached the same conclusion. At certain junctures in the evolutionary journey you perceive a change in the focus of your *sadhana*. In the first stage we grow ever larger through an accumulation of understanding about ourselves. As we become aware of our lower nature, we transform lust into devotion, pride into humility and fear into trust. We free ourselves from the 'no' that once inhibited us from connecting with life, and we feel more and more empowered to realize our goals and desires.

We go on growing, and when we have reached our zenith, the carpet is subtly pulled out from under us. A deconstruction process begins, where we are trimmed down to the point of letting go of all borrowed knowledge, and even of the knowledge acquired from spiritual experiences. I had learned much from spiritual schools, yoga, psychology, and shamanism, but there came a time when I understood that knowledge was of no more use to me. I saw that the only thing I could hold on to was the little spark of truth that I had perceived through personal experience. When I was with my Guruji again, I looked into his eyes and said, "All I know about life is your love. I know of nothing else, so please take me by the hand and bring me with you." This phase of the journey cannot be understood intellectually. I cannot even speak of it, for it is a phenomenon that happens in silence. I make a big sacrifice here in trying to transform truth into words. I speak because I know that few understand silence, but truth is too great and words are too small . . .

A GRADUAL PROCESS

Comment: For several months of doing this work intensively, I had been experiencing an almost constant state of bliss. I was feeling that I was able to love without demanding reciprocity. I was even making progress sending love to the guys around here who drive their motorcycles at night without lights. I knew that I hadn't arrived, and that this state couldn't last forever. And it was being in contact with people I thought I should feel closer to, but wasn't, that brought me crashing down, and I started to feel alienated from the community of people around you, the *sangha*. Suddenly their serene detachment started to appear to me like thinly veiled indifference or disdain, reminding me of the popular kids who had excluded me from their clique in middle and high school. I had done a lot of work on my childhood and my parental issues, but hadn't yet looked hard enough at the traumas of adolescence. It was like I had gotten the A and B of spirituality, but had tried to skip over the C and D to get to the E.

Prem Baba: It sounds like God and your ego have been playing hide-and-seek inside of you. There are two main points you bring up. First of all, realize that not everyone is going to love you. We need to give people the freedom to love us or not. They may have the inclination and the time to focus on us in a more personal way, or not. In any case, when we allow our own love to flow we do not feel separate anymore.

The second point is that the two phases of spiritual development are not completely separate, but are overlapping. Sometimes we're in the first stage and get glimpses of the second. Or maybe we are in the second stage and have to go back to the first. During the second phase, all the focus is on the divine presence – on consciousness. One is abiding in the present moment and entering into communion with God. Everything is alright, until we start to notice suffering approaching in the form of irritation, sadness or discomfort. Conditioning is calling us, suffering wants to catch us. The past is knocking on our door.

If you pay attention and observe the flow of thoughts in a focused way, you'll recognize the soundtrack. And as you identify the content – for example, being offended because someone didn't accept you – you will understand where, why and how you are getting triggered. You will realize that it's only the residue of a psycho-emotional pattern that you are projecting onto a new set of people. So what can we do about this kind of situation? Sometimes we may just ignore it and go back to presence by not feeding it. But if it keeps shouting at us, it means that something is still pending from the past, that we haven't fully finished the ABCs yet, and we'll have to revisit the first stage to complete the purification work. We must establish a definitive link between our present discomfort and our wounded child; from there we will be able to disassociate from the sufferer inside. This sufferer is but an image that makes us prisoners to the past, captives held by the lassos of rancor. Such rancor remains because of the pain we carry from having experienced humiliation, exclusion, or a lack of affection.

We can be surrendered to God in many areas of life, but there are areas in which we don't yield at all: we are blocked and are constantly revisiting old stories or emotions. This means we are still entangled by denied feelings – or at least one foot is still caught. We are still reliving the childhood wound in our adult life, taking revenge on our imaginary parents. When we are free of the past, our minds no longer project towards the future. We are in communion with God, meaning we live in the present moment. We become a channel for prosperity, health, joy and everything good. We can only make the breakthrough by recognizing the last identifications and uncloaking delusion – an essential stage that seekers might prefer to avoid. It is much easier just to be ecstatic, but this very joy brings the hidden layers to the surface; ecstasy is actually a great danger to the personality that still carries malice within.

I teach about the realm of higher consciousness, and also about the level of the ABC of Spirituality to give you the tools to deal with everything that emerges in your growth process. This transition can be difficult. You are finding it challenging just to go from one to the other and back again. Accept where you are right now as the observer. Sometimes you are still identified with the ego, and sometimes you abide in the higher self. Denial is the greatest obstacle to evolution. It is important to understand that the numbness of denial indicates that work remains on the psycho-spiritual level. Pretending otherwise is tantamount to donning the mask of "the enlightened one."

You can only deeply understand what I am saying by coming closer, by connecting your heart to my heart. This transmission is a spiritual revelation. You empty yourself completely to receive the transmission. When you become hollow like a bamboo flute, God plays a melody. I used to go to Maharajji with many questions, and he would sometimes answer them. In truth he only answered me three times, and afterwards always just told me to go meditate and find the answers inside myself.

Truth is a revelation. The fire is glad to warm anyone. You want to feel the warmth, but first you have to come close to the fire. Don't just stand aside and complain about the cold. This fire offers its warmth to absolutely anyone who may be feeling cold.

You are in the waiting room of enlightenment: now connect to my heart. Nothing else is needed. You'll know that your time has arrived when you can remain in equanimity amidst the ups-and-downs of everyday life.

20
Four Keys to Sustaining Ecstasy

Question: Yesterday I had one of the most profound experiences of my life. I saw myself dissolved. My body had no limits and all the suffering in me was consumed by love. But when I returned to the world to relate with people, this blissful state dissipated and sadness grabbed a hold of me. How can I maintain the state of ecstasy I experienced?

Prem Baba: It seems that you experienced what Zen masters refer to as *satori*, or a glimpse of the eternal. Many people experience the eternal without being aware of it. However, if you are attentive and determined, you may use this experience as an arrow pointing towards liberation. *Satori* is attained by emptying the mind. When you perceive the real being, you are present, and from presence springs truth.

Today we heard some beautiful live devotional music. Some of you sang along and thus co-created the music. Creativity, and even the ability to experience beauty, is only possible when the mind is peaceful. If the mind is loaded down with knowledge and thoughts, we can't create anything new, and we remain numb to beauty. Beauty is an expression of the fresh energy of Being.

When the mind becomes serene we experience a connection with the eternal that reveals beauty. The more intense the experience of Being, the more we are able to see the brilliance and the beauty around us. This experience of heightened beauty is a sign that we are in a state of Unity. We are able to realize Unity because we were never actually disconnected from the eternal.

Everything begins with presence, with quieting the mind. This is the foundation of the practice. It's from silence that truth is born. But to abide in this silence we must understand that compulsive thinking is a disease that we need to treat. Western culture conditions us to think compulsively, so that we lose our connection with beauty and truth. We may look at a beautiful view of the countryside without really seeing it, and we may hear music but not really listen to it – because our minds are busy classifying, labeling, evaluating and interpreting all that we see or hear. The most we ever do is mechanically interpret what the senses have registered: "How pretty!" But in truth we still aren't listening or seeing because for that to occur we need to be empty, we need a serene mind.

The mind can become so agitated that we no longer perceive our connection to the divine presence. When the mind is agitated, it prevents us from perceiving beauty. It blinds us to our own beauty and so keeps us from creating beauty. The agitated mind will produce more agitation, be it in the form of art, music, or any other means of expression. All the ugliness we see in the world is a result of this agitation. Fear, hatred, suffering, and people's stubborn insistence on having everything their way — all of these are automatic reactions caused by the agitated mind.

On the contrary, true action emerges from the heart. Heart is another name for presence, for serenity. The heart is Being. When the mind is serene, you perceive Being. You see that you are connected to everything, and that the body is but a small aspect of reality. You are life itself, and the first quality of life is love. What is the nature of a flower? It's to perfume and be beautiful. And what moves this flower to exude perfume and beauty? It is love, because love moves all of existence. Love is the essence of life.

When we get a glimpse of the eternal, we feel this love. We are engulfed in love. Naturally, we want to hold on to this feeling, and so we try to get love from others. In the process, we lose sight of our true nature, which is love itself. Maintaining presence when relating with one another is the human race's greatest challenge. Mental agitation and, at a deeper level, your imprints and *sanskaras* (the latent mental and karmic tendencies that shape your current life) prevent you from sharing your love with others.

The experience of the eternal will dissolve these imprints. Little by little you will be freed of selfishness, the master thief of consciousness. The freedom to be yourself and to love selflessly will help you sustain this enlightened state.

If you want to experience unity and sustain the ecstasy you have tasted, it may help you to think of your inner path as a series of phases through which you transition, one after the other:

PREPARATORY PHASE - HEAL THE WOUNDED CHILD

In the preparatory phase of the inner work you are going to learn how to deal with the shadow side of the personality. You will endeavor to integrate and free yourself from the defense mechanisms and hypocrisy that prevent you from being spontaneous and authentic. You need to use all your willpower to carry out this transformation.

The purpose of the preparatory phase is to face up to denied aspects of the personality in order to stop using masks. One frees oneself from hypocrisy, which makes one smile when one feels angry, appear courageous when one feels fearful, and appear charitable when one feels stingy. We create all of our masks in order to be accepted by others. As small children, we develop masks in reaction to the perceived threat of being denied love. All of us, especially children, need to learn that it is okay to make mistakes.

If we accept the challenge of being real, we will no longer need to put up a false front. We will accept our jealousy, envy and anger. When we accept what are considered to be imperfections, we eventually come to understand their root cause without needing to create a mask to hide them. Gradually, character defects lose their power over us. We stop seeing these so-called defects

– our own and those of others – as defects, and instead see them as "special effects."

The culmination of the preparatory phase involves renouncing pacts of vengeance, and being wary of our small-mindedness. Enough conflict, enough revisiting misery! If you want freedom from the past, cast a look over your shoulder and see whether you can really be thankful for it all. Look at your whole family, living and dead, and other key figures in your past. See if you can look into the eyes of your parents and be thankful to them for the part they played. If not, continue working to liberate yourself from the wounds and vendettas of the past. We liberate ourselves from the past when we come to peace with it. To go forward on our spiritual journey we need to close all open accounts and shred the statements.

When we are mature, having healed the wounded child, having purified and transformed the lower self, then we are ready to sustain ecstasy. Ecstasy is positively-oriented pleasure, the pleasure in seeing others happy, the pleasure of being a link in the chain of happiness and of using our talents for the common good.

First Phase - Practice Presence to Elevate your Energy

The *first key* to sustaining ecstasy is to *elevate your energy frequency through presence.* Recognize that you are living in a world full of divine presence, and consciously ask to connect to that presence. You will know that you have established a connection when you perceive beauty all around you. The stronger your connection to the realm of Truth, the more beautiful everything will seem to you.

When you feel that your heart is open, pay attention and see what, in particular, stands out in its beauty. It may be a tree, a flower, or a work of art that touches you. At that moment, breathe deeply. Your energetic frequency increases when you take in the beauty that surrounds you.

Go about your day in this state of expanded consciousness and heightened perception, and you will have no doubt that we are living in a spiritual world. You will notice that everything is divine and sacred, and that God is manifested inside every living being. Then, ask God to be able to sustain this perception. The divine presence is real, and it is always there; you just aren't able to perceive it all the time. However, you can ask to see it more often. Make a conscious internal prayer: "May I be one with You, and may our connection never be broken."

Aside from prayer, an important key to being able to abide in the divine presence is to practice feeling fully present in your body. You cannot sustain ecstasy if you are not present. There has to be someone "home" to have the experience. So as you go about your day, moving around in the material world, bring presence to all of your activities. In this way, each act becomes a *sadhana* in itself: whether it's washing dishes, driving your car or sitting in front of the computer, everything you do becomes a spiritual practice aimed at anchoring supreme consciousness. At the same time, observe all that is transient without becoming attached to it. Wholeness in action and serene observation together: that is what practicing presence is.

Here are some practical things you can do to anchor yourself in the divine presence:

1) *Practice remembrance of your true self from the moment you wake up in the morning.* As you awaken, slowly and consciously lower your feet to the floor. Let go of any lingering dreams or thoughts. If you experienced something significant while you were asleep, such as a truly meaningful dream, it will remain with you; the rest you can let go of. If you feel sleepy or can't shake off something that happened during the night, splash cold water on your face or take a shower. Keep your mind clear from the moment you wake up by letting go of thoughts as they come; what will help you do this is to connect with your *guru mantra* if you have one. This practice of leaving your thoughts aside should be repeated as often as possible during the day so that your mind stays calm, relaxed and fresh.

2) *Be present in your body.* Take your awareness into your body and really feel it; in this way you will be able to detect if there are any blockages in your body, and you may then do physical exercises to free up those blockages. As a preparation for the upcoming day, perform movements that draw the energy from the body's core to the extremities. You may choose to do *Qigong*, specific yoga *asanas*, or free movement and dance. These practices will help you identify where the energy is not flowing so that you can unblock it.

3) *Energize your physical and spiritual bodies* with breathing exercises, different *kriyas, hatha yoga, mantras*, and other practices to move the life energy through the *chakras*. Don't worry about figuring out which practice you should do: it will knock at your door in due time, according to your specific needs of the moment.

4) *Watch what you eat.* If you have done sufficient work at the earlier stages you will already be eating healthy food in moderate quantities so that you can sustain the increased energy. Of all outward practices, diet is the factor most directly under our control in daily life. It is also the factor that can most easily knock us down. You can accumulate a lot of energy through meditation and physical yogic exercises, but it gets stifled and wasted if you overeat or eat junk food. I keep coming back to this point because it is so important during this phase: if you want to sustain the energy you need, pay attention to what you put in your mouth. Move towards a healthy *sattvic* diet.

It's not so hard up to this point. If you are dedicated to your *sadhana,* you will take these teachings to heart and naturally start to put them into practice. Be committed, and you will have glimpses of divine connection. Soon enough, you will be able to sustain the energy for longer periods of time. However, for that to happen, you must share it with others. This brings us to our second key: consciously intend for others to vibrate at this increased energy frequency.

SECOND PHASE - SEND BLESSINGS TO ALL BEINGS

The **second key** to sustaining ecstasy is to **send out blessings and direct our talents towards serving others.** Our life then becomes a prayer for the happiness of all, and we become a channel for divine love. To sustain pleasure and the state of universal love, we must *want* to see the other shine. We pray: "May all beings be happy, may all beings be blissful, may all beings be in peace." The ability to give selflessly is the hallmark of real humanity. Understand this simple yet tricky point: the love that we so desperately want comes to us when that same love is flowing from us in abundance.

Learn to use the mind to help the energy reach others through visualization and positive intentions. It doesn't matter where you are – on the bus, in a restaurant or walking down the street: direct the loving energy passing through you towards others to illuminate them. "May you be happy; may existence provide you with all your needs; may you be realized in God." You can do this when you have awakened the sincere desire for the other to be enlightened. Then you practice making the other happy, not from behind the "pleaser mask," but because you know yourself to be an inexhaustible fountain of love and that love is the essence of the human experience. At this stage, loving is spontaneous; you no longer need to direct energy to it. You *become* your prayer and radiate those blessings wherever you pass. This occurs because deep in your heart you want everyone to achieve their full potential.

If you find that you cannot express love, return to the pre-paratory phase to identify precisely which situations you cannot embrace, and which people you cannot love. You will see that there are residues of the past to which you are still attached. You may still be acting from a pact of vengeance, trying to force your bad parents to become good parents. You may be feeling rebellious and angry at the world, hoping that those around you fail.

You came here because you feel the grace flowing through me. I have awakened in myself a sincere intention that you become self-realized, and I am determined to help you in any way I can. You can feel that I am really with you, really supporting you in your endeavor. It's true, I *do* want you to be happy, and I don't want anything in return. I don't judge you. I don't care whether you own this or that, whether you are wearing a heavy aura or a shiny halo. I don't love you because you are doing any particular thing. *I love you because I am love and my nature is to love,* just as the nature of fresh water is to quench thirst. I don't think about it: it happens naturally, because I have awakened the will to see you happy. Love has awakened. This is the meaning of the word "blessing": a profound heartfelt intention that the other's potential may awaken, wishing them the best. I'm rooting for you. I want you to shine. I want you to realize that you are a star and accept that a star should shine. May all beings in all worlds be happy.

Live your life sustaining the awareness that everything is divine by allowing your energy to expand and reach the other. Become a channel of blessings, helping all the buds blossom into flowers. This is the most important key for sustaining ecstasy: when you love, you experience presence, your energy increases, and you become a channel for the flow of love.

THIRD PHASE - NOTICE SYNCHRONICITY

The ability to sustain the positive intentionality that we cultivated in the second phase brings us to the ***third key: recognizing synchronicity.*** We develop a state of mindfulness and become able to recognize the signs that existence uses to show us the next step on our path. By being awake and alert, we can perceive those mysterious coincidences and let them guide us in the right direction. This key opens our eyes to the richness of human life. If we could learn to be guided by insight from the time we are children, how different life would be!

Stay connected, with your antennae out. If you can stay tuned to this frequency you won't fall from your serene state of mind. Your faith will be strengthened as you sense that you aren't alone, that there is a higher power at work guiding you and everything else in the world. This faith gives you fulfillment and the energy to live happily. It gives you the certainty that you can accomplish your destiny.

Nurture your mindfulness of synchronicity in everyday life. For example, you may dream about a certain person one night, and the next morning – *voila!* – there they are at the German Bakery having a coffee. Open your mind to the possibility of synchronicity. Go talk to the person, or at least be open to identify a possible message in any given encounter. All such mysterious coincidences bring messages. The message is not always pleasant, but there is always a message. When you get the message, you strengthen the most beautiful of qualities: trust in the great teacher, God. Synchronicity is the language of existence. It is the great mystery conversing with you.

Cultivate peace in your mind to recognize synchronicity. When you are willing to perceive synchronicity, you awaken your positive intentionality. You say yes to life, yes to realization, yes to unity. Trust puts positive intentionality in motion. It maintains the course of willpower by focusing on positively oriented pleasure.

Experience the depth of this teaching. When you recognize that synchronicity is the language of existence, and that existence is indeed talking to you, you free yourself of loneliness. This deep feeling of orphanhood is perhaps the greatest source of pain that a person carries inside. We believe that we are abandoned in this world, that no one out there cares for us. Since God appears to have forsaken us, we develop intense skepticism and dedicate ourselves to self-punishment. But when we start noticing synchronicity leading us towards fulfilling our destiny through various "mysterious coincidences," we rescue our long-lost faith. We discover that we were never alone, and that this orphanhood was but a myth of our mind. We are in awe as we behold a higher intelligence that guides us and guides everything in the world. This faith fills us with life force, giving us the certainty that we can indeed fulfill the goal that has been destined for us.

FOURTH PHASE - LET THE WISDOM OF UNCERTAINTY GUIDE YOU

The *fourth key* is nonattachment to a particular outcome. Without this key we will inevitably fall. I'm talking about acceptance, about **allowing ourselves to be guided by the wisdom of uncertainty**. This is the key to freedom and renewed enthusiasm through discovering the mystery of life. Life is a great adventure that provides no guarantees, so to use this key we need to *abandon the very idea of security and guarantees.*

For example, let's imagine that you hear the voice of synchronicity telling you to go to the *Kumbh Mela,* the great pilgrimage, in Haridwar. You call a taxi, but the taxi can't get to the pilgrimage site because the road is closed. So you have two options. Either you get irritated and fall into the frustration trap, dissipating all the love and spiritual energy that you have been cultivating in just one minute of anger; or you open up to the wisdom of uncertainty. If you really want to go to Haridwar, get out of the taxi and grab a rickshaw or walk. Maybe on the way you'll see something – and it could be something apparently mundane, like a billboard with words on it for example – that answers a question in your soul. God may have a specific reason for preventing you from arriving to Haridwar by taxi. But if we are closed and hell-bent on a particular outcome, life will not be able to guide us, and we won't be able to receive the message the universe is sending us. At the deepest level, these situations come to remind us and help us focus on the real purpose of our incarnation.

To be guided by the wisdom of uncertainty, release yourself from the ego's desire to know exactly how things are going to turn out. The ego is exasperated because it doesn't know. But how can the Great Mystery guide us if we have already decided on an outcome? It's vital to have the freedom to go with the flow. This key is helpful in relaxing the rigidity created by the ego.

When the ego appropriates an experience you easily get identified with form; your consciousness lowers and you return to the valley of weeping and gnashing of teeth. Then, you are the Infinite who has sought lodging in a closet. You are stuck and squeezed inside of yourself. You are far too vast to be confined in such a small space. A life of captivity is a life of suffering.

To be guided by the wisdom of uncertainty, we must let go of the idea that everything needs to be completely safe. The security we seek is an illusion created by the mind. Who can say that if things happen in accordance with the plans and expectations of the ego, we will be safe? This idea is but a trick of the ego, for such security does not exist. It's only when we open our arms to uncertainty, and the potential risks that go with it, that we experience the mystery.

We do need to accommodate ourselves to living in this body and to the laws of nature. One of those laws is that we need to have a plan; we have to take care of our affairs. So, for example, I can anticipate that we are going to finish our season here in Rishikesh on the fifteenth of April, and so we will have to book a taxi soon, and start packing. My travel companions and I have flights to catch and we need to know the logistical details. But something may happen all of a sudden that intervenes to disrupt this plan. If that occurs, it doesn't mean that the world is against us. Perhaps it's just the opposite. Maybe this is the way God has chosen to give us a present. But we can only receive this gift and enjoy it if we relax with the fact that things might not turn out exactly as we planned.

Letting things unfold naturally will open you up to your innate enthusiasm for life and help you recover your sense of freedom – and freedom promotes ecstasy. I could have jumped right to the heart of the matter and simply said that truth is ecstasy. But you need to take a path to get there, and I am showing you this path. I call it the Path of the Heart, the path that leads you back to the divine realm.

If our children learn these keys to sustaining ecstasy during childhood, they can avoid the arduous work of unlearning conditioned habits that we have to do as adults. In essence, we must teach them human and spiritual values. We must teach them to "fear no evil," and that the goal of life is to stay in touch with oneself. We must teach them to use their gifts in the service of global happiness arising from inner peace. The teaching is the same for adults and children. We just need to put it in terms children can understand.

If I teach you how to sustain a blissful life but your children continue to be raised based on fear, our work here will be endless, and we will never be able to move on from this world. We need to raise our children in ways that encourage them to stay in the divine presence from early on; this way we can close the circle and make the global transformation of consciousness possible.

So to summarize these four keys: *Silence the chatter, and silence will reveal its secret in the form of beauty. Beauty expands your energy, so that you consciously reach out to others and sustain positive intentions towards all. Begin paying attention to synchronicity, to the "mysterious coincidences" of life. Be mindful not to over-manage the course of events. Give yourself over to the wisdom of uncertainty. Let love carry you away. You will see that, little by little, you will be able to remain in the state of ecstasy for longer periods of time, until the day you can maintain it for good.*

21
Putting God in First Place

Question: I understand that I need to focus on knowing myself as the driver/passenger, rather than as the car that is my body. I need to contemplate my own mortality. Recently my best friend found out she had cancer. I am terrified of losing her. This drove home the point that I haven't wrapped my head around death. I can't imagine someone I really love dying, and of course then I am completely unprepared for my own eventual death. What can I do to both keep myself healthy in this body and to prepare myself for eventually leaving it behind?

Prem Baba: You are so afraid of death because you still believe yourself to be only the body you inhabit. You dread harm coming to it, out of fear that, if you were to be parted from your body, you would cease to exist.

YOU ARE NOT YOUR BODY

Only when we rise above our absolute identification with the body can we overcome the four big barriers to enlightenment, which are: *not to believe in God, not to speak the truth, to fear death, and to think only of ourselves.*

As long as we imagine ourselves to be the body, our access to divine reality will be blocked. Any purported belief in God will be a mere idea created in our mind. True faith can arise only from a direct experience of the Divine, and such an experience demands a disidentification from the body.

If we believe ourselves to be the body, everything we say will merely be a product of the intellect: borrowed knowledge that only serves to reinforce who we think we are and maintain our identification with the body. On the contrary, when we gain access to spiritual reality a deep comprehension of the truth blossoms within us.

An often unconscious dread of death drives people to devote every waking moment to the preservation of their bodies. It is true that your vehicle needs to be properly cared for so that it can easily take you where you need to go. To make it run smoothly, you need to be sure to put in only the right kind of fuel. If you eat right, you will have a more peaceful experience during your meditation. However, our concern becomes neurotic when all our actions emerge from a fear of eventually losing this vehicle. With this mindset, every thought we have will be self-centered. We become convinced that we are a water droplet that needs to protect its existence. In this way the droplet constantly flees the possibility of being dissolved into the ocean.

We can only dissociate from the body when we recognize ourselves as a manifestation of the Divine that is merely occupying the body for a finite period of time. This is what the guru does: reminds you that he and you are one, that you are *Atman* – you speak in all mouths and act in all bodies. This body is ephemeral. It can be severely injured or die at any moment.

Not long ago I went to Varanasi to perform some *pujas*, spiritual offerings, for our lineage of gurus. There I had the opportunity to meditate at a cremation ground where hundreds of bodies are burned every day. There were bodies of children, young people, adults, and old people being cremated. Having an experience like that is a stark reminder that our bodies have a very limited lifespan. We have an expiration date. If you don't learn who you are this time around you will have to return to another body and start all over again. You only escape this cycle of birth, death and rebirth when you know who you really are, when you recognize yourself as a manifestation of the Divine. This is a goal worthy of dedicating your life to. Until we give ourselves over to this Truth we will be bound by karma. To untangle ourselves, we need to focus all our energy on attuning to our divine reality.

Redirecting Your Energy towards God

It is the nature of the body to desire. It wants to reaffirm its own existence by stimulating the senses. Desire is a bottomless pit. It never ends. A particular desire may be fulfilled and provide a fleeting pleasure, but desire itself remains. As long as we are identified with the body we create desire so that we can remind ourselves that we are still alive, and have so far escaped death.

We stimulate our senses in many ways. We do so not only with tangible things, but also with more subtle stimuli. The senses are not limited to hearing, sight, touch, taste and smell. We also receive stimuli from our attachment to possessions, and even from our various arguments, power struggles and manipulative games. These dramas are addictive, and we can easily waste our entire lives starting fights.

Instead, put all your energy towards noticing the presence of God in your life. You may work in the world and make money, but just to create the conditions that enable you to dedicate yourself to focusing on the Divine. And always remember that this awareness of the divine presence is your real goal; so do not waste your life simply attempting to accumulate a lot of stuff. When we die, we will not be able to take our bodies, or even a single grain of dust with us. All that we take will be our consciousness, and the net weight of our positive and negative karma.

If you truly dedicate yourself to recognizing God inside yourself this time around, you will jettison that karmic baggage. On this path to freeing yourself of karma, you will not be tempted to accumulate new burdens through confrontations or competition. You will not have time for such distractions because you will be too busy being present. Your attention will be focused on contemplating God within. Everything you do will reflect this. When you recognize God in yourself you will also notice certain new imperatives, because God is the one guiding you now. God will use your gifts and talents to carry out the divine project of world peace. The voice of the Divine, speaking through your intuition, will tell you, often in a very obvious way, "Do this, and go there." Your life will become prayer and your professional life will be dedicated to serving God, because your gifts and talents are tools of divine manifestation.

It is still rare to find someone immersed in the consciousness of the true self, but it will soon become less unusual. We are going through an exceedingly fertile, though intense, period in the history of planet Earth. At this very moment there are certain divine beings who have incarnated on earth, and are working tirelessly to awaken all of humanity. A global movement of inner and outer change is in the works. One part of this divine project aims at bringing enlightenment to those who are already mature enough. The other aims at elevating the vibrational frequency of this earthly plane. This transformation cannot be achieved by any individual or small group, no matter how powerful. It can only be brought about by the simultaneous awakening of many seekers like you. As you surrender and give yourself over to the Divine, you become enlightened. As an extension of Divinity, you become a ray of divine light that illuminates everyone around you. All together we may gradually raise the energy frequency of the world.

I have an unshakable faith in Love, and I am at the service of Love. God will use your gifts and talents to spread the light. Together we will elevate the vibration of this world, inch by inch, in all places and situations. I want to see you shine, because I know that you can shine like a star. I know that you have the power of illuminating many others. But you can only realize this truth when you remember that *you are Love.* I love you, not because of anything you do for me. Rather, I love you because I am Love. My work is to help you recognize this truth, that you are Love.

22
Sanatana Dharma: The Path of Enlightenment

The rich spiritual heritage of India is sometimes called *Sanatana Dharma*. This term has been variously translated as "the way of life," "the path of enlightenment," and "eternal truth." Perhaps because the term *Sanatana Dharma* has so many subtle shades of meaning, it was easier for foreigners to refer to it as the religion of Hind, or India: that's how the term Hinduism was coined. But it is a mistake to think of *Sanatana Dharma* as Hinduism. The term "Hinduism" is laden with many cultural accretions: rites, taboos, the caste system, and so on; whereas *Sanatana Dharma*, as I see it, is the essence of religion itself. It is the essence of Buddhism, of Judaism, of Christianity, and of Islam. In its essence, truth is one and the same.

There is horizontal religion, which is religion as a social phenomenon created by the human mind to give some direction to the evolving human entity,[7] and to make it possible to live

---

[7] See glossary of psycho-spiritual terms for an explanation of evolving human entity.

amicably in society. But there is also vertical religion, which is what the true meaning of the word religion refers to. "Religion" comes from the Latin *religare*, meaning to reunite the individual soul with the Universal Soul. It is a synonym for yoga, the path of enlightenment, and the eternal religion: *Sanatana Dharma*. Vertical religion is not based on acquired truths. It has no dogmas. It is the religion that is born in your soul, a spirituality that is as natural as love. It blossoms as our consciousness expands. The more our consciousness expands, the more present we are, and the more we appreciate the sacredness of life. What I call authentic religion is the perception of the sacred — it brings us into the divine presence.

PERENNIAL WISDOM

Sanatana Dharma, as a manifestation of the eternal religion, has given us many important sacred texts. These include some brilliant gems such as the *Ramayana* and the *Bhagavad Gita*. The *Ramayana* tells the story of Lord Ram, one of the *avatars* of Vishnu, and his consort Sita. This story sheds light on many of the mysteries of the initiatory process. By reading this sacred text we gain insight into who Ram and Sita are inside of ourselves. It contains many keys to help us understand our own process of spiritual evolution. Another gem is the *Bhagavad Gita*, which is perhaps the most sublime treasure that *Sanatana Dharma* has bequeathed the world. It might also be the most objective sacred text of all: the wisdom presented is universal and goes straight to the essence, leaving little room for interpretation.

These scriptures impart a blessing on all humanity. When you feel ready to receive the blessing of these texts, open one up. Let yourself be touched by the moving stories and teachings. You may receive answers to your questions, and your consciousness will expand. Devotional chanting of the divine names is a powerful practice that also serves to remind us of these stories and the wisdom they contain. They are treasures of humanity, replete with messages and keys for the treasure map of consciousness. As your consciousness gradually expands, you will start to understand your role in the play, your calling in life.

According to the *Vedic* scriptures of *Sanatana Dharma*, everything we understand as reality is but a dream of Vishnu, the Sustainer of the universe. This life is a great cosmic theatrical performance in the mind of God. And in this play, planet Earth plays a very specific role. It is a school in which we learn to love consciously. But I am not sure if the word "learn" is the most appropriate one; actually, we are here to be *reminded* that *we are conscious love.* From the time that we first came here and became attached to matter, we have been generating karma. We have been perpetuating a vicious cycle that reinforces our false identity. Now, we are here to remember our true identity. This planet is a kind of power plant that transforms the suffering caused by our identification with matter.

These are divine mysteries that can only be comprehended if we go to the very core of the mystery. And the core of the mystery is our heart – the nucleus of our inner world, wherein lie all the answers. Is it an easy process? No: because in order to get to our hearts we first need to quiet our minds, which is a great challenge.

TURNING OFF THE RADIO

As people in evolution, we have undergone many changes, and survived mutations. One of the most recent evolutionary acquisitions we have inherited is the powerful instrument that we call the mind. Rare is the human being who has figured out how to use this tool skillfully and wisely. On the contrary, it's usually the mind that uses us. In order to use our powerful minds in the service of evolution, it is necessary to have discipline, time, and a great amount of patience.

In the New Testament, the mind, with its fixation on repetitive thoughts, is symbolized by a donkey. If you observe your mind during your daily life and work, you will understand how much it is like an ass! When the donkey refuses to move, there is no way to get it going. Try to force it and you will soon see. When the mind gets stuck, it really gets stuck! And it takes a lot of work to get it moving forward again.

What is the mind anyway? What is this entity? Is it an entity at all? Or could it simply be a stream of thoughts? This is an important question to contemplate, so that we may learn to control our minds and penetrate the core of the mystery. The mind is a vehicle. It is a channel, a passageway for our thoughts.

Our task is to learn how to observe these thoughts without identifying with them. They are simply passing by, like radio waves passing through the air. Our conscious-mind-radio is usually tuned into multiple frequencies. Each minute something different flashes by and we have no control over what we are picking up. These frequencies bring us messages from the networks of sadness, of hatred, of joy, of sentimentality, of possessiveness – a torrent of thoughts. When the anger network broadcasts its poison we become spiteful; when we are tuned into the romantics classic station we turn gushy – and so it goes. You identify with that frequency, become that thought, and then spend all your time trying to solve the problem that the thought has convinced you that you have.

Since you are identified with the thought and believe it to be real, you invest all your energy into overcoming the problem. But when you finally do, in reality you are only changing the frequency of the radio. The radio is still on, and still capturing frequencies. Not two minutes after you have solved your problem, another thought passes through you, and now you are identified with that one, and you have a new problem to solve. This goes on and on as long as you keep your radio turned on. You are not walking the dog – the dog is walking you!

To dominate the mind is to turn off the radio and learn how to turn it on only when you want to, and to the station of your choice. When you turn off the radio, thoughts cease to have power over you. To turn off the radio is to be present, to be whole in your actions. Then you will realize that your problems don't exist; it was only your identification with the thoughts that led you to believe they were real.

When you find yourself identified with a thought and believing that the problem is real, confront it head-on. If you need to take action to de-identify yourself, then take action. Remove yourself from the grip of your identification. Believing that your fantasy world is real will get you nowhere – you will only continue to walk around in circles.

Question: If the thoughts are not in the mind, then what is their source?

Prem Baba: They are circulating around the planet. From time to time, you generate thoughts yourself, but most of the time you are only giving passage to preexisting thoughts along with the world-view that underlies them and the emotions they generate. As I've said, the earth's role is to process suffering, which means that it transforms the ideas and thoughts that cause suffering.

As we say, there is nothing new under the sun. It is very rare for a person to actually produce an original thought or idea. People may think they are writing a book, or building a house, or composing a song; but all of that is just stuff passing through. As long as the person is not truly present, they cannot create. Creation arises from the union of the feminine and the masculine, and that union only manifests through presence, when the radio is turned off. When we leave it on, we are steered by unconscious forces, all the while convinced that we are the ones doing the steering – that we are the author of our thoughts.

A Step Towards God

Question: I understand that we need to cultivate our awareness through *sadhana* and, in this way, seek to follow the path of righteousness. How do we find the time to do *sadhana* without losing our spontaneity, and without neglecting our material responsibilities?

Prem Baba: This is the great challenge of the seeker born in the West. If you had been born here in India, you could go to an ashram and surrender your life if you felt called to do so. But if such was your karma that you were born in the West, you must find a way to balance your spiritual life with your material life. This challenge exists in India as well, but it manifests in a different way, as spirituality is interwoven into the material life. In the West, there is a stark contrast between the two.

When the Divine touches you, there is no going back. As much as karma may dictate that you work for a corporation and take care of a family, if you have been touched by the mystery, you will feel compelled to solve the equation. This happens to each person in their own time; it happens naturally. You will learn to tend to your responsibilities and still find time to meditate, even if it's in the middle of the night. If the middle of the night is the only time available for your spiritual practice, so be it. You will sleep less and meditate more, or wake up earlier in the morning to meditate.

Directing your will towards God will bring about a revolution in your life. Your inner processes will accelerate as you accumulate more energy. Your karmic bonds will start to loosen. New directions will emerge for you, presenting new ways for you to play the game of life.

Have you ever heard the saying that if you take one step towards God, God takes ten steps towards you? It is true. Nowadays, on this planet, I would say that if you take one step towards God, God takes a hundred steps towards you. At the same time, it has never been so difficult to take that one step. As Maharajji recently announced, God has never been available so cheaply. Even a little prayer brings great returns. This is a sign of the times.

Question: Sometimes I feel my consciousness changing, and I am able to let go of my ego and bloated self-image, which are identified with my story and my personality. I feel that I'm stuck somewhere between ignorance and enlightenment. I am not identified with anything: neither with my lower self, nor yet with love and light. Sometimes it's a very peaceful place to be, but other times it feels uncomfortable and unsafe, as if anything could invade this space. I don't know if this is the right place to be in, to not be identified with anything. Is it simply part of the process? Where am I?

Prem Baba: This is an important moment: you were already able to release certain identifications, but your higher self has not yet manifested itself completely. Who are you? If you can observe the ego, if you can observe this image of your-self that you have created, then you already have a clear idea of your true identity. The observer is the closest manifestation of the higher self that you have access to so far. It is not the higher self in all its glory, but it is a manifestation of the light nonetheless. If you are able to witness what is transitory without becoming identified with it, then that's where you should stay until, little by little, you are able to receive the grace of the higher self. It will come through your intuition, which will grow ever stronger, and through teachings that will arrive as insights. Many times the higher self manifests as a voice speaking inside you.

Each time you catch yourself identified with the ego once again, turn your attention back to the guru. You will slowly return to this space of observation and re-establish presence. This is how it was with me: when I noticed myself feeling encumbered, I would look at my Guru, and slowly presence would return. We have this deeply-ingrained tendency to believe that our thoughts are real, and this constantly lowers our level of consciousness. Even spending two minutes looking at the picture of the guru is enough to bring us back to our center.

DISCOVERING YOUR NO

Question: I am curious about your experience. What was your awakening like? How did you finally master your lower self and abide in the higher self?

Prem Baba: My guru Maharajji once told me, "During a certain stage of one's spiritual evolution, it is natural for God and the ego to play hide-and-seek inside the devotee. Wherever the seeker may be and regardless of how thick the veil of illusion, he or she should simply call upon God, and God will come."

Once, when I had fallen from grace yet again, I kept my guru's teaching firmly in mind. I walked down to the shores of the Ganges River, and entered a state of meditation. In deep prayer, I was able to perceive for the first time that my frenetic search for enlightenment was hiding a thin layer of self-deceit. I saw that my search for God was not authentic. Consciously, enlightenment was my greatest desire; but I wanted it not out of love for God, but to escape suffering. I could see the way I bargained with God, or rather with the projection that I mistook for God.

I went into the depth of my unconscious and saw a *no* to God, a *no* to enlightenment. A part of me was still very much attached to this world and to engaging in conflict. I saw a wounded child taking revenge on his parents for not giving him exclusive love; and I saw how I had been projecting this negative aspect of my parents onto a God that still resided outside of myself and that was only a mental creation.

At the same time, I was able to perceive that God is *life* acting through me and in everything that lives. At that moment, I could see that the only reason I was not free was because I didn't want to be, and that at the core of my being, I could simply choose to renounce attachment, conflict and my *no* to life.

That's when a song emerged from inside, from the depths of my sincerity:

I make a request now,
That I may be reborn
And awaken self-realized
Close to the power.

Divine and sovereign Mother,
You who have all power
Light up my life
I will eternally thank you.

In response to my request, I heard Mother Ganga speaking inside me: "See how I am free. I attach myself to nothing. I am always flowing." At that moment, I entered *samadhi* and was flooded by grace. I received many teachings about the spiritual journey. Those teachings later became the foundation of the method that I have developed and use today with my students and disciples.

The voices of the lower self came back once again, but this time I could clearly see that there was a false self and a real self and that the one observing all of this was the real self. I never fell into the trap of Maya again. At that moment I laughed in pure ecstasy. I said, "I've found the way! The doors of suffering have closed." I was once again flooded with grace, and walked up to Maharajji's room. He looked at me and gave a hearty chuckle. Then he said, "You are a guru. As a guru you are free to work as you wish. I ask of you only one thing: that you lead everyone to God."

Later, after I had left, he told a friend of mine, "Prem Baba is enlightened!" Some time later he told me, "Prem Baba, you are a holy man. I saw this in your face the first time I met you."

After reaching this state, all questions ceased. My heart opened and the love flowed freely. I saw myself as the sun, giving light without wanting anything in return. Desires and attachments dissolved. My mind became quiet. I stopped running after fleeting joys in an attempt to escape suffering. Equanimity and a profound peace began to manifest. Presence brought calm and silence.

PART SIX

Master Teachers

The mysterious workings of karma and the play of Mahamaya had created conditions that threatened the evolution of humanity. To pull humanity back from the brink and rescue the universe, God came to inhabit the Earth.

23
Rama, Sita, and Commitment to the Truth

The *Ramayana* is an ancient epic in the Indian tradition of *Sanatana Dharma*. It tells the story of Sri Rama, an *avatar* or incarnation of Lord Vishnu, the embodiment of the divine power of preservation and sustenance. The *Ramayana* is nectar that nurtures the soul. It is full of inspirational passages that awaken the soul's virtues. What may, at first glance, appear to be just a story of heroes and villains is really describing the cosmic drama that takes place within spiritual initiates on their journey towards enlightenment. As an incarnation of Lord Vishnu, Rama embodies pure God-consciousness. Rama's life story teaches us about commitment to truth and to both our worldly and spiritual responsibilities. It inspires us to fulfill the mission of our incarnation and to let go of all the attachments that hold us back on the path to enlightenment.

The Ramayana also contains beautiful teachings about the *lila* or play of the Divine. Rama shows us how to embrace life circumstances that may be difficult to accept. Instead of always opposing life, we must learn to relax and stay open to receiving the message that it brings us.

RAMA ACCEPTS HIS DESTINY

Lord Rama was a crown prince, the eldest son of Dasaratha, king of Ayodhya. Dasaratha was growing old, but still hadn't fathered any children, even though he had three wives. This lack of a successor filled him with anxiety. Through the practice of austerities and mystical rites, King Dasaratha and his wives were blessed with four sons: Queen Kaushalya gave birth to the eldest, Rama. Queen Sumitra gave birth to twins, Lakshman and Shatrugna. Queen Kaikeyi gave birth to Bharat. All were rays of the incarnation of Vishnu that mainly manifested in Rama himself.

Rama and his brothers came in answer to the prayers of the gods, the *Devas,* because *dharma* was threatened by dark forces led by a wicked ruler of Sri Lanka named Ravana. What made his rule so horrendous is that he persecuted spiritual people and prevented them from carrying out their work. Not only were the demons he controlled growing in number unrestrained, but they practiced ever more abhorrent acts of evil. Ravana was the very personification of evil and wielded absolute power that was growing beyond Sri Lanka and into India. He owed his worldly success to austerities he performed to gain mystical powers, making him a virtually invincible conqueror.

Only Vishnu Himself, by incarnating in the form of Rama, could stop Ravana and re-establish *dharma*. The mysterious workings of karma and the play of Mahamaya had created conditions that threatened the evolution of humanity. To pull humanity back from the brink and rescue the universe, God came to inhabit the Earth.

Rama was being raised to succeed his father, and was educated according to the customs of the age of *Treta Yuga*. Unlike our current cycle of *Kali Yuga*, the age of ignorance, the *Treta Yuga* was quite an elevated stage of humanity's spiritual evolution. Belonging to the *Kshatriya* caste of warriors and administrators, Rama and his brothers were trained to govern and to fight whilst upholding spiritual principles. As Rama's wisdom and benevolence were so evident, the king, queens, subjects, and Rama's royal brothers were all filled with enthusiasm over the prospect of having the very incarnation of divine wisdom as their next ruler.

But one night, when Rama was about twenty-eight years old, his father saw some bad omens. In order not to take any chances with the fates, he decided to move Rama's coronation up to the very next morning. But instead of being crowned the next day, Rama was forced into exile for fourteen years due to a dramatic turn of events. How did this happen?

King Dasaratha's youngest wife, Kaikeyi, had a maidservant named Manthara who, desperate to further her own interests, managed to convince the queen that her direct son, Rama's younger half-brother Bharat, should be the one to succeed his father, even though the kingship rightfully went to the eldest. Kaikeyi had a pure heart, and she and the other queens loved all four sons equally. To Kaikeyi, Rama was as much a son to her as his brothers, and since the law declared that the eldest should take the crown, she had never thought twice about it. Nonetheless, she still carried a grain of unconscious fear in her heart, and Manthara was able to poison her mind and convince her that if Rama became king she would lose her rights to her share of the kingdom.

Years earlier, after Kaikeyi had saved his life twice in battle, Dasaratha had promised her that he would grant her any wish. Since Kaikeyi had still not claimed her wish when the time came for Rama to ascend to the throne, Manthara managed to convince her to demand that Dasaratha fulfill his promise by giving the crown to Bharat and exiling Rama to the forest for fourteen years.

Upon hearing this unforseen, earth-shattering request the king experienced such extreme shock that he fell back and fainted. But in an era when vows and solemn promises were held to be inviolable, the king had no choice but to make good on his vow to Kaikeyi. And in an era of filial piety, the word of a parent was considered weightier than any contract. Rama obeyed his father without hesitation. He recognized that the will of the Divine had been expressed through his father. Rama was unwaveringly faithful to the truth, and he knew that this was all part of the divine play.

Rama subsequently endured many trials and tribulations, but he never strayed from his *dharma*, not for a single moment.

He was the victim of the trickery and manipulation of the shadow side when his rightful kingdom was taken from him and he was exiled to the jungle for fourteen years. Nonetheless, Rama accepted exile with exemplary equanimity because King Dasaratha had made a decision. Rama understood that his father had acted under duress, and to alleviate his father's suffering he calmed down Lakshman who was beside himself with righteous indignation and would not accept the situation. For Rama, his father's order was nothing less than the message of the universe sending him to the jungle for fourteen years. He renounced the throne and happily went into the jungle with his wife Sita and brother Lakshman.

Tragically, King Dasaratha's grief at the turn of events and the sudden absence of his beloved Rama was so severe that he died of a broken heart. The thought of having sent Rama to the forest had simply been unbearable, for this was a punishment meted out only to the worst of criminals who were condemned to die. Only a handful of extreme ascetics ever willingly chose to venture into the forest and face its sinister dangers.

When Rama's brother Prince Bharat, who had been acting as a governor for the king in a distant part of the kingdom, finally arrived, he found to his horror that his father had died, his beloved brother Rama had been exiled for fourteen years, and that he, Bharat, was to be crowned king! Bharat was a ray of Vishnu, and was totally committed to the truth that Rama represented; consequently, he refused to be crowned, and made a solemn vow that he would never accept Rama's throne. Bharat was so filled with disgust and shame at his mother's behavior that he refused to receive her and headed to the jungle to search for Rama and implore him to return and ascend his rightful throne. His mother Kaikeyi followed behind, lamenting and repentant.

Meanwhile Rama, Sita, and Lakshman were doing well in the jungle. They had made a nice little retreat for themselves. When Bharat's entourage found them, Bharat pleaded with Rama to return. Rama refused, saying that all of these apparent mishaps had occurred to fulfill a divine purpose that lies beyond the comprehension of the human mind. He was determined to fulfill his destiny by staying in exile for the determined period. Bharat argued that the kingdom could not remain without a king for fourteen years. He had vowed not to take Rama's place, so he could not reign. Then their spiritual teacher, Guru Vashishta came up with a solution: crown Bharat as Rama's viceroy until Rama returned from his jungle exile.

The real reason Rama needed to be in the jungle was that he was born to stop Ravana and re-establish *dharma*. Rama's troubles were only beginning. Soon after, Rama would be attacked by a legion of ferocious demons, and Ravana would manage to capture Sita through trickery. As the epic's drama unfolds, Rama and Lakshman set out to save Sita from the clutches of Ravana and meet the monkey-God Hanuman, who uses his miraculous powers and commands an army of monkeys and bears to help them rescue Sita and kill Ravana.

A PORTAL TO THE ETERNAL

This is a captivating story, but what is its significance? Rama represents commitment to the truth, whatever the truth may be. In the face of this greater truth we have to confront lesser, disagreeable truths about ourselves. May the commitment to truth awaken in you. May you put truth above all else; in this way you will be in harmony with *dharma*. There is no greater *dharma* than faithfulness to the truth. This is exactly what the story of Rama teaches us. Rama is the quintessence of integrity and of complete loyalty to the truth. He is the personification of *dharma*. If you emulate him you will experience inner peace and love, and this will allow you to develop the inner quality of *ahimsa*, non-violence.

Hanuman is a potent symbol representing the love for God. Many images of him show him pulling his chest open to reveal his heart, where Rama and Sita are enthroned. Once, Hanuman was given a priceless pearl collar. He began to bite into each pearl to see if he could find Rama and Sita inside; when he didn't, he threw the pearls away, because to him they were worthless. Hanuman is the embodiment of perfect devotion. He ensures victory to Lord Rama through his loyalty. Loyalty is the first quality a true disciple will manifest, and it is the fertile ground from which respect and humility may sprout.

When surrendering to God through your guru or any other divine manifestation, you are going to face some unexpected and difficult situations. Things won't always happen the way you would have wished. If, in the face of this "no," we renounce the truth by closing ourselves down or by starting a fight, we will inevitably suffer. Rama represents happiness and peace, but this state of equanimity and bliss was severely tested when Sita was abducted by Ravana.

Rama isn't just a name or a form, but the eternal itself. The name of Rama connects us to the eternal. It is sweeter than honey. You will experience this sweetness in chanting his name. You will enjoy prosperity and well-being throughout your life, because the name of Rama awakens the eternal in you. Understand that this whole story takes place inside of you: it is a deep and subtle initiatory journey in which you direct all your energy to God whenever you are being tempted to deviate from your path.

Today, on Rama's birthday, let us make the intention to "grow a virtue." Choose a virtue or a good attitude that you already practice or embrace, something that sustains your soul. Make the intention to elevate this good habit or inclination into a *sadhana* or spiritual practice. Follow through with this intelligent austerity, even if the demons in your head try to divert you from your intention. Call to mind Rama's deep commitment to the way of truth and his determination to follow the path of *dharma*.

May Lord Rama inspire you on the path of obedience, surrender, loyalty, respect and commitment to eternal Truth.

24

The Inner Mysteries of Shiva, Ganga and Durga Devi

We are approaching Mahashivaratri, one of the most important festivals celebrated in India. Literally, "the great night of Shiva," it honors the marriage of Lord Shiva and his consort, Parvati, and symbolizes the state of wholeness that is achieved through the perfect union between masculine and feminine. Many people mistakenly interpret this festival to be the celebration of the marriage between two external figures. In reality, during Mahashivaratri the matrimony occurs inside of us: it is an alchemical fusion that takes place when the mind is silenced.

A smaller festival called Shivaratri happens once a month during the thirteenth night and fourteenth day of the waning moon. The moon is the power that rules the mind: our brainwaves vary in frequency according to the amount of light being reflected by the moon. On the night of the new moon, the moon stops exerting influence over the mind, and the mind enters a calmer state. By focusing on Shiva, devotees take advantage of this auspicious opportunity for liberation. In addition to sending prayers and giving offerings in honor of Lord Shiva, the sages fast during the day and spend the night in vigil.

Although every month in the lunar Hindu calendar has a Shivaratri, the Mahashivaratri, the great Shivaratri, occurs in the month of *maagha*, which usually coincides with the month of February. On this day God fully manifests in material form: for the benefit of his devotees, Lord Shiva presents himself in the form of the *lingam*. The *lingam* is a symbol or form in the shape of an obelisk (phallus) inside an ellipse (*yoni*). It is the unsophisticated and unadorned representation of the featureless God. It is the material representation of the light of supreme wisdom.

On Mahashivaratri we contemplate this external symbol, but with the understanding that it resides inside of us. The outer festivities occur simply as a reminder that Lord Shiva lives inside.

THE TEACHINGS OF LORD SHIVA

As we worship Shiva, he removes our karma and transmits the teachings we need. Once I was in the Shiva temple connected to our ashram, and it was very crowded with devotees doing *pranam* or reverences, lighting incense, making *pujas* or offerings. People would perform their reverences, *pranams,* would light incense, and would offer their gifts, *pujas*. As I was walking in, I noticed a modest Indian man silently climbing the stairway that led to the raised area from which offerings could be made. When coming back down, he tripped on the stairs and landed face first on the street. He immediately raised himself up on his knees and bowed before the very steps that had sent him reeling to the ground – he did a *pranam* to the steps. At that moment I saw what had taken place inside the man: he realized that Lord Shiva had just removed one of his karmas. Instead of getting angry or annoyed that he fell, he went to his knees in appreciation for the unconventional teaching he had just received.

This scene touched me deeply. Through his intense devotion to Shiva, the man had immediate access to feelings of authentic gratitude that usually only emerge after one has made significant progress in integrating the lower self. When life knocks us down, it always has something to teach us. Any obstacle that emerges is an additional challenge to overcome. But we must have developed a staunch will to assume self-responsibility before we can truly comprehend the karmic reasons for attracting a personal stumble. When this comprehension dawns on us, we simply feel gratitude for falling down. We know that all the positive and negative situations that were sent our way contain their particular teachings. We understand that God is constantly taking us by the hand and giving us everything we need. At this stage of understanding, there's no further need for us to examine our self-responsibility. We simply thank the Divine for absolutely everything, and we continue humbly following the guidance as we contemplate this divine mystery.

God is one, but God manifests in different forms at different times to best help us with our particular needs. We may learn much about ourselves by meditating on the physical shape that Shiva chose to receive our prayers and worship. Lord Shiva is that particular aspect of the Divine that compassionately grants us wisdom. He is the manifestation of the Divine that comes quickest to answer the prayer of his devotees and *yogis*.

Shiva's body has many details we can meditate on. On top of his head he carries Ganga, the goddess with the power to purify our sins and to liberate us from all evils. In his matted locks, he carries the crescent moon, the symbol for equanimity and sovereignty over the mind. Cobras are constantly moving around his ankles, shoulders and neck; they represent mastery over the life-force and the breath and remind us of the cycle of life and death.

Shiva carries lethal poison that, if released, can bring about an immediate cataclysm; but out of compassion for humanity, he keeps the poison safely in his throat. By this act of mercy, he inspires us to learn how to transform the poison in our lives into nectar. Shiva has with him a *kamandalu*, which is the ascetic's bowl, representing the renunciation and detachment needed to approach God and to obtain liberation. He also has a trident, which among other things symbolizes his command of the influence of the sun, the moon and the stars.

Shiva's body is covered with ashes, which represent the last form of matter: nothing else can be done with matter after it becomes ash. The ashes represent the incineration of Kama, the divine form of desire. Shiva covers himself with ashes to extol the glory of defeating Kama, and thereby eliminating the passion that brings agitation to the mind. Only when desire has been burned up can *prema*, divine love, manifest itself.

Because he overcame desire, Shiva is also remembered as the one who has conquered death. He often lives in graveyards and cremation grounds in order to teach that death is a mystery to be understood. Death is an illusion that the material world wants to make into a reality. Cemeteries are actually not places of horror: they are auspicious reminders that death should be faced and deeply understood – for it is inescapable.

These are a few possible interpretations of the meaning of Shiva, which should merely serve as references for our own inner meeting with this manifestation of the Divine. Shiva is inside and outside – He is everywhere. Shiva is cosmic consciousness itself, which deliberately chooses to manifest itself in a specific form out of compassion. Shiva is the transformational power of the universe alongside Brahma, the creative power, and Vishnu, the power of preservation. Shiva means grace, good fortune, and prosperity. Because this is also the exact meaning of "Sri," this title is not placed before the name Shiva as it would be when referring to other divine beings. He is the personification of graciousness and of love itself. Shiva is *prema*, divine love.

It was on a day of Mahashivaratri that I awoke from the dream that I was a little droplet of water and realized that my true self in fact was the ocean. My life until then had been dedicated to proving that I was *the* droplet. Life was a rush. I was fleeing suffering and running after joy. I was always running until I remembered that I am not in fact the droplet, but the ocean itself.

The truth is, I never died and I was never born. I am not the body and you aren't either. We are but one, the eternal and changeless. We are divine love. When you wake up, you start working so that others may also wake up. You are love. You may not believe this, but you are love. You are capable of infinite goodness. Now slowly free yourself from the past and the idea that you are a droplet separate from the vast ocean.

SHIVA RECEIVES GANGA

The goddess Ganga represents mercy. As the story goes, Ganga was a star whose favorite pastime was to observe human beings living their lives on this planet. She found herself constantly enthralled by the beauty of humanity until she observed it begin to decay. She watched how human values began to be forgotten. She witnessed how again and again people would act on the whims of their lower nature, wasting their lives in useless conflict, competition and strife. Humanity was soon fully engaged in a terrible game of destruction.

Moved by this sorrowful sight, Ganga felt the urge to help. She sought out Lord Narayan to obtain permission to come to Earth in order to remind human beings about their inherent divine nature, which had always been so delightful to observe from above. But Lord Narayan told Ganga that if she were to go to Earth, she would destroy the planet altogether, for it could never bear the impact of her descent and the might of her power.

At this moment Lord Shiva came forth and offered a safe landing for Ganga on planet Earth. He took the shape of Mount Kailash, and Ganga turned into a torrent of water that flowed down from the top of the mountain. In this way Shiva buffered the impact of Ganga's descent and channeled the flow of water into what became the Ganges River with which we are familiar.

To this day, the Goddess dwells in the river and benefits us by washing away the sins and *sanskaras* of all those who enter with devotion. This is but a story, but the fact remains that to this day millions of people bathe in the Ganges as a sacred ritual. Many people claim to have experienced liberation thanks to the mercy of the goddess Ganga and say they have seen this celestial spirit manifesting itself in the form of the river.

DURGA DEVI OVERCOMES THE DEMON

The goddess Durga is a feminine form of Shiva. Like Ganga, she is the *shakti* of Shiva: she carries the power of Shiva. She is responsible for having overcome Mahisha, the most powerful of demons who is a metaphor for the ego itself.

Mahisha had acquired supernatural powers that allowed him to change forms at will. He could turn into a buffalo or a man, or any other creature he desired to become. To acquire such powers, Mahisha spent years in meditation, did a lot of *japa* – repeating God's names – and practiced severe austerities, practices of self-discipline. Finally, one day, Lord Brahma himself came to answer Mahisha's prayers and said, "Yes, Mahisha, you have practiced very severe austerities. What is it you want?"

Mahisha immediately answered, "I want immortality."

Brahma responded, "But Mahisha, all those who are born in this world must someday perish."

Incensed at the news, Mahisha thought, "What?! So I've practiced all these austerities for nothing?" But he didn't want to waste this opportunity, since he was face to face with the Lord of all creation. Mahisha sought power at any price – all his strength was directed at the effort. In a sudden stroke of inspiration, he said, "Lord Brahma, grant me then but one wish. If I must die, allow my slayer to be a woman." Lord Brahma consented, and Mahisha thought, exhilarated, "I have just received the boon of immortality! How could a mere woman, such a fragile and insignificant creature, possibly kill me?"

He quickly called on his vast legion of demons, and they departed for the heavens. When the guards at the gates of heaven saw Mahisha approaching with an army of demons, they informed Indra, ruler of the gods. Indra rushed to meet Mahisha, and said, "Mahisha, why have you come here again? You have already tried to assault heaven so many times, and have always failed. What do you want this time?"

Mahisha responded, "I didn't come here to talk. Prepare yourself to fight."

Hearing Mahisha speak so audaciously, Indra deduced that he must have something up his sleeve. He called all the *Devas*, the gods, to arms.

Thus started the greatest battle the heavens or the earth had ever seen. In fierce combat, the gods realized that Mahisha had indeed become too powerful, and that they would not be able to stop him. As the *Devas* gave up and fled, Mahisha took Indra's throne, presiding over heaven and earth. He immediately decreed to his army of demons, "From now on there will be no more worship of Brahma, Vishnu or Shiva. All beings must worship only me. If anyone disobeys, cut off their head." Through these commands, he transformed the cosmic order of the universe.

Mahisha's demons brought destruction and chaos to earth, initiating an age of darkness. Though outwardly humans praised Mahisha in obedience to his power, privately they continued to pray ardently that God would free them from this critical situation.

Finally Brahma, Vishnu, Shiva and the other *Devas* came together and, from their faces of fury, a feminine form emerged shining like a thousand suns: Devi Durga was born. After each of the *Devas* gave her their weapons, she said, "I will destroy Mahisha." At that very moment, Mahisha's heart skipped a beat. Devi Durga set out to confront the demon.

Mahisha had been worried, but when he saw Durga approaching and realized that she was the source of all the anxiety he had been feeling, he blurted out derisively, "Ha! A mere female."

She replied, "I am not a mere female. I came to fulfill Brahma's promise. Was it not your wish to die at the hands of a woman? Prepare to die."

Mahisha called forth his soldiers, and a great battle ensued. From the body of Durga emerged thousands of soldiers, and the battle raged until only she and Mahisha were left standing. Durga faced great challenges: Mahisha eventually transformed himself into a buffalo and Durga cut off his head, but each drop of blood that fell on the ground would grow into a new demon. Finally Durga transformed herself into the terrible goddess Kali, who drank every drop of blood that spilled from Mahisha before it reached the ground. In this way Mahisha was finally defeated. But drinking the blood of this awful demon drove Kali mad. Completely altered, she saw Shiva lying on the ground, and stomped on his chest. When she did so, Shiva absorbed all her energy and began to help her master and transmute all the evil that had just entered her body.

This story is rich in symbolism that we may interpret in various ways. At this moment I would like to focus on this avidity with which our egoism wants to assault heaven. We can see this in the zeal with which we try to go against the natural flow of life and stubbornly strive to make things go *our* way. Our minds eagerly try to strategize about every life situation. This rationalization process is the main defense mechanism we employ, and is precisely what prevents us from accessing our true nature.

It is a curious paradox that we force life because we want to possess everything, but it is precisely this forcing that prevents us from having what we want. Maharajji recently said, "It is not you who takes things. It is God who gives them to you." I myself take nothing, but rather let God give me what I need. I recognize that

I don't know what is or is not good for me – only God knows. Therefore I pray, "May Your will be done. May I fulfill what You have willed for me."

Why are you here, to realize yourself in God or to lay siege to heaven? It is impossible to become God by attempting to conquer heaven. This great battle between Durga and Mahisha continues today in the form of the struggle between our higher selves and our selfish selves: it is being fought inside each of us at every moment of our lives. This story holds out the promise that, just as Durga prevailed, so can we.

25

The Bhagavad Gita on the Struggle between the Higher and the Lower Self

As we progress in the practice of self-observation and we review our day, we will notice that at some moments we are more present, while at others we act mechanically because we are in a state devoid of any real conscious awareness. If we can identify the moments when we start to oppose life, we will locate specific areas in our psycho-emotional system that still need to undergo a process of purification, for they are the ones that put us to sleep.

If we can overcome resistance, and truly commit to putting these teachings into practice, we will notice that we are immersed in an intense inner battle between our higher and our lower selves. *Sanatana Dharma* beautifully describes this inner process in the poetic language of the *Ramayana* and the *Bhagavad Gita.* This inner battle of love is fought every day, from the time of our birth to the moment we draw our last breath, whether we are aware of it or not. When we can consciously observe the scene, we enable the higher self to achieve some meaningful victories. The greater the triumphs, the more we will attain the final goal of emanating conscious love. Our actions naturally become virtuous as we begin to walk the path of *dharma*. Virtuous action, or doing good, means doing anything that draws us closer to the Divine. On the contrary, "bad" or "evil," once we remove all judgment or moralism, is simply to do things that distance us from the Divine.

If you are not yet familiar with the story of the *Bhagavad Gita*, it is high time to pick it up. Though the poetic wisdom of its verses touches anyone with its beauty, the real treasure lies in the sheer depth of the text's mystic significance. Many believe that the war portrayed in the *Bhagavad Gita* was an actual event in India's history. And I affirm that this war is undoubtedly real: it continues to be waged to this day inside each person walking the earth.

THE BACKGROUND STORY

The story describes a royal family that was divided into two clans: the Pandavas were the five sons of virtuous King Pandu, while the Kauravas were their hundred cousins, children of Pandu's blind brother Dhritarashtra. The cousins underwent warrior training together under the guidance of Drona. They had always lived amicably together, but when Pandu died and the time came for the eldest of the Pandavas, Yudhishthira, to claim his deceased father's kingdom, rivalry broke out. Dhritarashtra had taken over his deceased brother's throne already before Pandu had died, and wanted to pass the kingdom down to his own eldest son Duryodhana, but had to relent to the will of the masses and rightfully nominate Yudhishthira as crown prince.

To try to get the kingdom back into the hands of the Kauravas, King Dhritarashtra conspired with Duryodhana and Shakuni, the evil uncle of the Kauravas. Following Yudhishthira's coronation, Duryodhana built the Pandavas a gorgeous palace as a residence, which he filled with flammable materials that caught on fire while they were sleeping the first night. Fortunately, the Pandavas managed to escape through a tunnel that had been secretely built by a paternal uncle who had discovered the plan.

To ensure their safety, they lived in disguise and only made their existence known again when Arjuna won the hand of Princess Draupadi in marriage. When he did, Arjuna took the princess home to show his mother what he had won for himself, and his mother replied, without turning around to see what it was, "Whatever it is, share it with your brothers!" Since to the Pandavas a mother's orders were law, the five of them ended up marrying Draupadi. Their Kaurava cousins eventually agreed to return part of the kingdom to them. They gave them only the most barren, hostile lands to rule, but the Pandavas were nonetheless able to develop this land into a great and luxurious city, the original Delhi.

Duryodhana was green with envy at the unexpected success and prosperity of the Pandavas. To cheat them out of their assets, he invited Yudhishthira to a fraudulent game of dice, knowing that this was his biggest addiction. Every time Yudhishthira played the loaded dice, he lost a valued possession. He played until he had lost everything. Gone were his riches, his right to become king, and even his brothers' and wife's right to remain in the territory. When Yudhishthira had nothing left to bet, King Dhritarashtra banished the Pandavas to the forest for an exile of twelve years. As an added humiliation, on the thirteenth year they would be allowed back in the city, but would have to scrape together a living by walking around in disguise. He did compromise by saying that, if the Pandavas happened to outlive their ordeal and managed to escape detection while in disguise, then they could claim back half the kingdom.

Thirteen years later, the five brothers were in bad shape, but had indeed survived and escaped detection in the thirteenth year. Faced with this unexpected turn of events, the Kauravas refused to give up a single inch of land. The ensuing clash of arms was unavoidable, and as the conflict escalated to involve India's greatest military powers, the Pandavas went to Krishna for help. This was the beginning of the awesome battle described in the *Bhagavad Gita*.

WHAT THE CHARACTERS MEAN

The tale is filled with spiritual meaning. Dhritarashtra represents *manas*, the blind mind; in other words, the mind ruled by the senses. The Kauravas represent all bad habits and addictions. They personify the lower self and its *nine matrices:* gluttony, sloth, greed, envy, wrath, pride, lust, fear and deceit. They also represent the primary distortions of the *divine qualities of love, power and serenity*, which become the masks of submission, aggression and withdrawal, respectively. When the Kauravas are in charge of the psycho-emotional system, the person derives fleeting pleasure from repeating negative behaviors and from giving free rein to their compulsions. Moreover, the person lives a materialistic lifestyle, addicted to the short-lived gratification provided by material objects.

In the story, the late King Pandu represents *buddhi*, or discernment. *Buddhi* is the highest intelligence, that from which wisdom is born. It guides us directly to the truth, and enables us to renounce all forms of attachment. Krishna is the higher self in all its glory. The third of the Pandava brothers, Arjuna, represents the conscious ego. He is the one who actually undertakes the great feat of defeating the Kauravas, the army of the lower self. To achieve victory, he willingly goes to Krishna, his Guru, to be instructed on how to detach himself from, and eventually destroy those who had been his friends and teachers. Indeed, Arjuna had spent his whole life among the Kauravas and learned everything he knew from them. The *Bhagavad Gita* is the story of how Arjuna learns and accepts the reality that his highest mission in life is to take up arms against those dearest to him. The epic war took place on the sacred plain of Kurukshetra. It is still being waged in the Kurukshetra that is your body. Witness the sheer scope of the vendetta as the armies mobilize and clash in your various physical, emotional, intellectual and spiritual bodies ...

It is interesting to note that, even though the eldest of the Pandavas, Yudhishthira, was highly virtuous, he succumbed to his weakness for gambling. When the time came for Yudhishthira to take power, the lower self deliberately hit at his Achilles heel, swindling him of everything that was rightfully his. This serves as a reminder to be aware of your own addictions, no matter how small, so that you do not fall prey to them. To help you identify the addictions that still plague you, I constantly emphasize the importance of dedicating yourself to the practice of self-observation and to the careful analysis of each moment of your day. In the beginning, don't try to tackle vices and addictions that seem impossible to change. It is enough to begin by breaking a seemingly trivial negative behavior, as this may reveal a swarm of negative tendencies hidden in the dark corners of the soul. As you practice self-observation and note the moments when you were engulfed in unconsciousness, pay attention to minor details, as they will unveil the blueprint of your lower self.

UNCOVERING YOUR ENEMIES

Self-realization, the ultimate goal in the battle of love, is attained through the practice of meditation. It can occur only in silence. Regardless of whether you follow the path of love or the path of meditation to attain the supreme aim, you will end up in the same place: the abode of silence. The recognition of our true being brings us to a state of calm and inner silence that gives us bliss. Inner realization also brings harmony to our outer lives.

Everything we need or do unfolds naturally, and every area of our lives flows smoothly.

If in some area of our lives the wheel is not turning, it means that the Kauravas have taken charge. The block may lie in our financial, professional, or romantic life, or in our sexual, physical or spiritual life. In that place, there is a point of hatred and fear that has still not been purified and integrated. An unconscious pact of vengeance continues to sabotage any possibility of success so that we consistently feel unlucky in that area. Only through committed self-observation and through a systematic daily review of our setbacks can we identify, dissolve and integrate any points of hatred. Eventually we will dissolve the overarching pact of vengeance.

Let's look at some ways that a pact of vengeance can negatively affect a person's life. For example, a person can be engaged in a pact of vengeance that results in other people repeatedly rejecting them. In every situation, they somehow manage to attract people who will give them the brush off. It seems ridiculous, idiotic even, that a person would unconsciously draw such people or circumstances to themselves. But such are the workings of ignorance; this is how it manifests.

Another pact of vengeance can result in a person being financially unsuccessful. An unconscious voice inside them says, "I will not thrive. I simply will not prosper and allow my parents to have even a little bit of pleasure at seeing me well off." Or the person may say, "I *need* to suffer. Since I did not receive their love when I needed it, I must continue to suffer." This too may seem foolish, but so it goes when ignorance has taken over the throne that rightfully belongs to higher intelligence.

On the path of integrating the lower self, we should not oppose anything. Although the metaphor of a battle is useful, remember that it is a battle *of love*. Don't misconstrue this analogy to mean that what is called for is an attack on some psychological behavior or addiction, undertaken out of your own fear or dislike of this characteristic. Taking the offensive in this way will never bring you to victory.

The method for sharpening our greatest weapon, which is self-observation, always begins with the ABC of Spirituality, the process of accepting our own shadow. First you recognize that the Kauravas are indeed in command of your psycho-emotional system. Identify who is the thief who robs you of your energy; then you can devise a way to remove him. Having located him, commit to studying his habits. As we observe our own negative behaviors and the undesired situations that emerge in our lives, we will understand the cause and effect relationship between our problems and this energy parasite. Only then can we take action to eliminate the addictive behavior. Although this whole process is fairly obvious and straightforward, the veil of illusion prevents us from understanding it and changing our patterns.

The first step towards liberation is to identify not only which particular Kaurava is in command, but also his underlying strategy. You will find that he likes to boast about his ingenious tactics; so you can simply ask him what his battle plan is, and he will tell you. As soon as we focus on a specific aspect of the lower self, we are given the information we need regarding its workings. It is very simple; nonetheless we need to really ask for it. We must affirm to ourselves, "I want to know what's inside; I commit myself to seeing it. May it come out into the open, even if seeing it may wound my pride or offend my vanity." When we ask truthfully, the destructive characteristic eventually comes out from the shadows and is laid bare before us. The answers to our pleas come when we least expect them.

ATTAINING VICTORY

Once we understand who we are up against, we will need to brandish the appropriate weapon. If we are tackling a bad habit or addiction, we can commit to intelligent self-discipline in order to redirect and strengthen our willpower. To practice self-discipline doesn't mean that we become masochistic, just smart in the way we use our life energy.

Let's imagine, for instance, that you realize that the energy you generate during meditation is dissipated by unnecessary conversation. Since you already know that your particular pact of vengeance undermines you through speech, you can commit to staying silent for a few days. Or, to give another example, perhaps you realize that the Kauravas' plan is to numb your body by having you overeat or eat junk food. If you observe yourself, you can detect exactly how this food makes you ill and lethargic, or perhaps disturbs your sleep and prevents you from entering a state of meditation. You can engage in intelligent self-discipline whereby you eat only *sattvic foods* for a few days. You can eat in lesser quantities or you can choose a day of the week for fasting.

So how is your battle going? Have you been listening to *buddhi*, the highest intelligence that allows you to renounce material attachments and to experience freedom and truth? Or have you been listening to *manas*, the sensory mind that imprisons you in material pleasures? Where is your willpower directed? Have you been using your available life force to perform *sadhana*? Or do you waste your energy trying to satisfy the senses?

The aim of these questions is not to make you feel judged. Rather, they should help you to take an honest look inside in order to locate yourself. Check on the progress of your inner battle: Do you find that you are committed and unswerving as you confront the enemy? Are you as relentless as Arjuna became after receiving his instructions from Krishna? Or are you weak and powerless as you struggle to renounce certain attachments?

Defeating the forces of the lower self requires a warrior's training. Then, once we have achieved significant victories against the Kauravas and made sufficient progress in our spiritual practices, we are ready for *Tantra*. *Tantra* is not, as is commonly thought, a form of sexuality; *Tantra* is spontaneity, the path of total acceptance. In order to practice *Tantra*, one must have already developed a measure of self-control through yoga. Yoga should not be understood to be limited to physical exercises; it refers to all spiritual practices that create a direct connection to the Divine. Yoga is the path of developing willpower through intelligent self-discipline. Once we have mastered yoga, once our willpower is sufficiently developed, then we can move on to *Tantra*, practicing complete acceptance of what is.

One's own will is perhaps the greatest power available to a person on the path of self-realization. Willpower is developed through consistent, dedicated practice. Certain realized beings have nurtured such tremendous willpower that they can perform what may be considered miracles. They did not acquire this willpower out of the blue or as a stroke of luck; rather, they deliberately built it up over many lifetimes.

Every determined spiritual seeker has already developed a certain measure of willpower. Some of this power is already being employed in the service of evolution, but the rest is still being used to fuel self-destruction through negative attitudes, addictions and compulsions that sabotage any possibility of attaining lasting happiness. In the battle of self-realization, rescuing our willpower from the hands of the Kauravas is an arduous but absolutely vital endeavor.

The higher self has triumphed when you, the person in evolution, finally realize who you really are. Until then you continue battling in an *ascending spiral:* your enemies become ever fiercer, your victories ever bigger. If you persevere, at some point you will be able to recognize your inner divine being. As you allow your soul to take command of your personality, you will naturally experience bliss.

The soul is the subtle particle of consciousness that contains within it the Divine and all its virtues. It usually remains inaccessible because the lower self and its entourage of bad habits and addictions have usurped the throne of consciousness. The lower self imposes its will on the senses in pursuit of instant gratification, and as a result we spend our lives focusing on the external and moving in a *descending spiral*. One clear indicator that the lower self is fully in charge and is pulling us down is that we have difficulty maintaining spiritual practices. We find that even if we try, we are unable to dedicate an hour of our day to do our *sadhana* or to meditate. When the time comes to sit in front of our altar, our compulsions emerge from the depths and we end up acting according to our old conditioned habits: we simply must go turn on the computer, do some chores, or eat something. We are pulled into a downward spiral, caught in the trappings of the external world from which we seek immediate gratification, and thus we create a snowball effect of negative karma.

When we truly dedicate ourselves to studying the tactics and strategies of the armies of the lower self, down to the smallest details, and we have achieved significant victories in integrating those negative aspects, then we are prepared to take on the leader of the Kauravas. The great General who secretly directs every destructive behavior is *negative intentionality*, that subtle part of ourselves that deliberately chooses to create negative circumstances in our life. At the mercy of this negative intentionality, we unwittingly choose to destroy and hurt ourselves. We say *no* to life and insist on opposing its flow, and as a result nothing seems to work out as we find ourselves having to cope with an unexpected illness, a professional setback, a financial failure, a sudden divorce, or being isolated. When we finally catch the

General hidden in his bunker, we discover that he has been in command of our personality this whole time. And we also realize that we have always had the choice to follow his orders or not.

As we redirect our energy and allow ourselves to follow the course the universe has laid out for us, we activate *positive intentionality*, the deliberate intention to move ourselves towards God. We live with the unwavering intention to bring light, joy, love, health, prosperity, and union into every moment of our lives. When we can resolutely say *yes* to all that is constructive and positive, then the Pandavas have finally defeated the Kauravas and can at long last reclaim their kingdom.

26

The Essence of the Teachings of Jesus Christ

In my view, Jesus Christ is the power of forgiveness. He is the power that cures us of all the negative characteristics which we carry in our psyches and hearts. He unties the knots that bind us to our karmic burdens. Forgiveness and gratitude give us access to this healing; and we can only open our hearts once we are healed. Forgiveness frees denied feelings from the psyche. Gratitude promotes elevation and transcendence. It reminds us that we are manifestations of divine love. Through gratitude we remember that we are an ever-flowing source of love, imbued with infinite goodness, able to forgive even one who hurt us gravely. We *can* feel grateful for everything that life deals us. We become thankful for all that we understand, and also for what we cannot yet understand.

How can we put these teachings into practice? How can we free our hearts from the resentment, the woes and sorrows we still carry around inside? A teacher is happy when a student puts the teachings into practice. We are here today to celebrate the birthday of master Jesus, so how can we best put his teachings into practice?

THE LORD'S PRAYER

One of the legacies Jesus left for us is the Lord's Prayer. All too often it is repeated mechanically. This is what the prayer means to me:

Jesus prayed,

"Our Father who art in heaven" – Father, You are the masculine principle that activates consciousness, the power of action that creates and that moves everything; "who art in heaven," the heaven of *anahata chakra,* the heart. You are the Truth; You are my real being.

"Hallowed be Thy name" – for Thy name is unpronounceable, and holy by nature. You are the Unmanifest. You are emptiness, nothingness in itself, from which arises everything that exists. May I always remember Your sanctity.

"Thy kingdom come" – Sometimes we pray, "To Thy kingdom we go"; but now I am praying for Your kingdom to come to us, for I find myself powerless and too weak to come to You. It is Your *lila* to reach me and liberate me. Please pour Your mercy on me. Illuminate each one of us – this whole realm – with Your light.

"Thy will be done on earth as it is in heaven" – for I have been trying to do things my own way, but I keep falling into the vicious cycle of suffering. Free me from selfishness, from the idea that I am separate from You. I have been stubbornly trying to do things the way I think is best. I have been trying to exercise control, and have repeatedly fallen into the traps of my own destructive repetitions. Thus, I ask: may I be One with You, and may our connection never be broken. May the words of my mouth be the pure expression of Your holy word. May every action I perform be the fruit of Your holy will. Act through me. Please come and inhabit my mind, my body, my heart, in such a way that no one can tell us apart. Tear away all of my vanity so that I can truly become Your instrument. May Thy will be done.

"Give us this day our daily bread" – Free me from the fear of scarcity. May I really trust that nothing will go lacking. Manifest through the power of *Annapurna Lakshmi*, the Goddesses of food and abundance, and enlighten us. May there be balance and harmony in our material lives.

"Forgive me my trespasses, Lord,"– forgive me my sins, for I recognize that I don't love as I should and that makes of me a great sinner. I am not a pure channel of You. I do wish harm onto my brothers and sisters, as I feel jealous and greedy. All of this happens only because I want to be distant from You. But if You come, all of this disappears, and I will really want to love my brothers and sisters. "I have a key; I hold it in my hand, but only one who is able to ask for forgiveness can use it."

"Just as I have forgiven those who have trespassed against me" – I am trying to forgive one who has offended me, but I have repeatedly flunked this test. I failed to integrate this holy teaching into my life, and so I continue to suffer. Help me to integrate this

holy teaching, help me especially to forgive those who have hurt me the most.

"Lead us not into temptation" – The distractions from You are so many; the sensory world and all its diversions drag me away from You.

"But deliver us from evil" – Release me from everything that leads me away from You. Today, I know that only love can free me from evil, including love for the dark side. Thus, teach me to "fear no evil." May I get to know my own shadow, so that I can come to understand that it is but a defense against the pain that I have experienced here on earth. May I transform evil, for that's the only way I can free myself from it. May I transform malevolence into goodness, *"for Thine is the kingdom, and the power and the glory, for ever and ever."*

Amen, amen, amen!

Another powerful prayer from this legacy represents the essential teachings of the master teacher, but is not even repeated mechanically. Its full meaning is often not understood. When he was being crucified, and in the throes of suffering, that blood-curdling torture, Jesus called out,

"Father, forgive them, for they know not what they do."

PUTTING THE TEACHINGS OF JESUS INTO PRACTICE

My beloved friends, I invite you to put these teachings into practice. Become mindful of all your karmic debts. Become aware of who you are still unable to love. Which people do you feel compelled to hurt somehow, either actively through your hostility or passively through your indifference?

On this Christmas Eve I invite you to remember your mother, who brought you into the world. I invite you to remember your father, who served as a channel for you to come here. I invite you to remember your siblings. I invite you to remember all those people who had any role in raising you, and towards whom, for any reason, you have held on to some bitterness or resentment.

If you feel that your heart is completely clean and at peace with these near and dear ones, then use this opportunity to be really thankful for that.

Try to remember what these people gave you, and what you gave them in return. Try to remember the difficulties and problems you caused them.

Today you may receive the blessings of Master Jesus in order to heal this resentment, to heal wounds caused by the absence of mommy or daddy, or by the mistakes they made. It is important that we understand that until we purify ourselves of our resentments, it is impossible for the heart to be opened. But how do we transform bitterness into empathy? How do we transform pacts of vengeance and destruction into compassion? We have to dive deep inside this question in order to understand. Until then, the inner voices clamoring for revenge will not leave us in peace. They will remain active inside of us, causing us confusion and causing us to stumble towards unconscious actions. We have become so accustomed to the din inside our heads that it has become background noise that we don't even notice, but the "disease" it causes shows up as anxiety, irritation, anguish, depression and in the various ways we fail in our lives.

Think about your extended families and departed loved ones. Examine whether there is anything left unsaid, tears that haven't been shed, protests that haven't been voiced, and whether you are still feeling suffocated by the past.

It is impossible to be reborn in spirit without first being free from the ghosts of the past. The only way to free ourselves from the past is to come to peace with it. We are only ready to be reborn in spirit once we can look back and be truly grateful for everything we experienced. We will then be ready to forget that we were ever born. We will be prepared to live and breathe the divine presence.

If you do not succeed in this quest to abide in the divine presence, it is due to these imprints that still mark your lower *chakras*. You cannot enter the kingdom of heaven in your heart with resentment and unhealed wounds. May this ray of light continue to shine and work its magic inside of you. When we make progress in this healing process, we naturally start to see beauty in life. We begin to be grateful. This is how we begin to become translucent, to give passage to the Light.

In closing, I would like to share a beautiful story about gratitude that a friend told me. It describes a twenty-nine year old woman who lost her baby after being pregnant for six months. When this happened, she went into a state of shock: the floor was torn out from beneath her, the world paled, her life seemed to be meaningless. She fell into a deep depression. One day she woke up and saw a present waiting for her at her doorstep. It was a basket filled with love: it contained croissants, Belgian chocolates, and many of the finest little delicacies in the world. It was decorated with a lot of care. When she saw this, she was able to acknowledge and appreciate the love that went into it. Her sister had given it to her. She was able to thank her sister from the bottom of her heart for this expression of love. Once she had attained real gratitude, she could start to notice the brilliance of life again.

This is a small example of the power of gratitude. Gratitude is your being able to recognize and acknowledge an expression of love. When was the last time that you let your gratitude show? When was the last time you expressed your gratitude in a tangible way? Meditate on these questions regarding forgiveness and gratitude.

PART SEVEN

Challenging Questions

My experience is that bhakti, devotion, is the faster way; but not everyone needs to follow the quicker route. It was my path, but I'm offering other tools as well. Regardless of the path you choose, notice that until you break through, this resistance to love brings suffering.

27

Is this Religion?

Question: Is this religion that you teach?

Prem Baba: That depends on what you mean by religion. If to you religion means *religare*, the reconnection of the soul with the Absolute, then yes, I teach religion. But if by religion you mean a certain sect or a collection of dogmas created by the human mind to control others, then I do not teach religion.

We are called upon to question the preconceived beliefs that we carry. Only through freedom can we experience true love. We need to allow ourselves to be spontaneous before our real being can manifest itself. Imagine a flower having to ask her father or her mother, or even a priest or a psychologist, whether or not she is allowed to exude her perfume. This is not to say that these people can't give good advice every now and then, but their recommendations are of little value if they do not echo the voice of our hearts.

RELIGARE

My religion is yoga. Yoga means to "yoke" the individual back together with God. Love is what enables this alchemical

246

union to occur. My religion is love. It is the path of enlighten-ment. If you let me, I can guide you until you are able to free yourself from all dogmas and concepts, from all acquired knowl-edge; so that only the purest truth blossoms in your heart.

Your dogmatic mindset compels you to always want to understand everything, because you want to get somewhere. This is what I mean when I say that the mind has usurped all the energy and left very little for the heart. You condemn whatever the current situation presents, and then keep wanting to move from wrong to right, and from right to even more right. In this way you exert a lot of effort, as you keep doing and doing and doing. You are conditioned this way. If I tell you that you do not have to do anything and to just sit here quietly, you will think something is wrong and you will rush to find something to do. You are addicted to doing.

The truth is, you are already perfect just the way you are. The only thing missing is for you to perceive this. You are a diamond who is trying at all costs to become the most precious gem, when in reality that's already what you are. You're just so busy all the time that you cannot stop long enough to see your own brilliance.

You are obsessed with trying to change yourself. You have fallen prey to the moralistic pattern that says you should avoid evil and do good. So you are constantly condemning and reject-ing yourself, making yourself miserable. This is what prevents you from perceiving that you are the most beautiful of flowers. Instead, you spend your time envying the flower next to you, whom you think is more beautiful than you are. You waste your life away in useless comparison and competition. All of this, because you are not able to sit quietly and observe yourself. If you can stop your compulsive doing and take a look at yourself, you will start to perceive that you emanate a certain brilliance and a certain fragrance. You already are the most beautiful of flowers.

THE WAY OF SIMPLICITY

The qualities I have come to value most are *silence, calmness,* and *simplicity.* These qualities blossom from the heart, and they will lead you to the goal. The mind and the intellect will never lead you to God – ever. You can only realize God through love, and God only manifests when you quiet down. *Love is the perfume of the flower that you are. Love is the shine of the diamond that you are. When you recognize this truth, you have realized the goal, because you recognize that you are an embodiment of the Divine.* Pay close attention to these words. Be aware of your mind wanting to indulge in complexity and engage in compulsive doing, for this is how it distracts you from the goal.

This is not theory: I am speaking from my own experience. I recognize that, in a sense, I know nothing. The path that takes us to God is the path of the heart, and the heart expresses itself in silence, calmness and simplicity.

I have had many teachers in my life, but I have had only two master teachers: Master Jesus and Maharajji. To me, they both vibrate on the same frequency: silence, simplicity, and calm equanimity. Maharajji says, "You surrender yourself and I transform you into what I am." That is essentially the method that I use: I touch your heart and you become me. There is no difference between you and me, we are different only on the surface. Inside, we are all the same. I sit here on this chair because love came to live in my heart, and so they gave me a teacher's chair to sit on; but if there was no chair I would sit on the floor with you. We are the same.

If the monster inside you can just quiet down, stop wanting so much, and stop trying to storm the gates of heaven, you will be able to experience what I am talking about. With a quiet mind you will be able to feel me instead of just trying to understand me. Life is not meant to be understood with the head. It is a mystery to be enjoyed with the heart. The mind will never understand God. God can only be accessed through the heart. What I teach is the way of the heart. It is the path to enlightenment, to realization in God.

The Essence is What Matters

Question: I am drawn to you and your teachings, but *I can't stand* all the outward forms: the rituals, the traditions, the practices... I just want to relax. How can we make what is right for us to do also feel good? What's up with all the forms anyway?

Prem Baba: The opportunity for us to be here together in *satsang* is a true blessing. You come here and we sit together as teachings are transmitted, and slowly you are bathed in the light of understanding. Your mind quiets down and you experience unity. The way in which this happens is not important. But since you, like some others, are distracted by forms, I will explain certain procedures and practices, and the nature of transmission, so that you can more comfortably receive these teachings.

Don't be distracted by what is impermanent. Look at my heart and not at the surface forms. If your heart feels like doing a certain practice, do it. If you want to do the rituals of our lineage, like a *pranam* or *puja*, you are free to participate or simply observe. But don't participate in anything you don't feel drawn to. What are you trying to prove to me? I want nothing of you. My only purpose is to remind you that you are divine light.

Why push yourself to please me? I prefer your true anger to your false smile. Truth is a flower that blossoms from the seed of freedom. Imposed truth is like a plastic flower – it has no fragrance. Instead of pushing yourself to sing *mantras* or to do *pranam,* question the recalcitrant voice inside yourself that refuses to do any practice from any tradition. Ask yourself whose ways you are trying to oppose, and why. "Please let me know the real reason for my closed-mindedness. I commit to seeing it, as much as this may hurt my personal vanity…" If you make a sincere request to understand, eventually the frozen image at the root of your opposition will be revealed to you.

The forms that we observe at this ashram are part of the tradition of this lineage; but the forms are means, not ends. These traditions help us sharpen our spiritual perception and achieve progress on our journey. For example, *pranam* is a practice in which you place your forehead at the feet of the guru to activate your *ajna chakra*, the third eye. One possible translation of the word *guru* is "heavy," because the guru is so filled with the presence of God that the divine energy overflows through the guru's feet. So aside from being an act of humility, reverence and devotion, *pranam* is a psycho-energetic transmission that awakens the *kundalini* energy. It is a practice that goes back thousands of years in this tradition. But know that I don't love you any less if you don't do it. I let it happen here because we have time while we are chanting at the end of *satsang*. In Brazil we have too many people in attendance, so we've stopped for lack of time. The only way I could receive everyone would be if we only did *pranam*, rather than talking, during *satsangs*.

My job is to help you understand. I don't want anything in return. I don't want followers or converts to anything. I'm just here to help you follow your heart. Don't let the others' devotion to me, or their interest in traditional rites, bother you. Be free and let others be free as well. Each person has their own circumstances and needs a specific medicine. No one prescription fulfills everyone's needs. On the contrary, the skilled physician prescribes on a very individual basis.

Although the world of matter that we live in requires these meetings to have a certain setting, schedule and form, our relationship is individual and unique – it is just between you and me. What I'm saying, I'm saying to *you,* although there are many people here. What I transmit to *you* is what will awaken *you.*

Some will receive it easily and go into an ecstatic state. Others will be annoyed and suffer in denial. Either reaction is what the seeker needs at that particular moment.

Calm and tranquility should be your watchwords as you go through this process. Soon you will understand the real reason for your negative attitude towards outer forms and why they bother you so much. Images from the past will come surface. You might be feeling a lot of anger, and want to fight with me. You might be projecting your father, mother and whole family onto me – that is my role. I just ask you to apply a little focus and determination to discover the real actors in your play. This is the difficult part of the journey, but I guarantee that if you hang in there, you will be celebrating. And if you aren't celebrating yet, it's because you are not done with your process. Seek steadiness to continue on the way to awareness. Ask God's mercy to help you heal and integrate this knowledge in your heart and mind.

28
What about
all this Devotion?

Question: The other day I brought a friend here to *satsang*. Afterwards he went charging out the door without even looking back. I was worried that he might be ill, so I followed him to find out what was going on. He told me that he had liked you, and that a lot of what you had to say resonated with him. However, he said that he had had an extreme reaction to the group, to the *sangha,* and had to flee from the sight of "so much melting ice cream." I pointed out that if you take ice cream out to the sun it will invariably melt ... But it seemed to him that rather than being in the front hall of enlightenment, we were in the waiting room of the insane asylum. This is a friend I have known for a while, and I respect his integrity. So since I have been coming here for a while now, playing in the band, and feeling good about the whole experience, I was bewildered by the strength of his negative reaction. What do you think happened?

Prem Baba: The first point is that it is indeed possible that your friend noticed some imbalance in the *sangha* or the exaggerated devotion that some people may express. Truth and falsehood walk around together, sometimes hand-in-hand, so there may well be false devotion co-existing with true. This is how it goes in this realm of spiritual development. Think of the seeker as someone untangling the cords of karma that encumber him. Ultimately his goal is to separate the natural strands from the synthetic ones. At times you clearly notice the Divine acting inside of me and you surrender in devotion, while at other times you project distorted mental images onto me. Oscillating between the false and the real is a natural process in this stage of one's evolutionary journey. It is my work to repeatedly guide you from the false to the real.

Now we get to the second point, the more important one: we are not here to judge whether someone is worthy or unworthy. Rather, we are here to pray and work towards our own and others' awakening. All your efforts should be directed at turning *your own* devotion into an ever more candid and potent prayer. Once you have awakened your own ability to express yourself to the Divine in an authentic way, you should pray that the other may reach this same truthfulness.

Your friend or anyone else bothered by the way people behave should ask themselves this most basic question: "Why am I so bothered by other people and whether they are exhibiting truth or falsehood? Why is it so important to me?" Meanwhile, if *you* are bothered by your friend's reaction, ask yourself, "Why do

I get thrown off center if by chance those around me do not like my master teacher or my spiritual family?" The answer will likely bring up some childhood memory regarding your relationship with your parents. For instance, you might find that you felt the need to protect your family's reputation in face of others' real or imagined disrespect towards them. If you still carry this insecurity inside, you will project your family onto the *sangha*.

Third point: why does the melting of ice cream seem so threatening? What makes it seem to be the "waiting room of the insane asylum?" It was perhaps a clever gibe, but maybe he needed to make fun of others melting away in love because he was scared that he too might melt. The fear of this apparent madness is a strong defense mechanism that precludes even the thought of giving in to love and ecstasy. "What might happen if I let my defenses down, let myself be taken by love?" That isn't just his or your issue, but everyone's. To some extent everyone is afraid of dissolving in love. What is the origin of this fear? So what if the ice cream melts? Only then can it become a tasty milk shake! Are you afraid of losing the previous form of the ice cream? Why do you need to remain in the shape that you were scooped out in?

Falling in love with the Divine is a dramatic event. Cultivating an authentic sense of devotion is actually part of a game – a cosmic game. If you have decided to play this game, then go ahead and play it out to the end. The name of the game is, "going from fear to trust." Some will surrender themselves and play with abandon, and some will just go through the motions. Either way, they're on the game board, and to get their playing piece there they must have already taken one solid step towards trust.

Fourth point: only a humble heart is able to give itself to love. If we use pride as a defense mechanism, we won't be able to get our playing piece on the board so we can practice going from fear to trust. Another name for this game is "the path of devotion" – *bhakti yoga* – and it calls for love and humility.

THE NATURE OF DEVOTION

Understand that the work we do here is individual work: it is between you and me. Everything I say, I say to *you*. The format of the group setting is just to facilitate this unique transmission. It would be impossible to attend to the needs of so many people in the form of one-on-one encounters. Each person needs to focus on their own process. If you notice that someone is spaced out, just pray for that person.

Bhakti, devotion, is the quickest way to get in touch with the inner master or the outer guru. The guru is an embodiment of divine mercy. The guru manifests in a human body out of compassion, so that humanity may have God's address to go to, but the guru is not that body. There is also the unmanifest guru, which is life itself, but it is very difficult to access what is not manifest. Ultimately, what the incarnate guru says, what your intuition tells you, and the direction that life shows you through synchronicity, are all the same golden arrow pointed directly at the truth. For there is only one truth; there cannot be two truths.

The refusal to surrender to an outer guru has a lot to do with this resistance to melting down in the Divine. Here we are practicing *bhakti, jnana* and *karma yoga*. Why does *bhakti* bother some people so much? If the effusiveness of *bhakti* doesn't suit your personal disposition, use the other two methods. Use *jnana* – and the ability of self-observation that *jnana* develops in you – to investigate the question of why you are *so* resistant to loving life. It doesn't matter whether the guru is internal or external. Use *jnana* to invoke your inner master and to identify your prejudices. Identify the emotional and mental imprints that impede you from becoming a lover of God. It doesn't matter whether you take the path of meditation or the path of love. Either path will eventually take you to the other. True silence will open you to love. Follow the path of love, and you will attain inner silence.

My experience is that *bhakti,* devotion, is the faster way; but not everyone needs to follow the quicker route. It was my path, but I'm offering other tools as well. Regardless of the path you choose, notice that until you break through, this resistance to love brings suffering. Here is a clear example of such unease. No matter whether your friend's perception of "madness afoot" is true or false, his reaction points to his unexpressed pain and unshed tears.

This will be easier to understand if we take it to the personal realm. If a person has such a visceral reaction to devotion, what will they do when someone falls madly in love with them? The other is the same as life. When the other unleashes a river of love in your direction, are you going to run away, get sick, or fall into confusion, just to escape from the experience of "yes," of love and union? In both your spiritual and personal life, identify the part of your personality that sabotages your happiness. Identify and transform the part that says "no" to pleasure.

Whenever you are tempted to focus on the faults of others, remember to look inwards. This is the *mahamantra* of transformation: "I searched the world for evil, but but didn't find any; I turned my gaze inwards and found all of the evil inside me."

Forget about criticizing the other; just pray that he may awaken his potential and shine like a star. Wherever he may be now, whether mired in falsehood, wandering blindly, or well-established in truth, don't worry. Focus instead on awakening true devotion to God in yourself.

God is One, but out of compassion God manifests in many different ways so that you can draw near more easily. I am a lover of God, but you don't have to be. My Guru is my altar, because that is the manifestation of the Divine that is easily accessible to me. I also worship at the altar of the unmanifest master teacher and the truth manifest in other masters. It can be Krishna, Buddha, Jesus or any other divine manifestation.

The human mind creates religious fanaticism, which is a distortion of devotion. Fanaticism makes us believe that only our guru can take people to God, or that only our religion leads to God. This kind of mentality is a distortion stemming from our identification with the wounded child and its imprints. It is a psychic disease that needs to be treated.

We offer methods of healing that should be used until all obstacles to devotion are removed. As the way of the heart becomes unobstructed, we feel more and more devotion to the flowers, to the wind, to the river – all are manifestations of the Divine. When our world looks divine, we are lovers of God, guided only by trust.

YOUR GURU SPEAKS YOUR LANGUAGE

Even though you already feel devotion for all divine manifestations, you continue to focus on your guru because he speaks the language you most easily understand. In fact, it is the guru's ability to share the mysteries of creation in a way that the disciple can readily understand that defines the true encounter between the guru and the disciple. You connect with a living guru so you can have access to the divine mercy that manifests through the guru. The guru knows you and can give you what you need. He speaks to you in the spiritual language that you can understand, and which calms your heart. Even if I don't speak your worldly tongue, I speak your inner language. Likewise, although Maharajji and I need to communicate through a translator, he reads me very easily and I understand him very well. In fact, Maharajji became my Guru precisely because we speak the same language of the heart. It is that simple.

The way of the heart is the simplest of all paths. Any doubts that emerge are minor and simple to overcome, for they are just caused by the fear of surrendering to love. You fear to become a madman of God, and to go around singing, dancing and celebrating life in a completely carefree way. The children of God dance in divine madness, for they know that God takes care of everything in their lives. I know it's scary to lose control. It's scary to be consumed by love, because then you control absolutely nothing. This is how it goes on a personal level too, isn't it? When you fall in love, you melt like ice cream. So can you imagine falling into divine love?

This is my wish: may you become a madman of God, a lover of the Divine, and may you be guided exclusively by trust. May you let go of any grain of fear that still inhabits your system, in the form of skepticism, doubts, or the need to control life. There's no need to protect yourself. May you be guided by the heart and love without fear. You will discover whether you are really free of fear and its allies, pride and stubborn self-will, when you no longer have to please anyone. If your friend tells you that the *sangha* is just a bunch of lunatics melting away, you can simply agree. I myself also think some people here are crazy, but everything is just right the way it is. I accept you just the way you are, with all your lies and your truthfulness, and regardless of how crazy or sane you are.

It's not because you do something a certain way, or because you do something for me that I love you. I love you because *I am love*; and the measure of love is love. That is my job and that is all that there is for me. Life is very simple. I have no worries.

Recently I was concerned about an issue regarding the ashram in Brazil, which simply became too small for the recent influx of seekers who want to stay there and participate in our activities. I decided to talk to Maharajji about it. The day after I told him, I thought it best to repeat myself to make sure he understood, because we speak different native languages. Finally he stopped me and said, "I understood it the first time. Now it's not your problem anymore, it's mine."

That very same day a disciple came to me to say that he had suddenly felt that he should donate a large property he owned in Brazil to the Sachcha Mission. The land turned out to be perfect in every way, and we will slowly start building on it. If everything goes according to plan we will definitively move there by 2015, the culmination of this transformative period, and will continue to build up and use our current ashram as a retreat for wellness and relaxation.

This is how I live, and this is the lifestyle I am teaching you to live.

29
What about the Guru-Disciple Relationship?

The guru is like an oasis in the desert, a window to the heavens, a bridge to eternity. There are very few such portals offered to humanity. They appear on Earth, remain here for a short period of time, then disappear. The emergence of a true guru is a rare occurrence, but the same can be said about true disciples: they are hard to find. Only a tiny segment of the human population ever becomes spiritual seekers, and of those only a small portion ever become true disciples. A true disciple is that extraordinary being who has developed spiritual receptivity: he or she becomes open enough to receive the transmission of the guru. The disciple becomes like a hollow bamboo-flute through which the master teacher can play a melody. A *sadhaka*, a spiritual practitioner, spends a lot of time being a seeker before developing this basic quality that defines discipleship.

Enlightened people are rare. Enlightened teachers are even rarer. The difference between the two is this: an enlightened person has compassion for all humanity, but only the guru knows how to guide disciples to enlightenment. Because there are so few true gurus and disciples, it is rare for a real guru and disciple to connect – but when it does occur, the encounter bears the sweet fruit of profound love. It is possible for the guru to pass by right in front of you and for you still not to notice. You will only notice the guru's presence if you are ready and mature enough to empty yourself so that the sweet melody of the guru may play through you.

A DEEP LOVE AFFAIR

When this encounter takes place, it is a deep love affair. The world loses its appeal. The disciple is swept away by love's grace. This is when the master teacher can tell the disciples, "Put aside your fishing rods, for you shall no longer be fishermen: rather you shall be fishers-of-men." Thus spoke Jesus to his potential disciples. When Jesus passed by and the disciples recognized that he was the oasis in the desert, the phenomenon took place. Jesus told them, "Put aside your fishing rods and come with me." And so they put aside their fishing rods and followed him. When they were already at the city limits, someone came running to inform that the mother of one of the fishermen had died. When this man asked Jesus whether he should turn back, Jesus answered, "Let the dead bury the dead." So he continued to follow Jesus.

This beautiful passage touches me deeply, because I understand the exquisiteness and uniqueness of such an encounter.

When the potential disciple is ready to meet the guru, it is like iron filings being drawn to a magnet. This is how it was when I met Maharajji. When I recognized him, my heart connected with him and that's where it stayed. The master teacher recognizes the disciple, but the disciple also recognizes the master teacher.

The encounter between you and the guru is a matter of destiny. You may think that you pick out your guru, but the guru already chose you a long time ago. Just as a mother keeps her child in the womb for nine months, the guru keeps you in his or her womb for many lives, until you develop the quality of receptivity. You develop receptivity when you trust; and trust is only possible when there is love. When this trust is strong enough, the master teacher starts chipping away at your ego, bit by bit. Finally, when you are mature, you disappear as an ego altogether, and discover that you and the guru are one. You discover that you are an ocean of love.

Until you meet your guru, you may benefit from the wisdom of many spiritual teachers. But you will recognize your true guru when you feel the grace flowing. When I came to India for the first time, I came in response to a voice that had echoed inside of me since I was a boy. When I was twelve, I had already started practicing yoga. When during a class they played the first *bhajan* I ever listened to, praising Sita Ram Narayana, I heard an inner voice telling me that when I turned thirty-three years old, I should go to Rishikesh, India. I then forgot about this message, but when I was almost thirty-three, I had a vision that reminded me of it. So I came here and started seeking. I met many master teachers, many enlightened beings. All of them were good for me in some way, and I was able to learn something from each of them. But I did not feel the grace. I did not feel myself totally overwhelmed by love. This happened only when I met Maharajji, so I surrendered myself to him.

I continue to love and sometimes visit other master teachers. I cannot even describe how much I love and admire them. But my Guru is Maharajji – the others are my Divine Allies. The reality is that the master teacher is only one and truth is one, but they manifest in different ways, according to your need. This encounter is based on vibrational affinity. When you asked me if it is possible to love two people at the same time, I answered that indeed you can love all of humanity at once, if you are able to love consciously. Likewise, I see the master teacher in everyone. I see the beauty and the light of God shining brightly in many spiritual teachers, even though I am married to Maharajji. I see my guru in many other gurus. The truth everywhere is one and the same, but the mission of my soul demands that I be here with Maharajji.

SURRENDERING TO LOVE

The encounter between guru and disciple happens when you feel grace flowing. The true guru emanates grace, a grace that gushes from the heart. You feel this intuitively, although doubts may arise in your mind. You live the encounter; as it happens you sense the truth of your intuition telling you that you have found what you were looking for. When you find it, you stop seeking it. You cease to be a seeker and you become a finder. At this point your work changes completely. You no longer look for a path, for you have found it. Now you will dive deeply into yourself through the grace of the guru. This is when you start working on the deeper layers of the ego.

I receive everyone because I am love. I love everyone. I do not choose you based on whether you are rich or poor, ugly or pretty, good or bad: none of this matters to me. I am like the sun that shines on everyone. I am like pure water, quenching the thirst of all. And you have come here because you are thirsty for a love that is selfless and doesn't judge. I don't demand anything of you. I love you, and I mirror your own love back to you. If you can't see love in the mirror, it is only because you haven't emptied your mind and you are still projecting things onto me. To truly see me, you have to become empty like me. When emptiness meets emptiness, the search is over.

If you feel that I am your guru, we can formalize our connection through an initiation, with a *mantra*. In truth, this initiation is a commitment you make with yourself. You commit to being receptive, to surrendering. You commit to playing your part in this divine play; while my part is to help you master your mind. When you really want to be taken, then I will take you. But you will see that I am very demanding. Know that the love of the guru often needs to draw boundaries so that you do not deviate from the path. Your mind has been out of control ever since you learned to listen to it rather than it listening to you. It has been in this rebellious state for many incarnations. This is why you open yourself to guidance and surrender, so that I may help you master your own mind. Sometimes this means that I have to let you suffer whatever you need to suffer in order for you to heal a wound or a part of your ego. You may think this is cruel; but in truth only a pure heart overflowing with compassion can be a conduit for these difficult life lessons.

All of these are elements of guru-disciple intimacy. The relationship only works if there is a great amount of love and intimacy. People from Western cultures who are unfamiliar with the process of spiritual mentoring may judge or be shocked by the intensity of love between guru and disciple. But this transmission of energy can only happen with someone that you truly love.

STAY ON YOUR PATH

If you already have another guru and you are here sitting with me, it's important that you evaluate why you are here. Perhaps you are running away from the teaching of your guru. Or perhaps you are no longer in love with your present teacher; you have learned what you needed to learn and that relationship is no longer bringing you growth. This means that you have not yet found your guru. These encounters with various spiritual teachers are passages you have to go through and learn from on your journey.

Evaluate this issue with a great deal of attention. If you felt that grace when meeting your guru and you accepted initiation, you might be going through a test of your trust. Your trust and your faith in your guru will be tested time and time again. You will only receive the transmission when there is no longer doubt in your heart. The essence of the guru-disciple relationship is *surrender* – in other words, giving yourself over to this love with your whole being. You need to trust in the same way that a child trusts a parent. The child often does not know where she is going, but she takes her parent's hand and goes anyway. They may be headed to see the doctor, and she may not be happy about that, but she still goes.

If you have not yet discovered the qualities of trust and surrender within yourself, you can still be a friend of the guru's. You can receive some help as a friend, but you are not a disciple. I have many disciples, and I have many friends. In truth, all the disciples are also my friends, but they are learning to surrender and to be guided, whereas those who are just friends come to see me, receive some energy, and then move on.

If you feel the deep connection of a disciple and are here trying to do what I suggest, don't fool yourself into thinking that you are just a friend, when the reality is that you are just lacking the courage to formalize your commitment. On the other hand, don't trick yourself into thinking that you are a disciple when you continue to resist surrendering yourself. It's important that you have the maturity to recognize what relationship you have with a spiritual teacher.

WHAT INITIATION MEANS

To receive initiation, it is essential that you first feel this wave of love – that you experience this feeling of merging. Maharajji once said, "When you look at the guru and feel the same love that you feel when you look at your beloved, then you are ready to receive initiation." This feeling may dissipate later on, because initiation will uncover deeper layers of doubt and bring your shadow to the forefront. This is how love begins to purify us. Love takes us in and embraces us; but it also squeezes us and wrings us out. The gateway to heaven is quite narrow: only *you* can pass through it. None of these psychological selves that you carry as internal baggage may enter; only you. But even though the passageway is narrow, simply knock at the gates and they will open.

If you would like to know more about my work, know that I use many tools for opening you up to yourself. I have said it before: Prem Baba is just a name – one that I believe even fits me well – but it is just a name, and I am not a name. I am the wind, I am the Light that manifests as the colors blue, pink and gold. On this Earth I manifest myself sometimes as an eagle, sometimes as a hummingbird, and sometimes as pure water. I move through many worlds, and I have many allies. I draw from shamanism, the essence of Christianity, the teachings of the East and my knowledge of psychology. I join all this together: knowledge, art, philosophy, mysticism, science and spirituality; the Amazon rainforest and the Orient. I am always working to find the One within the many. What is not truth, I ignore, but what is true I integrate and use to your benefit. My job is to awaken you.

I recognize myself as a divine manifestation, and likewise I recognize that you are a divine manifestation. But I know that you have forgotten this fact. My work is to remind you that you and I are the same. This is why you feel an attraction towards me: because I do not judge you. I love you freely, for I see this same love inside of you. You may not be able to express this love fully yet, but I won't stop working until you do.

Question: Do you ever feel that a person is not ready for initiation and therefore refuse to initiate them?

Prem Baba: Yes. When someone comes to me in a state of confusion, I tell them to wait on initiation until they have more clarity about what they really want. You need to be touched by the truth. You need to find this clarity, even if only for an instant. This glimpse is sufficient, because the initiation develops over time. I don't want to push you into a hasty decision. If I tell you what to do, you will become dependent on me, but I don't want you to be dependent on me. Rather, I want to encourage your self-reliance, I want you to get in contact with the truth inside yourself.

In the past I've used the word "follower," but it is a treacherous word, and I like being careful with my words. I do not want followers. The term "follower" can give the impression that you are following blindly. The idea is to help you open your eyes, not to put blinders on! I do not want to convert anyone or to indoctrinate anyone. I don't work like that, and I do not support that kind of mentality. All I want is for you to wake up. I want you to become master of your own house. I want you to be free.

You were born to experience freedom. I am working to help you find your inner guide. You will hear me speaking inside of you through your intuition and the insights that arise. There is no difference between your intuition and what a master teacher tells you. The teacher may even give you instructions that foreshadow something that your intuition has still not grasped, but with time your intuition would have led you to that same juncture. This is so because the master is one. There is no difference between the living master, the inner master, and life itself. The master is one and Truth is one.

PART EIGHT

Concluding Meditations

A person of the light has a good heart, and is always ready to lend a helping hand. A person of the light is able to see the dormant potential in others and help direct energy towards their awakening. When you live with loving consciousness, at some point God catches hold of you, and when you least expect it you will find that you are enlightened.

30
Redefining Enlightenment

On my way to *satsang* today, a chant from the people of the Amazonian rainforest of Brazil came to me:

From far, I come from far away,
from the waves of the sacred sea,
so that I may come to know the power
of the forest and to love God.

I live on this path,
I walk it for days on end,
so that I may come to know that power
and the holy light of the true God.

The power of the true God
is for us to have love
for the stars of the firmament
and for all of God's creation.

If the true God is pure love, we align ourselves with the divine will when we love. You heard the call of the saints. You heeded that call because you are ripe to align yourself with the truth. I have noticed that spiritual seekers are often fascinated with the search for enlightenment as their sole purpose, to the point where they forget that enlightenment means becoming love itself. Stubbornly focused on their *sadhana* with the one goal of becoming enlightened, they become blind to the plight of the person sitting next to them. Sometimes that person just needs a bit of attention, even if it's only some eye contact and a smile.

Maybe we need to redefine the goal: if enlightenment means realizing our true nature – which is love and light – then behaving with disrespect or indifference is a sign that we are nowhere near our goal.

THE GOAL IS TO OPEN THE HEART

On the contrary, we must respect all expressions of life, and all the ways that life teaches us. That example I mentioned earlier about the old man who fell down the stairs at the Shiva temple really marked me. Instead of getting irritated and blaming life, he bowed down in gratitude, thanking those very stairs for the teaching he received from them.

We need to redefine our goal: instead of enlightenment, we should seek to be able to forgive and love everyone and everything. Enlightenment happens through divine grace. It is beyond the mind's control. All we can do is make efforts to clear the way. So the goal of our practice is not enlightenment, but to open the heart.

It's good to cultivate our body's ability to sustain presence with psycho-energetic practices such as *hatha yoga, japa* meditation, and *pranayama* breathing exercises. But if on the way to yoga class you mistreat the dog who cuts across your path, what is the point of all your practices? By all means, do your practice and prepare your system for the awakening of the *kundalini* energy, but remain mindful of your motives and goals.

The spiritual quest itself can become a great distraction. It could be your own ego taking you on this journey. In that case, your journey is a way to escape God's gifts. Instead of striving for enlightenment, be content being a person of the light, a person at peace with life, a person who celebrates the gift of being in this body. Rather than trying to be *the* enlightened person in town, be someone who is thankful for all that life brings.

A person of the light has a good heart, and is always ready to lend a helping hand. A person of the light is able to see the dormant potential in others and help direct energy towards their awakening. When you live with loving consciousness, at some point God catches hold of you, and when you least expect it you will find that you are enlightened. Without loving awareness none of your practices will amount to anything, for they are not fulfilling the goal of opening the channels of your heart.

Observe carefully with whom and under which circumstances you are unable to express love. When was the last time you expressed your gratitude? Gratitude is the soul's response to a true expression of love. When we feel love being directed at us in a tangible way our hearts explode with gratitude. If you haven't been truly thankful, it may be that you haven't yet been able to recognize these manifestations of divine love. Maybe the door is still closed. This is the play of Mahamaya: to limit our ability to love and to recognize love.

Question: It seems that most of the time the people around me are not capable of mature love. How can I stop focusing so much on what is wrong with them, and instead focus more on their virtues?

Prem Baba: This is the essence of the divine play we call human life. What distinguishes human beings from other species is our capacity to find satisfaction through giving of ourselves. But how can we open up and give of ourselves when the other's faults are always staring us in the face? I'm not proposing that the solution is to blind ourselves. We still perceive the other's shortcomings, but we don't remain fixated on them, because we understand that character defects and even brutal demonstrations of cruelty are defense mechanisms. They are the soul's cry for help.

Look beyond the shadow. Contemplate the beauty of the sunshine that lies undisturbed underneath all that darkness. Maybe this person is in need of your attention. But you can only look beyond the other's shadow side when you can look into and beyond your own. Understand dark-side games as defense mechanisms rather than the final reality of this person. The more you perceive your own defects as "special effects," the more you can recognize and accept them as such in others.

As you work to integrate these aspects of the shadow side, the challenge may seem daunting. Remember that you are not alone. The person next to you is going through the same difficulties. So, before thinking about enlightenment, think about how you can be a real friend.

A New Understanding of Enlightenment

Remember the essence of the spiritual work you have undertaken. It's clear that you are moving towards enlightenment. The issue is that the ego appropriates the idea of enlightenment very easily: "I want to become enlightened; that's all that matters." When you think like this, you are missing the mark. It is self-deceit, because only love can bring enlightenment.

Another trick of the ego is to frame enlightenment as something supernatural or extraterrestrial. That's not how it is; enlightenment is here on earth, in this body. You become enlightened when you open your heart to your brother or sister. I'm not talking about fake love, but the real thing. Your main goal should be to realize yourself as an embodiment of divine love.

I know that the ego feels threatened by this discourse. It would prefer to hear about opening *chakras* and about which *nadi* or channel the *kundalini* energy is passing through.

Sometimes I even speak about such things, because that knowledge is authentic. But the danger is that it can feed our ego, and the last thing the bloated self-image needs is more food! What the ego needs is a diet. We are born into this world to learn to love consciously.

Question: When one lives in an enlightened state, does one still experience anger?

Prem Baba: There is a kind of anger known as "righteous indignation" that can be an expression of love, an assertive expression whose goal is to establish limits, like one does with children. This more intense expression of love could be interpreted as anger, but it doesn't leave residues or cause the same heartaches and resentment as ego-driven anger. It is a reprimand that is not rooted in past grievances or lingering wounds, but instead emanates from presence in order to put things back into balance. You will recognize this if you are awake. It is a form of conscious love, and it causes no karma or loss of energy.

Question: It doesn't leave residues in whom?

Prem Baba: It leaves scars neither in the person expressing indignation nor the recipient, but they will have to deal with the emotions that are evoked. If the person on the receiving end is awake, they will perceive it as an expression of love and give the other person a heartfelt thank you: "Dhanyavad." If they are not awake, they will struggle to understand.

The person who expresses this kind of righteous indignation doesn't lose energy. When, on the contrary, the anger that is being expressed comes from the wounded child, one minute of it is enough to drain your energy entirely. That's not to say that this egoic anger should be avoided at all costs; sometimes you will have to lose energy because you need to pass through the experience of anger to move forward. Anger plays its role; that's why true anger is so much more valuable than a fake smile.

BRINGING LIGHT WHERE THERE WAS DARKNESS

Question: This morning I awoke to the sounds of a man beating his son. There were many people around; the child tried to run away, but the father held him tightly and kept beating him. What can I do with this image?

Prem Baba: I am always invoking light to illuminate all these dark places, to shine the light of love on the lack of respect, on the cruelty, and on the violence inside us. May all seekers be cleansed of hypocrisy. It's not good enough just to speak of noble qualities like love and generosity. In this light we truly love, and we truly give of ourselves.

Let me share with you the story of a remarkable man I once met at a conference. He was extremely successful in life. He used to be a banker in his country, Pakistan. He was a very loving man and devoted father. He had a twenty-year-old son who was the apple of his eye. While his son was delivering pizza one night, he was caught in the crossfire between two gangs and was killed by a bullet fired by a fourteen-year old gang member. The father received the terrible news by phone. At that moment his heart stopped and he left his body.

Then in the space between life and death, he had a vision: he saw clearly that there were victims at both ends of the gun. After this revelation he was able to return to his body. He had made the decision to rise to the challenge of compassion and live, rather than letting his grief and rage kill him. He started an NGO to help youngsters who have strayed into delinquency. He invited the grandfather of the boy who had shot the fatal bullet to join in his effort (the boy had been raised without a father). He hoped that the boy who had killed his son might help out in the effort once he got out of prison. The last I heard, the young man had been released and was getting involved in the project.

I call the star:
the star comes!
It comes to teach me
the love of wishing others well.

The love of wishing others well
brings health and well-being,
consecrating this love,
so that we may never go lacking.

Forever, forever
friend of my brother and sister,
for they are my light
in this world of illusion.

This is the love that brings light where there was only darkness. This openness to reconciliation and friendship is a shining example. During the same conference I heard the Dalai Lama tell the story of a Tibetan Lama who had been imprisoned when China invaded Tibet. He had been locked up and tortured for eighteen years. When the Dalai Lama asked him what his greatest fear had been during those eighteen years, the monk responded: "My greatest fear was that I would stop feeling compassion for the Chinese."

In ending, let me offer you a song that I received as a culmination of my search for the light:

The path I go on following
with firmness and with love;
surrendering myself to the will
of the supreme Christ 'I am.'

Oh my brothers and sisters, this is the time
to pulsate pure love.
The path of the heart
is the one that gives us this flower.

Aligning myself with the truth
of what I am,
I can only say happily
that I am pure love.

My father is a marvel;
my mother is a beauty.
I am the blessed child
of the mystery of love.

I will sing all the glories
of the empire of love,
helping my brother and sister
who have not yet seen.

Here I conclude
this song of love,
surrendering to God
to the Christ 'I am.'

Blessed be each and every one of you. May you receive the blessing that helps you befriend your brothers and sisters.

31
Becoming a Channel of Light

As we bring these teachings to a conclusion, I would like to suggest a little practice that you may find helpful in opening your heart:

Sit up straight, but not rigidly. Get into a comfortable position. If someone is reading this to you, you may close your eyes and breathe softly and deeply through your nostrils. Calm your whole system and empty yourself of turbulent and discordant thoughts. Through the healing silence, take refuge in your true inner being, who is guided by the compass of love alone. There is no power on earth greater than love. It can heal all wounds, dissolve all separations, and resolve all conflicts.

BREATHE IN SORROW, BREATHE OUT JOY

Visualize yourself as a perfect *yogi* seated on a hilltop, with a heart overflowing with love. You see a very long line of people

284

coming towards you. These are people who bring their need for exclusive love, people wounded by the trials and tribulations of life. The souls at the beginning of the line are the people closest to you – they are your nuclear and extended family, those still with us and those who have passed on. They may still carry some resentment towards you, and you may yet hold some grievances against them.

This is the moment destined for forgiveness.

Allow each one of your relatives to approach. Breathe in all of their negativity, including any grudges you may have, and let it be illuminated inside your heart of infinite tenderness; then breathe out light and blessings.

Now internally chant the *mantra*, either in the original or in your own language:

> *"Prabhu Ap Jago, Parmatma Jago.*
> *Mere Sarve Jago, Sarvatra Jago.*
> *Dukhantaka Khel, Kaanta Karo.* [8]
> *Sukhantaka Khel, Prakash Karo."*
> "God, awaken. God awaken in me;
> awaken in my brother and sister.
> End the play of suffering,
> and bring light to the play of joy."

---

[8] This is the foundational *mantra* of the Sachcha lineage. As of 2011, we are no longer chanting the third line, as in this year the lineage holder, Maharajji asked us to stop singing the word "*dukhanta*" (suffering) and instead focus on "*sukhanta*" (joy).

Pray sincerely for your brother or sister, this being who needs so much attention, care and love at this moment. Pray for the divinity that lives inside him but is still asleep, enveloped by the veil of illusion that makes him feel deficient and believe that he is a single drop of water instead of the Ocean itself.

With the deepest humility that you can manifest at this moment, lift your gaze beyond the clouds, beyond the veils of illusion, and invoke the Divine Being in each and every person who approaches you: "Awaken, God awaken! Wake up!"

You breathe in the negativity, which is then transformed by the light of the *mantra Prabhu Ap Jago* inside your heart. You breathe out light and the fragrance of roses. One by one the souls come to you and you share your blessings. You will recognize the faces of some, and not of others – it makes no difference. Bring in friends, relatives, enemies... At this point, all labels fall away. Bring them all in: leave no one out. Bring into your healing presence anyone with whom you feel you have unfinished business. Remain some time in this active meditation, receiving all those who come to you. Feel love and happiness flowing through you so it may be transmitted to the other. You are an ever flowing source of love.

You may also personalize your prayers, especially when those people you know well approach, so that the prayer fits the needs of that individual soul. For example, you can say, "May you be happy," "May existence provide for all your needs," "May you realize yourself in God." Offer these prayers with utmost sincerity. Through this dedication to the well-being of others, may the fire of love incinerate all discord left in your heart. May its flame consume all sense of separation, all your neediness and the illusion of scarcity.

You are a blessed heir of eternal glory and universal treasure. You are love itself. Remember this truth. Allow yourself to be an instrument of divine love. Simply allow the people to come to you. They come closer, receive your blessing, and go. You continue inhaling the sorrows of the world and exhaling the purest joy.

BRINGING LOVE INTO YOUR DAILY LIFE

Little by little, bring your visualization to a close, but keep your heart open. If your eyes have been closed, slowly open them, bringing with you the awareness that this practice of transforming negativity into light continues taking place. If you practice this meditation regularly, it has the power to change your life. May you recognize that these same people pass by you every day, and that their sorrows constantly pass through you. We often identify with their pain, simply because we don't know what else to do with it. Rather than suffering with the pain of the world, our work is to illuminate it. So if this sorrow passes through you, sing to it, pray, offer your best to it so that this energy can be elevated.

This is the healing work that the Earth is undergoing right now. The vision of worldwide transformation is about the transition from fear to trust, from hatred to love, and from isolation and separation to union. I am speaking about moving from egoism to authentic altruism. Our altruism is authentic when we are able to recognize our egoism and intentionally redirect the energy. You are being healed at this very moment. You are also receiving tools that will enable you to help others. This will happen in a natural way. You will notice it come about in your daily life.

Love is meant to be shared. But I am not speaking about false love that can only cause us pain. If we feign love, we will find ourselves back in the Matrix, and things there are getting intense. When the illusions of sorrow or skepticism squeeze us, the way to expansive clear vision is to take refuge in universal love. As long as the veil of illusion, Maya, restricts our ability to love, the only way to transcend the pain is by stepping back and looking at the big picture. We need to stop looking only at our own belly buttons and start thinking globally.

Back in your daily life, when you go to the bank and notice the tormented look on the face of the teller, try smiling at her rather than complaining; or simply pray for her in your heart. Only by truly empathizing with others can we rise above suffering and so ease their pain.

Remember my message throughout this coming year. Your identification with illusion may still give you trouble. In general, the monster is well hidden – but it will show up in the form of despair and skepticism, as well as in the fear of scarcity. Learn to recognize fear when it comes knocking, and know that your anxiety is nothing more than a nightmare.

When you notice yourself identifying with such feelings, wake up! Drink some cold water, take a bath, and just remind yourself to keep giving.

In the course of this journey, always ask for "strength to carry on, faith not to falter, light to see, and love to offer thanks."

Namaste!

Glossary

Psycho-Spiritual Terms

Note: Below is a list of definitions and explanations of many of the psycho-spiritual terms that Prem Baba refers to in his teachings. Many of these terms come from the teachings of Eva Pierrakos, including the tripartite division of the self into lower self, higher self and masks, the distinction between positive and negative intentionality, the distinction between positively and negatively oriented pleasure, and the concept of images. For further reading, see Fear No Evil, Creating Union, *and* Surrender to God Within, *by Eva Pierrakos, Donovan Thesenga, and Judith Saly, and published by Pathwork Press (www.pathwork.org).*

ABC of Spirituality – A methodology developed by Prem Baba that guides the seeker through the process of purification of the lower self. The study of our own often-unconscious negative behaviors is the necessary starting point of any authentic spiritual journey. Prem Baba includes the study of the lower self in virtually all of his oral transmissions, and also offers intensive retreats and weekly gatherings that focus exclusively on the

ABC of Spirituality. These help seekers go deeper in the process of identifying, integrating and transforming the unconscious or semi-conscious negative traits of the personality.

Autonomous complex – A part of the psyche that has split off and acts as an autonomous being with a will of its own. Autonomous complexes are aspects of the lower self that cause us to act destructively and to attract negative situations. They come into being when we experience some shock or trauma in childhood where it is understood that some part of who we are is not accepted by others. This part gets repressed and embedded in the unconscious, where it feeds off of our vital energy and wreaks havoc in our lives. As long as our autonomous complexes are not properly identified and integrated, they continue to exert their power, and we are unable to make any durable, positive changes in that part of our lives which was taken over.

Code – Vibrations of energy that permeate the world and influence how human beings behave, react and experience reality.

Comprehension – Comprehension is an understanding that is beyond the mind, beyond intellectual rationalization. Through contemplation involving one's whole being, we arrive at a knowing that is much more profound and impactful than a simple understanding. This comprehension allows us to accept ourselves, our life situations, and our past without resorting to the use of the intellect, so that we can make peace with our lives and consciously move forward.

Conscious self or **Conscious ego** – The part of our personality that we are aware of and can consciously direct. Unlike the lower self that is usually relegated to the unconscious level, or the higher self, which mostly remains un-manifested and inaccessible, the conscious ego is what most people think of as who they are. The conscious ego is the one who goes out to the world to make a living or to build a family, but it is also the one who willingly goes to a master teacher to become absorbed into a higher form of existence. Seekers who are still misadjusted with material life must first undergo the work of consolidating and solidifying their ego. Only people with a mature and stable ego, who are well grounded and in harmony with society and material life, are prepared to undergo a spiritual journey that will dissolve the ego into the higher self.

Entity, **evolving human entity**, or **person in evolution** – As a spiritual being evolves over many incarnations through the realms of matter, plant life, and the animal kingdom, it eventually acquires a human body endowed with a human brain, so that it learns to live amicably in human society. Although it is now a rational being, it is still unable to express authentic human virtues such as love, tranquility, non-violence, humility, trust and selflessness. Rather, this being is still understood to be in a state of evolution, as it will invariably continue to manifest destructive impulses that stem from its animal nature. It remains an *evolving human entity* or a *person in evolution* until it develops its ability to express human virtues, sometimes over the course of many lifetimes. Only then can the entity rightfully be called a *human being*. Sometimes "entity" is also used in the text in order to indicate an "autonomous complex."

Eros – The feeling of passion that we feel when we are romantically attracted to another. In Greek mythology, Eros was the god of sexual love and beauty. Eros is the life instinct innate to all human beings that drives them to relate and create. This constructive force is the search for one's female or male counterpart that is experienced outside of us but actually dwells inside. Thus, Eros is an energy that takes us to the state of wholeness.

Evil – A defense mechanism that results in ignorant and destructive behavior towards ourselves and others. Every human being develops these layers of "evil" in response to painful experiences in their past and in an attempt to numb and shield themselves from further pain. When these protective layers are removed, our true nature is revealed. Note that this term should not be understood with the heavy moral connotations ascribed to it by certain religions and society, which consider evil to be sinful wrongdoing that requires punishment.

False self – A temporary reality composed of our lower self and the masks that we wear. When we are identified with the false self, we unconsciously sabotage all our possibilities of attaining lasting happiness. The feeling of insufficiency leads to the compulsive desire to be accepted and loved. So as to receive attention, we consistently act through masks, which have nothing to do with our true nature. When we begin to remember who we really are, we remove these masks and begin to get in touch with the lower self. Compared to the masks, the lower self is already much closer to our true nature, but it is still a temporary reality that will at some point be transformed into our ultimate reality: the higher or real self.

Higher self – The higher self is the true self or soul, the aspect of the human being that expresses divine qualities such as love, wisdom, purity, humility and truth. It is the divine spark within each living being. The higher self is the finest and most radiant of the subtle bodies, and has the highest frequency of vibration. In most human beings, it is covered with numerous layers of less developed and denser forms of matter, most notably our masks and the various aspects of the lower self.

Image – An unconscious erroneous conclusion that becomes a generalization about life, usually formed due to painful events experienced in early childhood, and which attracts continuous hardships throughout our lives. This is not to be confused with the personal self-image which is a pretense shown to the world, or any more superficial kind of image that is a residue left in the mind coming from what the senses have captured throughout our day. Instead, this image remains frozen deep in our emotional world, and it makes us repeatedly fail at overcoming recurring problems that show up in our relationship or career, or related to our financial or physical well-being. An image is only dissolved through a dedicated and courageous study that usually takes months or years, examining all the undesired circumstances in our life until we find the common denominator between them. It involves overcoming shame and a long process of re-educating ourselves after years of repeating specific habits and emotional reactions.

Imagination – The constant, passive thinking process that the human mind engages in, which we are unable to control. A person in evolution spends the vast majority of their time having thoughts that simply act as background noise, and are not actually necessary or constructive. These thoughts differ from that rare, active creativity process, which can only emerge from a still mind.

Law of Giving and Receiving – A universal law based on the law of cause and effect that states that energy must flow, otherwise it stagnates. If we do not give openly and free from expectation of rewards, we do not participate in the dynamic exchange through which the universe operates. This in turn prevents us from receiving the affluence, love or joy we are seeking. Abundance circulates in our lives only when we give bountifully what we seek for ourselves. "Give and it shall be given unto you." (Luke 6:38). The law of giving and receiving is also the principle behind *Guru dakshina*, which is the financial contribution we make to the guru in acknowledgment and gratitude for everything that we receive from him or her.

Lower self – A layer of matter that is not quite as dense as the human body, but that is infinitely denser than the higher self, which it surrounds and confines. Usually commanding the person from an unconscious level of the psyche, the lower self consists of all destructive impulses and negative tendencies, as well as the negative intentionality that directs them. Although each person in evolution is purifying some particular aspect of the lower self more intensely than other aspects, everyone has a lower self that manifests ignorance and selfishness. The lower self proudly and stubbornly refuses to change or develop.

Lust – One of the more subtle of the nine matrices of the lower self, lust is a distortion of devotion. It is commonly defined as strong sexual desire and considered one of the Seven Deadly Sins, which has given it a heavy connotation of moral wrongdoing in traditional Christianity. As used in the context of this book, lust is a natural defense mechanism developed by the wounded child in response to a perceived lack of love. When we grow up, we unconsciously use sexual energy to manipulate and have power over others, as well as to take revenge and punish a partner or anyone else who is attracted to us.

Mask – An image we subconsciously create and use to get attention from the world, and that is superimposed on the lower self in an attempt to hide it from the people we relate with. The creation of this superimposed mask is usually unavoidable, because we are often not ready to pay the price of facing all the negative characteristics of the lower self until they are integrated. Instead of embarking on the arduous path of self-discovery, we simply hide all this negative content with a mask that has nothing to do with the temporary reality of the lower self nor with the lasting reality of the higher self – it is a totally artificial creation.

Matrix or **Matrices of the ego** or **of the lower self** – The nine matrices are the primary aspects of the lower self that breed all other bad habits and destructive tendencies. Every person has all nine matrices in their system, but incarnates with the mission of purifying and integrating one or two matrices specifically, which act more strongly in that person.

The matrix – Prem Baba also uses the term matrix – in reference to the movie *The Matrix* – to name the dream world that we are convinced is "reality" until we step out of it and realize that it is only a product of our false perceptions.

Negative intentionality – The deliberate choice to act and be hateful, destructive and negative. Spiritual seekers only become aware of and transform their negative intentionality at a very advanced stage of development. It is challenging enough to become aware of our general faults, negativity and destructive attitudes and to discover the pleasure we invest in being this way. But we eventually reach a stage where we acknowledge that if our life is not the way we want it to be, it is because we are choosing to negate life and to suffer because of it; it may be a means of punishing our parents for their inability to love, for example, or of blaming life for not providing what we want. But even when we begin to recognize the senselessness of holding on to this primary source of suffering in our life, we are unable to change. The key to transitioning to *positive intentionality* is to recognize ever more clearly that we aren't just victims of destructivity passing through our psycho-emotional system; we confront the denied feelings that have been causing us to choose to act this way, and then consciously de-identify from the destructive lower self and identify with the constructive higher self instead.

Negatively oriented pleasure – The pleasure that is attached to negative intentionality. A person derives energy and a feeling of aliveness from indulging in destructive feelings and situations, even as it causes them to suffer. Because they usually live in a state of numbness, oftentimes this negatively-oriented pleasure is the only pleasure they experience in their life, and so they become addicted to it.

Person in evolution – *See entity.*

Points of hatred – Pockets of unacknowledged and unexpressed hatred in the psycho-physical system that keep one tethered to the past and stuck in negative patterns. When a child does not receive the attention he wants, or is prevented from having things his way, he perceives this as rejection and evidence that he is not loved. Feelings of frustration, hatred, rancor, bitterness and a desire for retribution naturally arise. The child comes to despise his parents, the very people he loves the most, which creates a deep conflict in his psyche. With time, the child learns to numb the pain caused by this conflict, pushing the feelings of loathing deep into the subconscious. In every part of our psycho-emotional world that experienced this painful conflict, we keep these feelings of hatred that were not yet properly dealt with. As we become adults, these areas of the psyche become unconscious "points of hatred" that excrete their poison slowly and unpredictably, causing endless destruction.

Positive intentionality – The will to be a channel of divine love and joy, and thereby sustain happiness, prosperity, creativity and all that is constructive and good. As the spiritual seeker comes to the disturbing conclusion that they are attracting and attached to the negativity that rules their life, they enter into a deep existential crisis. Though the realization is unpleasant, it also provides the seeker with the conviction that liberation is possible, since they can theoretically choose positivity instead. But for this, they must confront their unconscious belief that they will cease to exist if they abandon the negative self that they have become so identified with, and must consciously choose to identify with their positive self instead. Spiritual practices can then help them increase their willpower and awareness as they begin to redirect their energy and resources towards all that is positive and constructive.

Purification – The process of reorganizing and integrating the fragmented parts of the personality. This is an intense inner housecleaning whereby we address any character distortions that may have emerged over time. During our life the various expressions of the mask, and of the lower self and the higher self become mixed up and intertwined. Purification means to disentangle, understand and rearrange all the aspects of the psyche according to their original nature. We distinguish the underlying motives of the ego for striving for any given objective. For instance, if we are striving to be faultless, the lower self may be pushing this effort as a way of being admired and obtaining recognition; but the higher self may also be seeking perfection out of love for God. On a spiritual path we purify our motives until we can consciously choose what part of us guides our life.

Sadomasochism – The desire to hurt the other, or to be hurt by them. In a loving relationship this manifests as the aggressor-victim dynamic: one partner plays the aggressor who inflicts emotional pain, and the other partner plays the victim, unconsciously asking to be hurt in order to punish the other through guilt – the victim blames the aggressor for all of the victim's suffering. The roles we use vary with each person we relate with and each area of our life: we may be masochistic at work and sadistic with our family, or vice-versa. The stronger the emotional bond between two people, the more intensely the sado-masochistic dynamic is experienced.

Wounded child – An aspect of the lower self that forms as a result of the traumas and painful experiences of childhood. Specific beliefs and images are frozen into the child's system, and self-defense mechanisms are put into place to protect him from further pain. As the child grows into an adult, these beliefs, images and mechanisms continue to dictate the person's view and behavior, even though their life circumstances are completely different. As long as the person does not identify and integrate their wounded child, they maintain the emotional maturity of that child, behave in the same predictable patterns, and are unable to develop into a truly autonomous adult.

Terms from Sanskrit and the East

Ananda – The feeling of bliss that arises when one is immersed in the Divine.

Ahimsa – Acting with *ahimsa* means acting in a way that does not harm others physically or emotionally. Examples of violence towards another person, the opposite of *ahimsa*, include: acting cold and withdrawn; speaking in a way that hurts the other, even subtly; and simply keeping one's heart closed to the other.

Annapurna, or **Annapurna Lakshmi** – Annapurna is the Goddess of physical and spiritual nourishment. She is a manifestation of Parvati, and like Durga and Ganga, she is a *shakti* of Shiva. *Anna* means food and grains, and *purna* means wholeness or perfection. She is often associated with Lakshmi, who provides for abundance and prosperity.

Arjuna – The third of the five Pandava brothers. During a twelve-year exile, Arjuna prepared himself for a possible war with his cousins, the Kauravas. Arjuna was already the most accomplished warrior of his age, but knew that even his extraordinary human skills would likely not be enough to vanquish the Kauravas. He thus spent these years practicing austerities in a holy place in the Himalayas so as to acquire the knowledge of divine weapons. When his austerities drove him to sheer exhaustion, the *Devas* elevated him to the celestial realms, replenishing his life force and personally teaching Arjuna the secret art of divine combat. Arjuna was also a close friend and the brother-in-law of Lord Krishna. During the War of Kurukshetra Arjuna recognized that Krishna was actually his Guru, and Krishna gave him spiritual instruction that became recorded as the *Bhagavad Gita*.

Asanas – Specific postures of the body that are practiced in *hatha yoga. See hatha yoga.*

Ashram – A spiritual hermitage where a guru and his or her devotees live and perform their spiritual practices. Because the guru's energy field envelops the ashram, it is believed to be a nexus of spiritual power. This means that anything that takes place inside an ashram influences and is a reflection of what is happening in the outside world.

Atman – One's divine essence. *See higher self.*

Avatar – While a guru was born as a common human being who eventually awakened and became enlightened, an *avatar* is a divine being who took on a human body and incarnated on Earth, and thus was born already enlightened. A guru has a personal relationship with his or her disciples, and is guiding a relatively small number of people towards enlightenment. In contrast, an *avatar* is an embodiment of a divine being who incarnates in a time of need to reestablish the *dharma* and to uplift humanity as a whole. He or she may elevate millions of people, in a more impersonal relationship.

Bhagavad Gita – The most highly treasured and widely read spiritual text in India, the *Bhagavad Gita* is also one of the most important texts in the history of world literature and philosophy. "*Bhagavan*" means Lord, and "*Gita*" means song: it is the song of the Lord. A part of the *Mahabharata*, its roughly 700 verses are the conversation that took place between Krishna and his disciple Arjuna on the eve of the great War of Kurukshetra, where Krishna teaches Arjuna how to become a perfect *yogi*. The teachings are a response to Arjuna's dilemma about having to fight his own family and prior mentors. Krishna affirms that Arjuna must fulfill his *dharma* as warrior and ruler, and he delves deep into the cornerstone philosophies of yoga and the *Vedas*. Thus, the *Bhagavad Gita* not only shepherds a person through the intricate Hindu theology, but also serves as a practical guide to living a balanced life and achieving liberation. Like the *Ramayana* before it, the *Bhagavad Gita* shows how a guru or *avatar* reaveals his or her concealed divine nature to a devotee in an often subtle and gradual way, sometimes only after years of service and preparation. Towards the end of their conversation, Krishna revealed to Arjuna his transcendental form as ruler of the whole cosmos. The vision was too much for even Arjuna to bear, so he soon asked Krishna to return to his normal human stature. The "*Upanishad* of the *Upanishads*" or the "Scripture of Liberation," the *Bhagavad Gita* details the way in which, age after age, the divine being comes to Earth and interacts with human beings, guiding them towards their own realization through a divine *lila*.

Bhakti Yoga – The practice of devotion undertaken by a *sadhaka* towards a guru or other manifestation of the Divine.

Brahma – The first aspect of the divine trinity in Hinduism, representing the creative power.

Brahmacharya – Celibacy as a practice of devotion to spiritual life. The *Brahmachari* conserves his or her sexual energy and directs it upwards towards God instead of dispersing it outwards.

Buddhi – The combination of wisdom and discernment that allows the person in evolution to overcome *manas*, the compulsive mind, and thereby eliminate one's identification with the material world. Only by developing *buddhi* can someone be freed from worldly desires and obtain liberation. *Buddhi* should be in charge of the personality. The *Katha Upanishad* (I.3) uses the analogy of the horse-drawn carriage: *buddhi* is the driver who holds the reins; the reins are the lower mind, or *manas*; the horses are the five senses; and the carriage is the body. The driver must direct the horses with the reins, not the other way around.

Chakras – The *chakras* are wheels or vortexes of energy that exist in the subtle body and interpenetrate the physical body. In the physical body, they are located near the seven major nerve ganglia that emanate from the spinal column. Each *chakra* is associated with different spiritual abilities and levels of consciousness, from the grossest at the base of the spine to the more subtle at the crown of the head. Especially from the third *chakra* onwards, it is exceedingly difficult to successfully open, purify and bring each *chakra* into balance without the help of a fully awakened master teacher. *See kundalini energy.*

Cycle of Birth, Death and Rebirth – The continuous flow of a being through various bodies and incarnations. It is widely understood in India that life does not begin with birth and end with death; rather, after death the soul eventually takes another body. The balance of karma accumulated during one's current life determines the characteristics of one's future lives.

Dhanyavad – "Thank you." An expression of deep gratitude.

Darshan – A vision of the Divine. A guru is able to transmit the experience of spiritual freedom through his or her eyes. Being in the physical presence of a guru is considered to be a blessing, because looking into his or her eyes, or observing the guru's facial expressions and other movements allows a seeker to have a direct experience of the Divine.

Deva or **Devi** – A god (Deva) or Goddess (Devi) that embodies some aspect of divinity.

Dharma – One's righteous duty. The Sanskrit term translates to "that which upholds or supports," or simply "law." It is the supreme law of life. To fulfill one's *dharma* is to carry out the original purpose or mission that was destined for one's lifetime.

Durga – An expression of Parvati that represents the power of destruction and transformation. Seated on a lion, Durga has many arms, each carrying a weapon that is used in battle against ferocious demons. Durga is the aspect of the Divine Mother that helps her devotees defeat their inner demons and transcend the ego. She does this through the purification of the lower self and through the love of the Divine Mother.

Ganga – The name of the Goddess who out of compassion for mankind descended to Earth and took the shape of the Ganges River. It is believed throughout India that a devotional dip in the Ganges grants a seeker the blessing of this Goddess, who has the power to free people from the bondage of their karma and to grant them liberation. Ganga represents the aspect of the Divine Mother who purifies everything that comes her way.

Guru – An enlightened master teacher who has the ability to guide spiritual seekers to enlightenment. *Guru* in Sanskrit means "the one who dissipates darkness." *See master teacher.*

Guru mantra – The *mantra* that is given to a seeker by his or her guru at the moment of initiation into the guru's spiritual lineage. The *sadhaka* then repeats this *mantra* until he or she becomes enlightened.

Hatha Yoga – A system of yoga based on *asanas* or physical postures, and *pranayama* or breathing techniques. *Hatha* literally means forceful or willful; *hatha yoga* is a discipline that strengthens and purifies the body and mind in order to prepare the practitioner for deep states of meditation. It is also widely practiced just for the health benefits that it provides.

Indra – The chief of the *Devas* or gods.

Initiation – A transmission of energy that a guru imparts on a spiritual seeker when he or she is ready to become a formal disciple of this guru. During initiation, the *sadhaka* receives a *guru mantra* amidst specific rituals, and is formally accepted into the guru's lineage. It is a common saying in India that there are three truly important days in the life of a human being: the day one meets one's guru, the day one becomes initiated by this guru, and the day one becomes enlightened. Prem Baba provides initiation into the Sachcha lineage in his Guru's ashram in Rishikesh, India, after a seeker comes to him there and asks to be initiated. As of 2012 Prem Baba is beginning to offer initiation in other countries to people who are ready to be initiated but unable to travel to India.

Japa – The practice of repeating a *mantra* to enter into communion with the Divine.

Jnana Yoga – The yoga of knowledge and wisdom. The spiritual seeker gains spiritual knowledge and self-knowledge through meditation and through teachings imparted by a master teacher. There are two main meditation techniques practiced in *jnana yoga*: analytical meditation aims to give the individual insight into the workings and tendencies of his lower self, while meditation focused on emptiness is used to anchor presence and abide in a state of detached observation.

Kali – One of the forms of Goddess Durga, she is the destroyer of evil. Kali helps seekers integrate the most destructive aspects of the ego.

Kama – *Kama* literally means sexual desire, pleasure, and fulfillment. It refers to passion, longing and the ability to enjoy life, and Vedic scriptures consider it as one of the four main goals of life. Kama is also the name of the god of love who awakens these qualities in people. He was sent by the gods to disturb Shiva in his meditation and make him notice and then marry Parvati and have children, as only a son of Shiva would be able to defeat the demon Tarakasur. In response Shiva incinerates Kama and spreads this energy of love throughout the universe, which does also end up affecting Shiva and bringing about his union with Parvati. Their son Kartikeya eventually grows up and defeats the demon.

Kamandalu – The ascetic's bowl, where he or she receives food and water given in charity.

Karma – A Sanskrit term meaning "act" or "deed," karma is the sum total of one's actions and accompanying reactions. More generally, karma refers to the law of cause and effect, which brings about negative consequences when a person's actions are intentionally destructive, and also when they are well-intentioned but rooted in ignorance. Selfless actions, on the other hand, create positive results. Karma is not to be considered punishment or retribution meted out by some higher or divine authority; it is simply the natural consequences of our acts.

Karma Yoga – The yoga of action. By practicing selfless service for the benefit of society or a spiritual cause, one's karmic baggage is dissolved.

Karma Yogi – A person who serves a higher cause and has eliminated all expectations and desires for reaping personal benefit associated with their actions.

Kauravas, or **Kurus** – The hundred children of King Dhritarashtra, all of whom were killed during the War of Kurukshetra. Duryodhana was the eldest, and often plotted to get the Pandavas out of the picture to clear his way to lordship of the Kuru Dynasty. There was constant debate regarding the right to rule, because although the Kauravas represent the senior branch of the family, Duryodhana was younger than

Yudhisthira, the eldest Pandava, so that both claimed the right to the kingdom. *See Pandavas.*

Krishna – An *avatar* of Lord Vishnu who incarnated on Earth at the time of the great War of Kurukshetra. Krishna is widely worshipped in all the stages of his life on Earth. When he was a prankster child, Krishna delighted everyone with his contagious spontaneity. Later, he set an intriguing example of the alluring lover. Although he was always surrounded by *gopis*, young maidens who would do anything to be with him, Krishna married Radha, the embodiment of perfect devotion. Krishna defeated the most ferocious of demons, and is exalted as the Supreme Being, having revealed his universal form to Arjuna in the *Bhagavad Gita.*

Kriya(s) or **Kriya Yoga** – The science of the breath. The term *kriya* means a complete action with a specific, intended result. *Kriyas* are advanced yogic techniques that have a powerful cleansing effect on the physical and subtle levels and can quickly take the practitioner into higher states of consciousness. These techniques combine postures, breath, *mantras*, and focus points in a very precise way in order to achieve the desired outcome. *Kriya yoga* is said to have been known to Patanjali and Jesus, and taught to Arjuna by Krishna. Nowadays, the term Kriya Yoga most commonly refers to the yoga techniques taught by Paramahansa Yogananda and practiced by the students of that lineage. *Kundalini yoga* as taught by Yogi Bhajan is also a practice of *kriyas.*

Kumbh Mela – A mass pilgrimage performed every three years to one of four specific locations on the Ganges River where it is believed that the gods pour the *amrita* or nectar of immortality – Allahabad, Haridwar, Ujjain and Nashik. Bathing in the Ganges during the *Kumbh Mela* is considered highly auspicious and is said to wash away a person's karmic debt so that they may attain liberation sooner. The *Ardh* ("half-complete") *Kumbh Mela* takes place every six years, the *Purna* ("complete") *Kumbh Mela* takes place every twelve years, and the *Maha* ("great") *Kumbh Mela* happens after twelve *Purna Kumbh Melas*, or once every 144 years. The festival attracts millions of *sadhus*, sages, holy men and women, pilgrims and spiritual seekers who come together in prayer, making it the world's largest gathering ever recorded in history.

Kundalini or **Kundalini Energy** – The life force or *shakti* of each human being that, in the majority of people, lies dormant in the *muladhara* or root *chakra* at the base of the spine. Through spiritual practices or contact with a guru, this latent power is awakened and rises through the central *nadi* or energy channel along the spine. As the *kundalini* energy rises it pierces through the *chakras* located along the spine, activating specific experiences, powers and states of consciousness. When the *kundalini* energy reaches and abides in the *sahasrara* or crown *chakra* at the top of the head, the person becomes fully enlightened.

Kurus – *See Kauravas.*

Kurukshetra – The sacred land where the epic war between the Pandavas and the Kauravas took place, and where Krishna recited the words transcribed in the *Bhagavad Gita*. It is located in the state of Haryana in Northern India.

Lakshmi, or **Mahalakshmi** – Lakshmi is the Goddess of wealth and abundance, the one who makes everything grow and prosper (*Maha* in her title means great). She is the *shakti* and consort of Lord Vishnu. Lakshmi manifests in eight primary forms: the Goddess who bears the power of Vishnu; the Goddess of wholesome food; of animals and nature; of children or offspring; of money and wealth; of personal courage; of victory and success; and the bestower of wisdom and knowledge.

Lila – The great cosmic play of the Divine. The *Vedas* describe the human experience on earth as a divine game. People get disconnected from their divine source, and over the course of many lifetimes, learn to reconnect to it. All experiences human beings go through, including the painful ones, take place to remind people of their original divine nature. An enlightened master or guru also has his or her own *lila:* the guru often acts in a way that bewilders the mind of a disciple, but leads to his or her awakening.

Lingam or **Shiva Lingam** – A phallic symbol in the shape of an obelisk inside an ellipse, it is a representation of Shiva and his power. It is revered in countless temples and shrines as a reminder that each human being holds the potential of attaining perfect union of the masculine and feminine principles.

Mahabharata – One of the two major sacred epics of ancient India (alongside the *Ramayana*). Spanning one hundred thousand verses (ten times the length of the *Iliad* and the *Odyssey* combined), the *Mahabharata* describes the War of Kurukshetra and the fate of the Pandavas and Kauravas in their struggle for the throne of Hastinapura. Aside from the teachings of Lord Krishna transmitted in the *Bhagavad Gita*, particularly noteworthy sections of the *Mahabharata* are the lessons conveyed through the various short stories about the Pandavas and the other remarkable characters they relate with. Specifically, the teachings of Sri Bhisma, the great grandfather of the Pandavas, describe the quest for virtue, prosperity and emancipation in great detail, and thoroughly explain all matters of *dharma*. During the War of Kurukshetra Bhisma was fighting against the Pandavas. On the tenth day of battle, when with the help of Krishna Arjuna conjured the inner resolve to defeat Bhisma and finally shot the fatal arrows, both sides ceased fire for the day in reverence for their fallen forefather and mentor. Bhisma mustered enough strength only to die after transmitting all his wisdom to Yudhishthira, the oldest Pandava. Although Krishna was entirely omniscient as an embodiment of the Divine, Krishna told Bhisma that he should be the one to transmit this rich knowledge on *dharma* to the recently crowned Yudhishthira, so that Bhisma could be remembered throughout history for his spiritual merits, as Krishna himself needed no further honors. The *Mahabharata* is rich with teachings on many other philosophical issues, including the four goals of life: *dharma* (right action), *artha* (purpose), *kama* (pleasure), and *moksha* (liberation). The last three of the eighteen *Parvas*, or books, of the *Mahabharata*, relate how Krishna disincarnates and how the Pandavas ascend to *svarga*, the spiritual world, which marks the beginning of *Kali Yuga*, the Age of Ignorance.

Mahalakshmi – *See Lakshmi.*

Maha Kumbh Mela – *See Kumbh Mela.*

Mahamaya – *See Maya.*

Maharajji, or **Sri Sri Sachcha Baba Maharajji** – The Guru of Prem Baba. Born in 1922, Maharajji became enlightened on October 3rd, 1955, the day after he first met his Guru, Sachcha Baba. For decades he remained in constant *samadhi,* almost never leaving his room at Sachcha Dham Ashram, in Rishikesh, India, where Prem Baba also stays and teaches for a good portion of the year. Until recently Maharajji went by the name he had before becoming enlightened, Hans Raj, to which his disciples appended the term Maharajji. Hans Raj means the master of the nature of the Self, and Maharajji means great king ("*Maha*" is great and "*raj*" is king, while "*ji*" is a term of respect). In 2011 Prem Baba requested his permission to refer to him as Sachcha Baba Maharajji, and this has been adopted as his new name. Maharajji left his body, entering the state of *mahasamadhi* on October 23rd, 2011.

Mahashivaratri – A yearly festival celebrating the great night of Shiva. *"Maha"* means great, and *"ratri"* means night. The festival celebrates the marriage of Shiva and Parvati.

Manas – The thinking mind. If properly used by higher intelligence, *manas* can facilitate the experience of higher consciousness.

Manifestation of the Divine, divine manifestation or **embodiment of the Divine** – Representations of God. Although God is One and indivisible, God may express different qualities at different times, through a specific divine being with specific characteristics, or through an enlightened human being who is able to sustain the divine presence while incarnated in a body.

Mantra – Sounds of power. *Mantras* are sacred words and phrases in Sanskrit and other ancient languages that are repeated either internally or out loud to produce a meditative effect. The perfect mathematical organization of Sanskrit phonetics, along with the specific combination of rhythm, sound and tonality of each *mantra*, activates *chakras* and higher states of consciousness whenever the *mantra* is vocalized or listened to. The effect is further enhanced when one is aware of the meaning of the *mantra* and makes it into a prayer.

Master teacher or **master** – The pure spiritual energy that guides a person's footsteps. The master teacher can be the voice of *intuition*, it can be an *awakened teacher* who knows how to guide others to enlightenment, or it can be the *flow of life* itself, which constantly beckons us to follow a specific course of action. Each person is free to either listen and follow the guidance of the master teacher, or to obey the mind and ego instead. *See Guru.*

Maya or **Mahamaya** – The great cosmic illusion that acts as a veil, blinding human beings to their true reality and causing them to view the world through the lens of duality: night and day, sadness and joy, yes and no, etc. *Maya* also refers to the Goddess and aspect of the Divine Mother who governs this illusion and all of our actions within it. In the *Bhagavad Gita* Krishna says, "The sovereign Lord dwells in the heart space of beings and moves them to act by His divine *Maya*, as though controlled by a machine" (ch. 18, verse 61).

Mirabai – A sixteenth-century princess who composed over a thousand *bhajans* extolling Lord Krishna, devotional songs that are widely sung to this day throughout India. Though she married Prince Bhoj Raj, she consistently affirmed that in truth she was only ever married to Krishna. Her devotion to Krishna eventually turned into such an intense mystical experience that she spent the rest of her life dancing in the streets, going from one city to the next. Through this pilgrimage that took her across Northern India, she touched thousands of people with the sincerity of her devotion for this aspect of the Divine.

Murti – Literally, "an embodiment" in Sanskrit, a *murti* is a representation of some aspect of the Divine made of wood, stone or metal. Though a *murti* may appear to be just a statue, it is bathed, clothed, adorned and worshipped as if it were the body of a divine being. This type of ritual activates in the devotee the same divine qualities as the ones that are embodied in the *murti*.

Nadi or **Nadis** – The channels through which subtle energy flows in the body. There are over 72,000 *nadis* in the human body, connected at the *chakras*. Yogic practices for raising *kundalini* focus on the three main *nadis*: the *pingala* is the solar energy channel, the *ida* is the lunar energy channel and the *sushumna* is the central channel through which the *kundalini* ascends.

Namaste – A gesture often used in greeting and in parting, whereby one puts both hands together in reverence and says *namaste*, meaning "The Divine in me greets the Divine in you."

Narada – *See Sage Narada.*

Pandavas – The five sons of King Pandu, the younger brother of King Dritharashtra (father of the Kauravas). Upon stepping down from the throne, Dritharashtra had to appoint the oldest Pandava brother, Yudhishthira, as his successor. This filled Dritharashtra's son Duryodhana with envy, so he plotted a trap to kill the Pandavas. He failed and the Pandavas were eventually given some land to rule over. They developed their land into a thriving city, but their success and prosperity fueled Duryodhana's wrath and caused him to devise a fraudulent game of dice through which he stole everything else that rightfully belonged to the Pandavas. Following their twelve-year long exile and year in concealment, the Pandavas claimed their right to have the kingdom back. When the Kauravas refused to share the kingdom, the devastating War of Kurukshetra became inevitable. One particularly challenging duel was between Arjuna and Karna. Though Karna was fighting on the side of the Kauravas, almost no one knew that he was actually the oldest son of Kunti, the mother of the Pandavas. Krishna revealed this fact to Karna on the eve of the war as a last prevention effort, since with Krishna's backing both the Pandavas and Kauravas would accept Karna as king. But Karna refused the offer of the empire due to his loyalty to Duryodhana, who had for many years granted him shelter and attention when everyone else had spurned and rejected him owing to a mistaken understanding of his family line. Karna also knew that he was the only person on earth with the skills to resist Arjuna in battle, and was eager for the honor of taking up arms against him. The duel was indeed unprecedented, and all the other warriors stopped fighting to watch as Arjuna and Karna used weapons charged with the supernatural powers of secret *mantras*. In the end, destiny favored Arjuna: Karna's carriage got stuck in the mud, providing Arjuna with the opportunity to defeat him. Arjuna won not because of skill, but because he had strayed fewer times from the path of *dharma*, having always associated himself with the virtuous Yudhishtira rather than Duryodhana.

Paramguru – The guru of one's guru, one's spiritual "grandparent."

Parvati – The *shakti* or consort of Shiva. She represents the aspect of the Divine Mother that brings about transformation. Two of Parvati's best known manifestations or aspects are Durga and Kali, aspects of the Goddess that have the power to destroy or transmute our inner demons.

Pranam – An ancient act of reverence, whereby one bows in honor of the divine being that inhabits another person. When performed to a fully awakened being, such as a guru, one may bow down to his or her feet. *Pranam* is not only a practice of humility, it is also performed to receive a direct transmission of spiritual energy.

Pranayama – The practice of regulating the breath as a means to still the mind and attain higher states of awareness. *Prana* is the life force that is accessed through the breath, and *ayama* means to suspend or restrain – *pranayama* is literally "the control of the life-force" in Sanskrit. It is one of the eight limbs of yoga as described in the *Yoga Sutras* of Patanjali.

Puja – A type of ritual performed throughout India where a person makes an offering to divinity. The offering may consist of food, flowers, flame and incense, or other every day objects, and is usually accompanied with the recitation of *mantras*. During a *puja*, one invokes some aspect of divinity through a *murti* or some aspect of nature, and in doing so, awakens that same quality in oneself.

Qigong – A Chinese practice of movement, breath and awareness that is used for martial arts training, exercise, health and mindfulness. Like *hatha yoga*, this is a powerful way to get the vital currents of the body flowing and to physically prepare oneself for entering into deeper states of meditation.

Rama – An *avatar* of Lord Vishnu who preceded Krishna, and is held with equal regard. Rama represents man in his state of perfection, and is the embodiment of virtue, strength and *dharma*.

Ramayana – One of the two great epics of India, next to the *Mahabharata*. It tells the story of Rama, and teaches how to live in accordance to one's *dharma*. The characters demonstrate what it means to be the perfect ruler, husband or wife, sibling, and disciple.

Religare – A Latin term meaning "to reconnect." This is the same meaning as the word yoga, to "yoke" back together. *Religare* is the root form of the word religion, and means to reconnect the individual soul with its original universal source.

Rishikesh – The "town of the *rishis,*" the great "seers" or sages of antiquity who lived in seclusion on the banks of the Ganges. Rishikesh is a city in the Dehradun district of Uttarakhand State, in Northern India. At the foothills of the Himalayas, Rishikesh is the first larger province that the Ganges River flows by on its way down from the mountains. It attracts thousands of pilgrims and tourists each year from across India and the world. Sachcha Dham Ashram, where Maharajji lived and Prem Baba spends the winter months, is located in Lakshman Jhula, a subsection of Rishikesh. The number of enlightened beings and ashrams that have emerged over the millennia in Rishikesh makes it a place that vibrates in a high spiritual energy frequency.

Sachcha – The irrefutable Truth.

Sachcha Baba – The Guru of Sri Hans Raj Maharajji, and *Paramguru* of Prem Baba. It is said that on the day that Sachcha Baba, the "Father of Truth," was born as Kulanandaji, the Ganges River deviated significantly from its course and flooded his whole village, reaching the front steps of Kulanandaji's parents' house. After they blessed Kulanandaji by placing his feet in the water, *Ganga* immediately receded back to its normal level and continued its regular course. Sachcha Baba left the world in 1983, transmitting his powers to Maharajji.

Sachcha lineage – The lineage of gurus in which Prem Baba is a spiritual master, where one guru transmits powers to the next. In this lineage the transmission occurred from Katcha Baba to Girinari Baba, onwards to Sachcha Baba, then to Maharajji, and finally to Prem Baba. Girinari Baba was commonly believed to be an embodiment of Sage Narada himself. Although he was a *sadhu* (ascetic) who would walk around in old rags, even kings would bow down to his feet in respect. He was committed to uplift humanity, but in order to fulfill his work he realized in deep meditation that he would require the cooperation of another very powerful *yogi* who was trying to transform the world through its destruction. This *yogi*, Katcha Baba, believed that humanity had strayed so far from *dharma* that it could no longer recover. He was working to dissolve the current reality to allow for a new, spiritually advanced civilization eventually to take its place. After submitting Girinari Baba to a series of difficult tests Katcha Baba became convinced that humanity could indeed be rescued, and transmitted his powers to Girinari Baba. Girinari Baba eventually entrusted his disciple Sachcha Baba with the mission of creating a golden age within the current *Kali Yuga*. Out of deep compassion for humanity, Sachcha Baba received the *mantra "Prabhu Ap Jago"* and formally established the *sankalpa*, the promise of the Sachcha lineage. Sri Hans Raj Maharajji was a family man and an employee of the Indian government. Upon meeting Sachcha Baba he surrendered and became enlightened on the same day. Sri Prem Baba went to India in 1999 in answer to an inner vision. He had already taken teachings from various spiritual masters and schools, but only felt that he could fully surrender when he met Maharajji. He became enlightened after three years of discipleship and continued with the mission of fulfilling Sachcha Baba's *sankalpa*, now focusing especially on establishing it in the West.

Sachcha Mission – The mission of establishing truth in all of humanity. This is the name that Maharajji gave to Prem Baba's ashram in Brazil, and it is the purpose of Prem Baba's work.

Sadhaka – A seeker who follows a certain *sadhana* or studies under an enlightened master teacher in order to obtain self-realization. Although nowadays *sadhaka* is used to denote any religious practitioner, the original Sanskrit term was a technical reference to someone who had undergone a specific form of initiation.

Sadhana – Spiritual practice. A seeker's *sadhana* can involve any combination of practices, such as repeating or chanting a *mantra* or performing specific rituals, practicing meditation, studying sacred texts, doing yoga or *seva*. But when Prem Baba refers to the practice of "the *sadhana*," he is referring to the repetition of the specific *mantra* that a disciple received during his or her initiation, in the way it was instructed to them.

Sadhu – A person who has renounced material pursuits in order to live a more contemplative life. *Sadhus* are either nomadic or live in caves, forests and temples; in any case they have few belongings and eat only the food that is given to them in charity. Some people attempt to lead the life of a *sadhu* but in reality are only concealing their inability to harmonize themselves with material life. One can only renounce what one already has.

Sage Narada – A divine sage who was known for his remarkable compassion for human beings. Narada assumed responsibility for the regeneration of humanity after the devastating War of Kurukshetra. When Krishna left his body and the earth entered into the Kali Yuga (estimated to have been in the year 3102 BC), Narada is believed to have remained on earth through countless incarnations to ensure that a Golden Age would be created within this Age of Ignorance.

Samadhi – A state of deep meditation in which one experiences unity. As a spiritual practitioner integrates the lower self and is able to get into an actual meditative state, he or she may experience *satori*, which is a flash of sudden awareness and a glimpse of spiritual reality. This experience is fleeting, and the person soon returns to ordinary states of consciousness. After having experienced many *satoris*, one learns to sustain that energy and may experience *samadhi*, a prolonged absorption in this state of bliss. One may enter and again fall from a state of *samadhi* many times. As one learns to sustain *samadhi*, one may experience permanent enlightenment.

Sanskaras – Karmic imprints on the subconscious mind. A person's *sanskaras* arise from childhood experiences or earlier, and shape their current life. A person's personality traits, unconscious or semi-conscious habits and patterns of behavior, and responses to life circumstances are all the result of their particular *sanskaras*.

Sanatana Dharma – The eternal religion, or the path of enlightenment. *Sanatana* means "eternal," that which never begins or ends; *dharma* as used here refers to "*dhri*," which means "to hold together" or "to sustain." *Sanatana Dharma* is the eternal law. It is the essence of religion; although over time religions might have lost their original intent, *Sanatana Dharma* preserves the teachings and practices that connect the human being directly with God, their higher self.

Sangha – A Sanskrit term that literally means "company" or "good company," the *sangha* is the group of disciples and devotees that surrounds a master teacher or guru.

Sankalpa – An intention, purpose, or mission that is established through prayer. The *sankalpa* is a resolution formulated by a saint for the attainment of a spiritual purpose that benefits all.

Satori – *See "samadhi." Satori* is a flash of sudden awareness and a glimpse of spiritual reality. The experience is fleeting, and one soon returns to ordinary states of consciousness.

Satsang – "*Sat*" means truth, and "*sang*" means company; "*satsang*" is to sit in the company of the highest truth, that is, to sit with a guru and to receive his or her *darshan*. This is a meeting between an enlightened master teacher and his or her group of devotees, where the devotees may sing and play devotional music, as well as ask questions that the teacher will in turn answer.

Sattvic Diet, or **Sattvic Foods** – A diet of foods that *Ayurveda*, the ancient Indian science of health, classifies as benefiting the body as well as leading to clarity and equanimity of the mind. These foods include most fresh organic vegetables and fruits, as well as many beans, cereals, grains and nuts. Foods that do not lead to a *sattvic* state are either *rajasic* or *tamasic* in nature. A *rajasic* diet consists of foods that heat up the blood or agitate the mind. This includes various peppers, spices, coffee, sugar, nightshades (crops that grow at night), acidic fruits and pungent vegetables (i.e. tomatoes, onions, garlic, and eggplant). A *tamasic* diet consists of foods that lead a person to a numbed or lethargic state of mind, and may make the person physically ill and emotionally "dead." These include reheated or expired foods, processed foods and candies that contain ingredients or chemicals fabricated by humans, artificially-conserved and canned foods, as well as any dead animal (pork, beef, chicken and poultry, and fish). White flour, potatoes, mushrooms, and eggs are also *tamasic*. Regardless of the type of food one is eating, overeating makes the meal *tamasic*. Milk and dairy products are often considered *sattvic* in India, but *tamasic* in the West, depending on how cows are treated and on whether or not they are slaughtered for beef consumption in that region.

Seva – The practice of selfless service. *See karma yoga.*

Shakti – *Shakti* is the creative power of the universe, the primordial energy, the divine feminine and the cosmic Mother. *Kundalini* is a form of *shakti*. More specifically, *shakti* is the spiritual power of a god, saint or guru. The *shakti* of a realized or divine being is expressed in their counterpart of the opposite sex. For instance, Brahma's *shakti* is Saraswati; she carries out the power of creation through the wisdom of the *Vedas,* and through music and the arts. The *shakti* of Vishnu is Lakshmi; she implements the power of conservation by providing for the material needs of all beings. The *shakti* of Shiva is Parvati, who implements transformation by destroying demons and transforming the lower self. A guru also has one or more *shaktis*, a close devotee who gives sustenance to the guru's work by regularly performing the practices of that lineage or fascilitating some other aspect of the work.

Shiva – The third aspect of *Parabrahma*, the absolute God. Shiva destroys ignorance and brings about the transformation of the universe. He is also considered to be the first *yogi*.

Shivaratri – The night of the month dedicated to Lord Shiva. *See also Mahashivaratri.*

Siddhi – Supernatural or extraordinary powers that are acquired by discipline, *mantras* or spiritual attainment, or that a person may have from birth. They include faculties like clairvoyance and knowing the past, present and future; being able to read minds; levitation or teleportation; and having power over other beings and the five elements.

Sita – An incarnation of Goddess Lakshmi who became the consort of Lord Rama.

Sri – A title of respect for an enlightened or divine being.

Tamasic Food – Food that numbs a person's ability to feel emotional or spiritual realities, and that is often physically harmful. *See Sattvic foods* for a list of those foods.

Tantra – The path of spontaneity, of total acceptance. *Tantra* is commonly misunderstood to refer to sexual rituals and techniques for attaining spiritual bliss. In reality, *Tantra* is a complete spiritual path in which no aspect of life is denied or repressed, and everything is considered to be divine, as opposed to more austere paths which require giving up material life and enjoyment of the senses. This method is often contrasted with that of the *Sutras,* which provide more specific guidelines: "Do this, and then that, but not that."

Treta Yuga – The second of the four main ages that humanity moves through, when spiritual values have started to be forgotten, but still play a dominant role in human society. To uplift humanity and destroy demons, Lord Vishnu incarnated three times in the last *Treta Yuga,* namely as *Vamana, Parashurama,* and *Rama. See Yuga.*

Vedas – Perhaps the oldest of sacred texts, this large collection of scriptures is the first recorded example of Sanskrit literature. The *Vedas* are divided into four main *"Samhitas"* or compilations of poems, songs, *mantras* and prayers: The *Rigveda* is the sacred science of reciting hymns; the *Yajurveda* is the science of performing sacrifices; the *Samaveda* is the science of chanting;

and the *Atharvaveda* is a collection of incantations used for healing purposes.

Vishnu – The second aspect of Parabrahma, who governs the preservation and sustenance of the universe.

Yoga – Physical, mental, and devotional disciplines that reconnect (or "yoke" back together) the human being with his or her original source, or higher self. The physical exercises of *hatha yoga* are well known in the West for producing a state of peace and for their health benefits. Other prominent forms of yoga are *jnana yoga*, the way of spiritual knowledge; *bhakti yoga*, the path of devotion; *karma yoga*, selfless service; *raja yoga*, meditation and control of the mind; *kriya yoga*, the science of the breath; and others.

Yogi – One who has mastered one or more types of yoga.

Yoni – The *yoni* is the abstract representation of *shakti* and *Devi*, the creative force that animates the universe. Its counterpart is the *Shiva lingam*. *Yoni* is the Sanskrit term for the female genitalia: it is the divine passage that leads to the womb, or the sacred temple. It is the source of all life.

Yuga – An epoch or era that defines the collective human experience on earth. According to Hindu philosophy, the universe endlessly cycles through four stages from the moment of its creation to its destruction. These four *yugas* are like the four seasons, but instead of being defined by the amount of sunlight that is present, they are defined by the amount of spiritual energy that humanity is able to sustain at that stage. Each *yuga* lasts for thousands of years. During the *Sachcha Yuga*, or Golden Age, humanity is guided by the highest spiritual truths. As the solar system starts to orbit further away from *"Vishnunabhi,"* considered a universal center of creative power, humanity starts a descending cycle. The *Treta Yuga*, or Silver Age, comes next, followed by the *Dvapara Yuga*, or Bronze Age, and culminating with the *Kali Yuga,* the Iron Age or Age of Ignorance. At the peak of the *Kali Yuga*, when humanity has completely forgotten authentic spiritual values, the solar system starts to cycle closer to *Vishnunabhi* again. It then starts an ascending cycle through the *Dvapara Yuga*, followed by the *Treta Yuga*, and culminating with the *Sachcha Yuga* again. The *sankalpa* of the Sachcha lineage in which Prem Baba is a spiritual master aims at creating a minor *Sachcha Yuga* within the current *Kali Yuga*.

If you are interested in learning more
about the work of Prem Baba
and the Path of the Heart,
please visit the websites
www.prembaba.org
and
www.pathheart.org